PETRA

'It seems no work of Man's creative hand,
By labor wrought as wavering fancy planned;
But from the rock as if by magic grown,
Eternal, silent, beautiful, alone!
Not virgin-white like that old Doric shrine,
Where erst Athena held her rites divine;
Not saintly-grey, like many a minster fane,
That crowns the hill and consecrates the plane;
But rose-red as if the blush of dawn
That first beheld them were not yet withdrawn;
The hues of youth upon a brow of woe,
Which Man deemed old two thousand years ago,
Match me such a marvel save in Eastern clime,
A rose-red city half as old as Time.'

From Dean Burgon's Newdigate Prize Poem 'Petra'

The Khasneh (The Treasury)

PETRA

By

IAIN BROWNING

Chatto & Windus · London · 1973

Published by
Chatto & Windus Ltd
42 William IV Street
London W.C.2

*

Clarke, Irwin & Co. Ltd.
Toronto

ISBN 0 7011 1881 4

© Iain Browning 1973

Printed in Great Britain by
Fletcher & Son Ltd, Norwich

To
B.W.B. *and* A.M.B.
with love

Acknowledgements

WRITING this book has brought me into contact with a great many people, in many countries and walks of life. It is my pleasure to acknowledge their unstinting help, interest and encouragement. Particularly I should like to thank Mrs Crystal-M. Bennett, Director of the British School of Archaeology in Jerusalem, not only for writing the Preface to this book but for having given much valuable advice on the preparation of the text. The support and very real encouragement of a person of her standing in the world of archaeology has been greatly appreciated. Mrs Helbaek (Diana Kirkbride) kindly advised on the section of this book which deals with her excavations at el Beidha. Mr Peter Parr generously gave permission for his plan of the Temenos to be incorporated into Map 4, as well as answering many questions on the Nabateans. The Abbé Starcky likewise generously verified the King List of the Nabateans for me whilst Mrs Jill Webster drew my attention to current thinking in anthropological matters.

I am most grateful to the Jordanian Department of Antiquities for their help. Mr Suleiman Mousa, the noted Arab historian, is an old friend and through his thoughtfulness I have received much help and kindness in Jordan. On my visits to Petra I enjoyed the company and knowledge of Mr Mohammed Murshed of the Department of Antiquities; through him I visited many sites which I might otherwise have missed.

At home, the encouragement of all my friends is gratefully acknowledged. They are too numerous for me to be able to mention individually but I hope, none the less, that they will accept my thanks. I should, however, like to thank specially Ann McCaig for her invaluable help in correcting proofs, Satani el Mufti who translated Arabic texts for me and Christine Povall for her advice and much practical help, including the preparation of the Index.

South Kensington,   Iain B. Browning
London

Contents

Illustrations

COLOUR PLATES

OTHER ILLUSTRATIONS

The monochrome illustrations may be found from the Index, where their page references are set in italics.

MAPS

TABLES

All illustrations in this book are by the author except for the following which are reproduced with the kind permission of: Mrs Crystal-M. Bennett, Figs. 4, 109, 110, 111, 112. Diana Kirkbride (Beidha Excavations), Figs. 177, 179. Mrs Jill Webster, Fig. 151. Mark Webster, Fig. 45. David A. Collins, Figs. 69, 88, 134, 168. Karl Schmitt-Korte, Frankfurt, Fig. 6. Eric Hosking, Frontispiece. The Trustees of the British Museum, Figs. 23, 24, 25, 27, 28, 29, 58, 65, 93, 115, 139, 184. The Jordanian Department of Antiquities, Figs. 3, 11, 19. The Palestine Exploration Fund, Figs. 21, 40.

Preface

CRYSTAL-M. BENNETT

DEAN BURGON, a relatively unknown cleric in the nineteenth century, elected to describe Petra as a 'rose-red city half as old as Time'. Had it not been for this famous but erroneous statement, the worthy Dean would lie dead in holy obscurity. Edward Lear's talented chef, Giorgio, was much more accurate in his description of the colour of Petra, and, being a cook, expressed his amazement at what he saw in culinary terms. Thus, he exclaims to his master that they have come into a land where everything is chocolate, ham, curry powder and salmon. He had forgotten the vanilla ice cream and blueberries. Apart from that, no more telling description could be given of the multicoloured striations in the sandstone rocky cliffs which engirdle Petra and give it such beauty. This is enhanced by the play of light, changing subtly and constantly the tones of colour in the sandstone. Perhaps, Burgon had the good fortune to emerge from the Stygian gloom of the seemingly endless path, the Siq, which leads into Petra just as the rays of the morning sun bathed the façade of one of Petra's most beautiful monuments, the 'Khasneh', in a rose-red aura.

Every visit to Petra is unforgettable, but none more so than the first, because one's thoughts wing back to that day, 170 years ago, to the emotions which must have overwhelmed the young Swiss explorer John Burckhardt, who had penetrated the fastness of this weird, fascinating place, of which he had heard so many rumours and all memory of which, in the Western world, had been lost for more than six centuries.

Petra is unique. In saying this, I am not forgetting the comparable rock-carved monuments at Medain Saleh in Saudi Arabia. There, they are dispersed so widely that one loses the violent, visual impact of those which flank the northern approach and surround the actual city of Petra, capital of the Nabateans, whose origins and history are discussed in this book.

Once Petra had been discovered, it was inevitable that it should be a focus of study, particularly for students of architectural history, for nowhere else could be found such a synthesis, and confusion of influences, Syro-Phoenician, Egyptian, Hellenistic and Roman as in these tombs, houses and stelae cut from the living rock. And, added to this, was the all-important question—what could be ascribed to the Nabateans, those mysterious people who had erupted almost volcanically from the desert in the two centuries before and after Christ?

Many studies have been made of the monuments in Petra, initially by the
Germans, who fell into two camps. Brünnow and von Domaszewski thought that
they should be regarded in the context of the architecture of the Antonine and
Severan (second century A.D.) periods of the Roman Empire. Wiegand,
Watzinger and Bachmann argued for a date during the reign of the Nabatean
King Aretas IV (9 B.C.–A.D. 40). Both sides have had their adherents subsequently among the French and the British. No doubt they all took into account
two factors: the activities of the Nabatean Kings, Aretas III, called Philhellene,
who lived in the first half of the first century B.C., and Aretas IV, who reigned
during a period when the Nabatean kingdom was extremely sensitive to the
activities of Rome, particularly in Palestine; and secondly, the annexation of the
Nabatean kingdom by Rome in A.D. 106. The debate continues to this day and
we are still not completely sure at which point in the history of Petra it changed
from a Hellenistic to a Greco-Roman city and which of its monuments can be
dated positively to a given period.

Epigraphical studies have helped. Fortunately, the Nabateans have left innumerable inscriptions in Petra and elsewhere in Saudi Arabia and Syria. Their
language was Aramaic and their calligraphy, initially of the same genre, evolved
gradually into a typically Nabatean style. In recent years, two important discoveries have been made in Petra. A group of stelae, in pyramid form, influenced
by Egypt and Syro-Phoenicia, was found at the entrance to the tunnel in Wadi
el Muzlim, a branch of the Wadi Mousa where the Siq, the eastern approach to
Petra, begins. One of them is of particular consequence because, for the first
time, we have the Semitic name for Petra, Reqem (Nabatean Raqmu), which
hitherto had been known only in literary sources. The dedication on this stelae
shows that the person mentioned was buried at Gerash; thus the 'nefesh' is
essentially commemorative and does not mark the actual burial-place. This
group of stelae has enabled the Abbé Starcky, one of the world's foremost
Nabatean scholars, to interpret the whole complex of 'nefesh' or minor funerary
monuments which are engraved on, or cut into, many of the rocky crags
surrounding the Petra basin. But, perhaps, more important was the discovery
of an inscription *in situ* in the south wall of the Temenos leading up to the temple
known as the Kasr el Bint. It belongs to the first part of the reign of Aretas IV
(the Augustan period), and as this section of the wall is an integral part of the
original building of the temple, the inscription has given precision to the dating
of one of Petra's most important free-standing monuments.

But studies of architecture and epigraphy are not enough. They must be sup-
plemented by detailed archaeological field-work. This was pioneered in Petra in
1929 and succeeding years by the British archaeologists, George Horsfield and
Agnes Conway (later to become the wife of Mr Horse as he was affectionately

known in Petra), and by Margaret Murray in 1937. However, their work was not in the centre of Petra and it was not until 1958 and thereafter that archaeological investigations under the directorship of Mr Parr and myself, of the British School of Archaeology in Jerusalem, were concentrated in this vital area. These excavations have done much towards giving a more solid frame, as well as filling in the details of the canvas of the picture, for the history of the central core of the city, from the second century B.C. to the end of the third century A.D.

Although many of the outstanding monuments in Petra are memorials to the dead Nabateans and uniquely a Roman Governor, Sextus Florentinus, it would be wrong to consider Petra as one vast necropolis. Stand in the Temenos of the Kasr el Bint, west of the Triumphal Arch which spans the Colonnaded Street, and look to the north-east. There will be seen street upon street of house buildings with façades ranging from the simplest to the most ornate carved from the rock in ascending terraces. It was one of these that Margaret Murray excavated.

And, too, one can find evidence of Christianity in Petra. An inscription in the great Urn Tomb attests to the adoption of Christianity in this place, which by then, in A.D. 446, was but a shadow of its former glory though for the Christians it could still boast of a Bishop.

Naturally, because of Petra's place in Nabatean history and the overwhelming visual testimony of their civilisation, be it in architecture or pottery, on which I have not commented but which once seen and felt is ever to be remembered because of its thinness and beauty, it is often forgotten that an earlier people enjoyed its remoteness and safety. The agile and venturesome reader of the Old Testament may climb up Umm el Biyara, the great rock massif dominating Petra from the west and which gives an eagle's-nest view of Petra, 1,000 feet below. He will find no evidence to prove that this was the Rock from which King Amaziah of Judah cast down his 10,000 (!) Edomite captives. But he will see for himself some of the stone buildings of the seventh century B.C. village of the Edomites, that elusive, enigmatic people who flit intermittently across the pages of the Bible, who refused Moses passage through their territory on the return from Egypt, who invoked the wrath of the later prophets, notably Jeremiah, and who ultimately were dispossessed of their land by the Nabateans. Until such time as we archaeologists can mount large-scale excavations in Petra, which finally is the only way to unravel the intricate threads of all the influences which have been woven into the fabric of Petra's history, we must be grateful to the author for producing a much-needed book which gives a well-reasoned and fascinating general insight into the history of an unique capital of a phenomenal people.

1 May 1972   Crystal-M. Bennett
The British School of Archaeology in Jerusalem

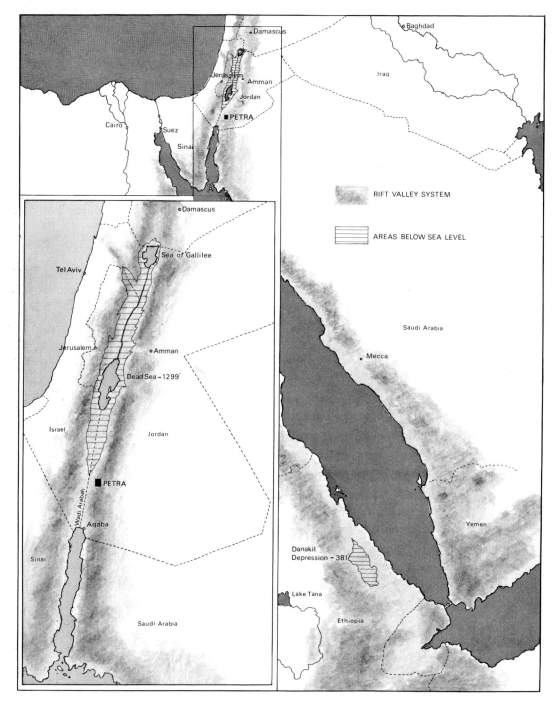

Map 1.   The Rift Valley System

CHAPTER ONE

The Beginning

PETRA lies hidden in the mountains which overlook the eastern side of the awesome Wadi Arabah, that part of the Rift Valley which runs between Aqaba and the Dead Sea. This Rift Valley is the dominant feature in the division between Palestine and the great bulk of the Near and Middle East and forms a natural frontier (Map 1). It is protected on both its sides by parallel ranges of high, rolling hills which extend far beyond the area of the Wadi to distant regions in the north and south.

To the north, the hills form a distant frame to the course of the River Jordan, encompass the Sea of Galilee, and ultimately draw close to face each other across the narrow Bekka valley in Lebanon. After the Bekka they dwindle away into the Syrian desert.

Southwards, the distance between them widens almost imperceptibly until the hills glower at each other across the head of the Gulf of Aqaba. From that point onwards they stand guard over the bright waters until the western range plunges into the sea at the tip of the Sinai Peninsula.

At Aqaba the eastern range turns lazily south-eastwards and arranges itself as a backdrop to the eastern shore of the Red Sea. About half-way down, in the distance between Medina and Mecca, it begins to gather momentum and becomes the barren highland whose jagged file runs through the Yemen and into the sea at Aden.

This simple geographical formation was known to the ancients, who found along the protecting mountains on the eastern shore an ideal route for the trade between Palestine, and thereby the Mediterranean, and the hinterland of the Hadramaut and the more distant world (Map 2). It is thus with the eastern side of the Red Sea, the Gulf of Aqaba and the Rift Valley that we are here concerned.

The Dead Sea (1,299 feet below the level of the Mediterranean) forced trade to travel up both sides of the valley. As there were more fresh-water springs on the eastern flank, a route became established on that side very early on. It is still in use today and carries the proud and ancient name of the King's Highway. At Petra, the trans-Arabian routes met the trans-Negev route to the great coastal emporium of Gaza.

The trade coming up the Rift Valley from Aqaba was not the only trade that

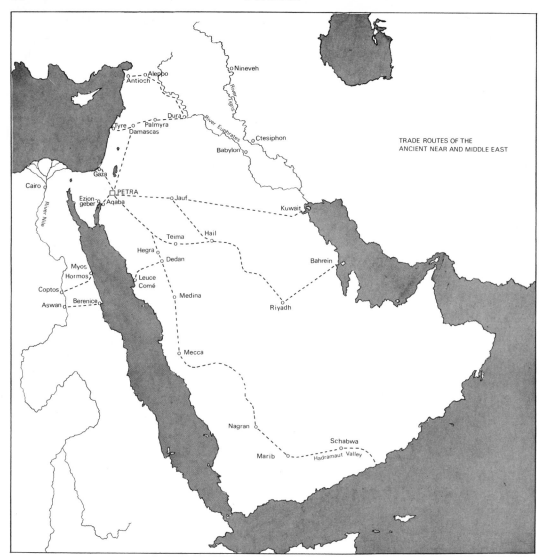

TRADE ROUTES OF THE
ANCIENT NEAR AND MIDDLE EAST

Map 2.   Trade Routes of the Ancient Middle East

plied in this part of the ancient world. The two great cradles of ancient civilisation, Mesopotamia and Egypt, needed by their very natures to make contact
even if it was only hostile rivalry. This was not easy however. Except for the early
Phoenicians, Man had not yet mastered the art of sailing other than for close
off-shore trips, and so land communications were the only practical means available. From the Mesopotamian alluvial flats of the Tigris and Euphrates valley
the land rises westward until it approaches the eastern edge of the Rift Valley.
At this point it has reached an altitude of something in the region of 3,000 feet
above sea-level—Mediterranean level—but it then suddenly sweeps up to

approximately 5,000 feet to form the long, high ridge which was the mountainous spine of the ancient kingdoms of Edom and Moab, and which still today dominates the tens of miles of desert stretching interminably back towards the east.

There is, in this mountainous ridge, an intrusion of two smaller parallel ridges, each of no great width. The one in the west is of Archean granite and it runs from just west of Petra, in the shape of the Porphyry Ridge, southwards to flank the sea on the eastern side of the Gulf of Aqaba, and thence along the coast. Between this granite ridge and the limitless Cretaceous sand and pebble desert that disappears into the heat haze in the direction of Mesopotamia, or as it is called today, Iraq, is a second ridge composed of the soft, dramatically coloured Nubian sandstone. This ridge begins as surface stone just south of the Dead Sea but soon becomes the succession of wind-swept, lofty hills that extend for as far as the eye can see. They are with you most of the time as you drive today along the Desert Highway, a long, rather sinister undulation which, if nothing else, adds a slight touch of variety to the soporific landscape that shimmers in the white sunlight.

This twin, and frequently interlocking couple of ridges, would have been a major obstacle athwart the lines of trade and communication between the peoples of the Nile and the Tigris/Euphrates valleys. If real contact was to be made, therefore, a convenient and practical route over or through the barrier would have to be found and thus permit the laden caravans to descend from the high deserts to the east into the Rift Valley. Just such a route was found near where the Wadi Mousa corkscrewed through an ancient fault in the rock barrier before releasing itself into the Wadi Arabah. This is the site of Petra. It marks, therefore, the cross-roads of two important trade routes of the ancient world.

Quite when the first organised trading establishment came into being is uncertain; it could possibly date as far back as the fifth century B.C. Trade would almost certainly have passed this way before then, using the site as a watering-place rather than as an emporium. Communications were still too irregular for the provision of organised facilities. Meetings by merchants were nothing more than chance encounters.

Water, however, was an essential which often determined the location of a major city or trading-post, and Petra's supply was beyond the wildest dreams of the most optimistic caravaner. The physical configuration of the mountains at this point would enable Man, if he was prepared to apply himself, to create a natural reservoir for the storage of water against even the harshest circumstances. The high, rolling limestone ridge in the east describes a wide semicircle, with parallel arms stretching out westward in the direction of the Wadi Arabah. It is subtended by two parallel folds of the exotically coloured Nubian sandstone, about a mile apart. The northern and southern ends are tipped up slightly, thus forming a natural basin. The Wadi Mousa flowed, and still does during the torrential winter rains, into this basin, but instead of being held there where it could be put to some good effect, it escapes down the spectacular Wadi Siyagh and spends itself wastefully in the hot sands of the Wadi Arabah.

The early settlers did nothing to undertake such necessary large-scale conservation but there is evidence that a limited provision was made for the long dry summers in the form of catchment channels which fed cisterns cut into the rock. The site is liberally scattered with cisterns of all ages and sizes but it is difficult to determine their age without associated evidence, and even this is not always wholly reliable.

The area known as Edom was occupied by a succession of tribes, some of which are recorded in the Bible. The Edomites, however, are the people of whom we must first take particular note. (The word 'Edom' means red; surely no name has ever been better given to a place unless it is the later name of 'Petra' which means 'Rock'.)

Unlike the Edomites who had mastered the arts of primitive metal-working, the Israelites, though habitual traders, were remarkably backward. Even when they entered the Promised Land they still could not make or sharpen their implements, let alone provide for domestic and decorative needs: they certainly had little metallurgical expertise, for this they learned from the Kenites.

The Wadi Arabah is liberally dotted with ancient copper slag heaps denoting extensive mining and working of the metal. The Khirbet Nahas site in particular, a name which in Arabic means 'Copper Ruin', was a great mining and smelting complex dating from well before Solomon. The recent 'Arabah Expedition' of Dr Beno Rothenberg, apart from establishing the great age of many of these sites, also showed conclusively that at least the Timna mines were of interest to the Egyptians. Under Seti I and Rameses III, mining expeditions were dispatched into the Arabah to develop the mineral resources. It should now be possible to identify the actual mines opened by Rameses III, an event described in the famous Harris I Papyri. Most of the Wadi Arabah sites were well guarded by forts and walls, either to keep foe out or slaves in. Copper and iron at so crucial a stage in Man's history were vital commodities, and it might be that the riches of the Arabah were originally as much the cause of the Edomite/Judean wars as the desire to control the trade routes.

Along these routes, despite the generally dangerous conditions, the merchants had continued to ply their trade to the obvious advantage of those who controlled the land over which they passed; here it was the land of Edom. The

Israelites, newly arrived in their Promised Land, no doubt saw this and realised that the wealth such trade brought would be an invaluable asset to their struggling economy. Unfortunately, this idea led to the subjugation of all potential, but weaker, rivals and the annexation of their sources of wealth: the fact that Egypt was stronger on land and the Phoenicians were stronger on sea was the reason why they were not engaged in conflict by Israel.

The conquest and enslavement of Edom did, however, provide the Israelites with a bonus. They won control not only of the trade routes but also of a large supply of an important commodity of trade, slaves. The Jews had a reputation as slave-owners and slave-traders. Joseph being sold by his brothers was nothing exceptional in their annals; our childhood familiarity with the story, and the fact that all ended happily ever after, has deprived us of our capacity to see objectively its true significance and horror. A happy ending was one case in a million, and a turn of real bad luck for the brothers who had had every reason to expect that they were rid of their tiresome kin for good: with most other poor unfortunates things went according to plan and they were never seen or heard of again. The merchants to whom Joseph was sold evinced no great surprise at the spectacle of some Jews selling their younger brother into slavery.

This was no doubt an expedient and profitable way of getting rid of an unwanted member of the family, but as a source of supply one's family and 'friends' were strictly limited. Prisoners of war, on the other hand, were quite another proposition. An almost constant state of armed conflict seems to have existed between the Jews and their neighbours, be it a local skirmish or a full-scale war, and this would have meant that there must always have been a batch of prisoners somewhere. Prisoners of war fetched good prices, for the majority were strong, powerfully built men with several years of useful labour ahead of them.

Such a fate was the most that the soldiers of a vanquished army could expect; the same would have applied to the civilian population of any race that had been subjugated. When the Jews took possession of the Promised Land they immediately enslaved the native population, looking on them as having been given to them by God; one only needs to read Leviticus 25, 44 : 46: 'And as for thy bondman, and thy bondmaids, which thou shalt have; of the heathen that are round about you, of them shall ye buy bondmen and bondmaids. Moreover of the children of the strangers that do sojourn among you, of them shall ye buy, and of their families that are with you, which they have begotten in your land: and they shall be your possession. And ye shall make them an inheritance for your children after you, to hold for a possession; of them shall ye take your bondmen for ever . . .'

The amount of incoming trade that passed through southern Edom can be

judged from an entry in the First Book of Kings 10, 14 : 15 : 'the weight of gold
that came to Solomon in one year was sixhundred threescore and six (666)
talents of gold. Beside that he had of the merchants, and of the traffic of the spice
merchants, and of all the kings of Arabia, and of the governors of the country'.
Here is Solomon importing gold as well as receiving it in taxes from merchants
and as tribute from subject princes.

No evidence was found by Dr Rothenberg to suggest that the mines on the
western side of the Wadi Arabah were being worked during the reign of
Solomon. Whether this was the case with the mines on the eastern side we do
not know; Mrs Bennett's forthcoming excavations should go a long way to
finding out. But from present information it would appear that there was no
great traffic in copper during his reign, at least in metal derived from the Wadi
Arabah.

Once he had control of Edom and its trade, Solomon went all out to develop
it to its maximum capacity. The old port of Eloth which had sufficed the
Edomites was totally inadequate to handle the tonnage he wanted to see passing
through, nor had it the facilities on a scale large enough to accommodate his
navy. Recent researches, however, make it probable that Solomon's port of
Ezion-Geber was not Eloth but Jeziret Faroun (the island of Pharaoh) further
down the Sinai coast of the Gulf of Aqaba.

Solomon imported luxury stuffs for the 'sweet life' to which the Hebrews
became accustomed during the palmy days of his reign. It is recorded that the
Queen of Sheba brought gifts of gold, spices and costly stones; the navy of Hiram
arrived with costly stones and almug trees—Solomon was famous for his gardens
—while the Tarshish fleet brought gold, silver, ivory, apes and peacocks. The
prophet Jeremiah refers to sugar as 'sweet cane from a far country'.

The whole Mediterranean basin at this time was waking up to the comfortable
side of civilisation and there was a considerable demand for luxuries. The opulence of Solomon's court was furnished to a remarkable extent with imported
goods and these had to be paid for: it must have been a staggering expense even
with his wealth and after discounting all that he received in taxes and in kind
from merchants and by way of tribute. This illustrates very clearly the value of
the trade passing up the Wadi Arabah: the Promised Land might have been
a dream of fertility to the Israelites after what they had known in their wanderings, but its natural products would hardly have amounted to very much in the
open market of world trade.

Goods arriving either by the land route or by sea at Ezion-Geber would have
been dispatched up to the Petra area where they would have been forwarded on
to other centres which were either 'next-stages' or terminals. Apart from becoming centres of manufacture and fabricated goods these terminals also became

established as slave markets. If we turn again to the prophet Amos we find him levelling complaints against the city of Gaza. It would appear that that city had a very well established, indeed famous, slave market. This contention is borne out to some extent by the fact that when Hadrian suppressed the Jews' revolt in A.D. 119, he sold the rebels into slavery at Gaza where, presumably, he was sure of getting the best possible sale price. Being the Mediterranean terminus of the eastern trade routes nearest to Egypt, it was natural that Gaza should become established as a great commercial centre akin to Alexandria, Tyre and Seleucia (the port for Antioch). There would, in fact, have been considerable rivalry between Gaza and Alexandria. The two were in direct competition as emporia from which the whole of the Mediterranean could be supplied with the trade that came up the Red Sea from the east. Gaza gained by being so close to Petra, where the two trans-Arabian routes converged with the coastal route up from the Hadramaut. From Petra there was also an extension of the route right up to the terminus of Damascus in the north. With all this chance of trade and variety of markets available it was natural that the merchants should direct their caravans through Petra, with the result that Gaza received the best of the Mediterranean-bound trade.

Alexandria, for all the greatness and power of Egypt, had no such variety of opportunity with which to attract the all-important merchants: the Egyptians were not averse, however, to forcing the merchants' ships sailing up the Red Sea to put into Egyptian ports such as Berenice or Myos Hormos, from where the cargo would be transported overland to the Nile at Koptos below Aswan and then floated downstream to Alexandria. This tactic would have further discouraged merchants from using sea routes in the early days, until their fleets and the nations which supported them had grown sufficiently strong to fend off the grasping Egyptians. Again, it was very much a case of who was powerful at any particular time when it came to deciding which way trade was going to be directed: the Ancient Near and Middle East saw the rise and fall of a succession of mighty empires which brought a constantly changing centre of emphasis both politically and economically. For centuries the Egyptians had it all their own way: that amazing civilisation which rose in the valley of the Nile dominated the Near Eastern scene in a way which few other empires have ever done. With the rise of Hebrew power and their short dominance of the area, and later under the Nabateans, the eastern route came into its own with all the attendant benefit for Petra and the land that had been known as Edom but which was now called Arabia Petraea—Rocky Arabia.

There is considerable evidence that trade with China was being conducted by the Near East well before the first century A.D. Chinese records refer to the place at which trade was transacted as Li-Kan, which it has been suggested could be a corruption of Rekem, the name by which Petra was originally known according to the historian Josephus and other writers. However, it could also have been Leuce Come on the coast just west of Dedan and which was the southernmost port of the Nabatean kingdom.

One route would certainly have been round the coast of the Indian sub-continent, where possibly the Chinese would have transshipped from their own vessels into Arab ones, and then on until the Straits of Hormuz, which connect the Gulf of Oman and the Persian Gulf, were reached. The ships could then either coast round the Arabian Peninsula to the Hadramaut ports or proceed up the Gulf and discharge at Bahrein or Kuwait. The vessels that went to the Hadramaut had the choice of either proceeding through the Straits of Bab el Mandeb and up the Red Sea to Aqaba, or of discharging their cargo and sending it up the long valley of the Hadramaut *en route* for Mecca via Beled Najran. By this latter route the whole of the Aden/Yemen massif was skirted. From Mecca the route went northwards to Medina and the great caravanserai of Dedan which was located in a deep and spectacular valley, reminiscent in some ways of Petra itself. It was either here, or at Hegra, now called Medain Saleh, seven and a half miles to the north, that the Nabateans would have taken over the merchandise and forwarded it through their lands on the next leg of the journey which would have taken in Petra with either Gaza or Damascus as the final terminus.

The cargoes discharged at either Bahrein or Kuwait were sent over the Arabian Desert, below the Jebel Shammar range, direct to Petra. This was a hazardous route involving many days' journey across most inhospitable desert. Whichever route was taken, be it by land or by sea, it passed through Petra. Nature had blessed it with abundant water of which the traders very naturally took advantage.

The only remaining principal trade routes of the ancient Middle and Near East were those by which cargoes were discharged at the head of the Persian Gulf—possibly at Spasim Charax—and transported up the banks of the Tigris to Ctesiphon. From here two routes were open to the traveller and his goods. One was across the Mesopotamian lowland desert in the direction of Palmyra and thence on to the Levantine ports. Alternatively, the Euphrates was followed as far as Dura or Thapsacus, before crossing the Syrian highlands to Aleppo with Antioch as the final call. It was the development by the Romans of these alternative routes which avoided Petra, in particular the Palmyra passage, which led to the ultimate decline and vanishing prosperity of Petra with the final consequence of its disappearance as a trading-post.

It is curious that, although the evidence of trade with China is so strong, no articles of Chinese manufacture have ever been discovered in Petra. This, however, rather than disproving the argument, suggests that all imports from that quarter were perishables such as spices, and above all silk thread and cloth, none of which could have stood the test of time in that climate.

By the time the Nabateans were in control of erstwhile Edom, about the beginning of the fourth century B.C., trade was well established. It was these tough Arab people who lifted it, and no doubt the revenue from it, to unprecedented heights. The Hellenistic world would have been able to absorb most of the available supply and China in its turn is recorded as importing 'henna, storax, frankincense, asbestos cloth, silk gauze, damask, glass, orpiment, gold and silver'. The export of silk gauze and damask to China of all places might at first seem rather like sending the proverbial coals to Newcastle, but in fact it indicates that the Near East had developed certain new techniques of weaving silk which were not practised in China at that date. These techniques were peculiar to certain cities, bringing them a great reputation which has to some extent persisted even into this twentieth century; Damascus gave its name to that fabric known as damask while Gaza, or so it is said, gave its name to the manufacture of gauze. Both cities were terminals of the eastern trade routes.

Imports were also received from India; Pliny in his *Natural History*, mentions a few commodities such as ginger and pepper, sugar and cotton as well as a medicament called Lycion which was shipped in leather bottles. Perfumes, chief of which was frankincense, were also on the list.

When one thinks that all this trade frequently passed through Petra, it is hardly surprising that the city became wealthy. Peace, however, precedes prosperity and the area was seldom peaceful. It took the genius of the Nabateans so to protect the trade routes that they were able to draw the maximum benefit in terms of revenue from the traffic which passed along them.

CHAPTER TWO

The Peoples of the Wadi Mousa

I

WHEN discussing the peoples who have successively inhabited the Wadi Mousa, in which Petra lies, it is not possible to give a continuous history. Far too little is known. Episodes erupt suddenly and unheralded into the limelight, only to be followed as quickly by long periods of total silence. A complete catalogue of historical fragments would be out of place here, therefore only those events which either bear directly on Petra or indicate something of the character of its people are mentioned.

The site has certainly been frequented by Man from prehistoric times, but the first people of whom we must take note are the Edomites. It is thought that they never occupied the actual site of the city of Petra (Fig. 1) but preferred to stick to the hills which are set so magnificently about it. Throughout the Old Testament there are terse mentions of them: these are nearly always critical and damning, for a state of ferocious hostility persisted between them and the Hebrews. The reasons for this mutual hatred are not known. Perhaps it was that during the Exodus the Edomite 'king', Rekem, refused the wanderers passage through his lands, necessitating a vast detour before they could reach their Promised Land. And yet the future King David went to a friendly Edom to hide from the fury of King Saul.

One would have thought that when David eventually became king, in about 1,000 B.C., he would have shown some gratitude and favour towards the Edomites who had protected him during the previous reign. Not a bit of it, he promptly attacked Moab and Edom and subdued them, exterminating two-thirds of the former and leaving his general, Joab, to massacre every male Edomite he could find. Admittedly the Edomites had been raiding Palestine on a regular basis for a very long time but the ferocity of the retribution was somewhat extreme. A Song of Triumph seems to have been in order on such occasions, and King David did himself proud on this particular one if the sixtieth Psalm is anything to go by: the Jews revelled in their Songs of Triumph—indeed made something of an art form of them. But when the tables were eventually turned, they took grave exception to the terms of the Edomite Song of Triumph. God was called upon to witness their suffering before such a display of uncharitableness.

Fig. 1 The desolated city area of Petra from the Urn Tomb. By the first century A.D. the low hills on either side of the Wadi were thickly covered with buildings. Most of the area still awaits excavation.

The whole history of the Edomites after this appears to be a continual state of hostility with the Hebrews—particularly Judah. They suffered from a succession of disastrous confederacies with their northern neighbours Moab and Ammon—or both—all of which were ruthlessly smashed by their oppressors.

It came to such a point that during the reign of Solomon, the people of Edom were not enslaved as they had been in the reign of David. Finer feelings for a relative people are unlikely to have been the motive for this: it is much more probable that during the previous reign the population of Edom had been so savagely depleted that it was necessary to release them to prevent the land from going out of cultivation altogether and returning to the desert.

There were moments when Edom regained her independence for a short while, but this required that they wage a ferocious and unrelenting war against the Judeans in order to keep it. No doubt the Judeans looked upon a free Edom as a very real threat to its control of the trade and copper of the Wadi Arabah. One is amazed at the pluck and sheer-dogged determination of the Edomites in their efforts to remain their own masters against ever-pressing and considerable odds. The almost constant massacres they seem to have suffered lead one to wonder where their forces came from: each time there was a battle it was recorded that the people of Edom were virtually exterminated.

An incident in this blood-stained fabric of ancient history is often quoted as having taken place in Petra. It is a gory tale which adds no end to the inventive virtuosity of the local guides today, but the sad truth is that in all probability it did not happen at Petra at all.

The Edomites had been on a raiding party, marauding and pillaging in southern Palestine, when they came up against the king of Judah, Amaziah (796–781 B.C.). A great battle ensued in which the Edomites were roundly beaten. It should be noted that at no stage in the chronicle is the size or strength of either party given; it could have been the confrontation of armies or just of small bands. Hotly pursued by Amaziah, the Edomites, or what was left of them, fled back across the Wadi Arabah to their refuge in their 'last stronghold', the great Biblical Sela—which means 'a rock'. Before the enemy had a chance to reorganise themselves, Amaziah launched an attack and took the stronghold by storm. 'He slew of Edom in the Valley of Salt (that part of the Wadi Arabah immediately south of the Dead Sea) ten thousand and took Selah by war' (11 Kings 14, 7), and as is frequently told, proceeded to throw the remaining ten thousand Edomites from the top of the rock to their deaths below. 'And Amaziah strengthened himself, and led forth his people, and went to the Valley of Salt, and smote of the children of Seir (Edom) ten thousand. And other ten thousand left alive did the children of Judah carry away captive, and brought them unto the top of the rock, and cast them down from the top of the rock, that they all were broken in pieces' (11 Chronicles 25, 11 : 12).

The general and popular idea is that Sela, the rock mentioned in these accounts, is the towering, sinister mountain Umm el Biyara (Fig. 2) which dominates almost every aspect of Petra. There is certainly an Edomite settlement on the top but the excavations conducted by Mrs Crystal-M. Bennett revealed evidence of only a small unfortified settlement dating from not earlier than the seventh century B.C. It appears also to have been occupied during the sixth century B.C. but was then abandoned by the Edomites after destruction by fire. The Amaziah story took place long before the settlement was founded. As there is no evidence whatsoever of a 'stronghold' on the top which could contain a whole nation or even a small part of one, one is forced to the conclusion that this is not the Sela which Amaziah took 'by war'. Scholars are still uncertain as to

Fig. 2 Umm el Biyara, the mountain which dominates the site of Petra.

exactly where Sela might have been, for in the kingdom of Edom many sites would have justified so graphic a name as the 'Rock'.

On closer inspection there are other inconsistencies in the two accounts. Both record the battle in the Valley of Salt, but the Book of Kings version goes on to relate that Sela was taken 'by war', whereas the Book of Chronicles just mentions that the Edomites were 'brought unto the top of the rock' for the enactment of this grisly pantomime: there is no mention of any battle to capture it. For those who do not know Umm el Biyara, reference to the photographs in this volume will show the utter futility of trying to take the mountain by storm: a modern platoon or even a section, armed with conventional weapons could hold off almost indefinitely the bellicose attentions of a whole army. It is one of nature's most impregnable fortresses. Likewise, it would seem an almost impossible task, quite apart from being a ludicrous exercise, to bring ten thousand captives, all most unwilling travellers, up that tortuous and perilous climb just to have the satisfaction of throwing them off the top.

An important fact to remember is that the Hebrew word 'alaf' meaning 'thousands' can also be translated as 'families', 'clans' or 'tents'. There are several instances in the Bible where the early translators opted for the more spectacular number, but on reading the context in which they appear one becomes aware that one of the other meanings would fit much more sensibly and appropriately.

The denial of Umm el Biyara raises questions of what happened, how many people were involved and where the incident took place. The last is actually quite an unimportant question in the present context, which is fortunate because still nobody is very sure. Various suggestions have been put forward as to the site of Sela. To answer the other two questions it is necessary to have a look at the Edomites themselves and to try to visualise the structure of the Edomite state and the nature of Edomite society. This is not easy, for detailed information is still very limited.

We know that they had a great reputation among the Jews for wisdom, so much so that even Jeremiah, who was sparing to a degree with his praise, was heard to comment 'Concerning Edom, saith the Lord of hosts: Is wisdom no more in Teman (Teiman?), is council perished from the prudent? is their wisdom vanished?' Other writers in the Bible tell us that the Edomites knew writing though it may not have been much practised; this was almost inevitable considering their proximity to Egypt with its huge cultural tradition. Cloth was manufactured in Edom, which means that spinning and weaving were practised. Women seem to have enjoyed a decent place in the society, which is always an encouraging sign. As masons they were poor workmen but when it came to the manufacture of pottery they excelled in a way that put them well in the lead.

Their pottery was of a quality and fineness equal almost to the later Nabatean work, with a creamy slip much decorated with bands of colour which makes it very distinctive. Of their religion we know only a little. It would seem that they were idolaters, with their gods approximating very closely to the early gods of the Hebrews. As it is, we do not know of any Edomite places of worship in Petra which would justify an exposition on Edomite religion in this work.

Of their social laws and customs we also have only a limited amount of information, but we can hazard some calculations as to the structure of their society. In the early days the Edomites had been conquered by Pharaoh Rameses III. His victory is recorded on the walls of his great temple at Medinet Habu and shows the chief of the Shasu (Seir), along with six other captive chiefs, kneeling before the Pharaoh. Over his head is written 'Chief of the foe of the Shasu'. The use of the word 'chief' is interesting for it gives us a clue to the type of leader in Edom at that time. He is not referred to as 'king'. It seems likely that the Edomite state was something in the nature of a confederation of cities or communes tied together very closely by their bond of common blood. Each commune was ruled by a 'Chief' and acted and existed economically very much on its own. The size of each commune varied enormously, ranging from a full-scale city such as the capital to a local village which accommodated only a few families. It has been suggested that Tawilan (Fig. 3), which overlooks Ain Mousa and the entrance to the Siq of Petra, might have been the southern provincial capital, which would equate with the Biblical Teman which is cited as being one of the main Edomite cities. The site has recently been partially excavated under the direction of Mrs Crystal-M. Bennett, the project being sponsored by the British School of Archaeology in Jerusalem, and it is upon material found there that much of our revised knowledge of the Edomites is based. The occupation of the site was from the end of the ninth century to the sixth century B.C., if not later, which would make it a Middle Edomite Period settlement. Evidence of occupation dating back to about 4,000 B.C. was found on and near this large and impressive site, which makes it a vital link in the ancient history of Jordan.

To return to the Amaziah story, it can be said with reasonable certainty that the event did not take place on Umm el Biyara however much this may deprive the Petra tour pundits of a good story. At this stage any reconstruction of the event is bound to be conjecture but the following appears to fit the known facts. A commune of reasonable size, say a dozen or so families, sent their menfolk off on a raid into Judah, leaving their families at their 'stronghold'. This would probably have been sited in a good defensive position on one of the innumerable cliffs overlooking the Wadi Arabah. The marauding party ran into trouble when King Amaziah appeared on the scene with a sizeable body of troops—news of unwelcome visitors travels fast in the desert. A skirmish took place in which

Fig. 3 The site of the Edomite settlement at Tawilan, overlooking the barrier ranges which hide Petra.

virtually all the Edomites were wiped out by the vastly superior Judean force. Those who did manage to escape fled back to their commune and thereby gave its position away to the pursuing army. Although the position was a good one from the point of defence, it was not good enough to withstand the avenging Judeans who swept in and drove the 'families' they found there back to the edge of the protecting cliff. The story needs no further elaboration. This would have been a total disaster for that particular commune but would not have meant the destruction of the whole Edomite race as is so often implied, and so often construed from Biblical accounts. Other Edomite communes would have been left to fight the Judeans another day.

Much of the history which we have been able to piece together is based on Biblical accounts. So long as the Jews were masters of their own fortunes we have records of their dealings, peaceful but more often warlike, with their neighbours such as Ammon, Moab and Edom. When, however, a much more serious threat is presented to them, their chronicles become too preoccupied with the greater perils to dwell over much on the irritations caused by the Edomites. The result is a marked decline in the amount and quality of information concerning the neighbour states. Just such a greater peril was the advent of the Assyrians in the early part of the eighth century. This does not mean that there was any lessening of the hostilities between the Hebrews and their neighbours—particularly Edom: the mutual hatred was too deeply founded and their suspicion of one another too intense to permit any rapprochement.

Edom seems to have been considered the richest of the transjordanian trio, Edom, Moab and Ammon, for Esarhaddon, King of Assyria, is recorded as

receiving from the provincial governors the following tributes which they would
have collected:

   Two mannas of gold from King Pudiel of Ammon
   One manna of gold from King Musuri of Moab
   Twelve mannas of silver from King Qaush-gaber of Edom.

In addition, Edom is recorded as having paid part of their tribute in 'costly
stones'. Quite what is meant by this we cannot be sure but these could have
included minor gem stones like garnets and topaz or small pieces of the gor-
geously coloured and veined mineral, malachite, which is a close associate of
copper. 'Costly stones' could also mean building stones of bright colours and
striking appearance such as are found in abundance in the valleys around Petra.

   Mention of King Qaush-gaber of Edom brings us direct into Petra—indeed
to Umm el Biyara. During the excavations of the Edomite settlement on the top,
a seal-impression, which would have been attached to a letter or proclamation
addressed to the inhabitants of the rock, was found (Fig. 111). This was the first
royal seal-impression ever to be found in Jordan or Palestine. Apart from being
interesting in itself, it is significant historically because it denotes that the Umm
el Biyara settlement, though small, was considered not unimportant. This seal-
impression must not be confused with the scarab bearing possibly the symbol
of the Edomite deity, Qaush, which was found at Tawilan (Fig. 4).

   The last of the Edomites is a sad, irrevocable
coda to their whole history. As usual it is poorly
documented and it is only the written records of
others' hate which tells us of the part they played:
the Edomites' records have either not survived or
been found, that is if they kept any, and they left
to posterity few of the evidences which are associated with civilised people. To refer to them as
barbarians on the strength of this would be to do
them a grave injustice for they achieved, in their
own terms, a remarkably high degree of cultural
attainment which was matched not only by their
considerable prosperity in the face of dishearten-
ing odds, but also by the mental, if not intellectual,
stature of the people themselves. To have held on

Fig. 4 The scarab found in the
Tawilan excavations; possibly repre-
senting the symbol of the Edomite
god 'Kaush'.

to their way of life and to have developed it over so many centuries without
giving in to all the ferocity of the archaic Near East was something nearing a
miracle.

   The once all-powerful Assyrian Empire lay in ruins, shattered by the new star
of the Middle East, the second Babylonian Empire. Nineveh, the hated capital

of the Assyrians—yet one of the most wondrous cities of the ancient world—had fallen to the combined forces of the Babylonians and the Chaldeans (a people from the Persian Gulf) in 612 B.C., leaving the Near and Middle East in a state of shock after so many years of firm—if harsh—control. Rebellion on all fronts had broken out into the open, with Egypt, as usual, endeavouring to make the most of the opportunity: their main aim was to prevent Babylon moving into the place of power vacated by the fallen Nineveh. Their greed caused them to fail lamentably when matched with the clear purpose of the Babylonians who ultimately drove back the Egyptian armies in 605 B.C. to the place from which they had come. Babylon took over from Assyria, replacing a harsh, rigid, tyrannous but brilliantly organised regime with a more generous attitude alongside equally firm control. Judah would have none of it: for too long they had called the tune and now hated the idea of dancing when someone else called it. Within seven years they were in full revolt against Babylon with Moab and Edom as allies. The end came when, after a two-year siege, Jerusalem fell in 587 B.C. All buildings, including Solomon's fabled Temple and Palace, were burned to the ground and all remaining walls levelled to one vast pile of rubble. The land on both sides of the Jordan was full of fleeing, broken men seeking refuge from the holocaust. Many made their way to the comparative safety of the high hills of Edom and hid there. King Zedekiah of Judah was led away with his court and all Jews of any consequence into captivity in Babylon, leaving only the poorest and simplest of the people to watch the walls of Jerusalem come crashing down.

The Edomites, to whom Jerusalem had been a symbol of Judean tyranny, revelled in the sight, and although they had had no hand in the exercise, they produced their own Song of Triumph. 'Down with it, down with it, even to the ground', they sang jubilantly and the Jews remembered the humiliation. In the 137th Psalm they called on their God, 'Remember, O Lord, the children of Edom in the day of Jerusalem; how they said, Down with it, down with it, even to the ground.'

The land of Judah lay empty and unprotected but for a few peasants. The Edomites gazed down from their inhospitable hills on to the green valleys and rolling hills of Judah. Tentatively at first, as though not daring to believe their luck, they came down, a few at a time, to take possession of their enemy's land. When they found that the way was clear they flooded down in their scores, out across the inviting landscape into a new life without the Jews.

Little is known of the next few decades but it is believed that about 580 B.C. the Nabateans were beginning to move into erstwhile Edom. Whether it was that they were pushing the Edomites out or not we do not know. Present indications are that they arrived and intermarried with those who had remained after the bulk of the race had gone down the hill to the pastures of Judah (see pages 32–33).

The Edomites who had gone to Judah set up a new kingdom of Edom which the Greeks called Idumea—a straight corruption of 'Edomea'. They obviously made little or no provision against —attack who was there to attack them, for the focal point of history had moved over to the Mesopotamian Valley. There, however, things had changed again; Babylon in its turn had fallen to a new empire which had risen further to the east, Persia.

In about 500 B.C., the Persians allowed some of the captive Jews to return to Palestine and their arrival triggered off further trouble. The Idumeans and the Jews, though so closely related, lived separate lives but no doubt plagued each other with raids. Ultimately the new Judeans were strong enough to contest Idumea and this they did when John Hycanus (135–105 B.C.) crushed the old Edomites and forced them to integrate into not only the Jewish state but also into the Jewish religion. This was the end of the Edomites.

The great old kingdoms of Edom and Moab had ceased to exist as organised entities in that period after the fall of Jerusalem, when chaos reigned. Weakened irretrievably by centuries of war, they had at long last no more stamina to resist and just vanished from the face of history.

We do not know the cause of the bitter enmity between Israel/Judah and the Edomites. Various suggestions have been put forward including the copper mines of the Wadi Arabah and the value of the trade passing through the country. Undoubtedly both these were contributory factors even if they were not the actual cause, but the real hatred seems to have started when King David repaid the hospitality and favour of the Edomites with a savage and brutal attack. Not content with this he had aimed at genocide. If an attempt at racial extermination is not a good start to souring mutual good relations with that country one wonders what is.

II

Before passing on to the Nabateans, with whom Petra is quite rightly so firmly associated, it is worth taking a brief look at the last few years of the Chaldean or Neo-Babylonian Empire before it fell to the Achaemenians, or Persians, in 539 B.C., for they inherited not only the imperialistic policies and power of the Assyrians but also the remnants of Mesopotamian culture. The Assyrians had developed certain architectural characteristics which the Neo-Babylonians hastily adopted: this amounted to a taste for monumental architecture—the famous Istar Gate with its guardian lions is an example. This cult of the massive had a certain impact on the more refined sensibilities of the Babylonians whose only intellectual diversion or occupation at that time was 'to contemplate its past glories'.

The Neo-Babylonian Empire, like all empires in the archaic Middle East, depended on trade. With the Medes controlling the trade routes to the east it was necessary that they maintain control of those in the west, hence Nebuchadnezzar's campaign in Palestine and the sack of Jerusalem. He even attempted to invade Egypt but without success.

In the last two or three reigns, the Empire was getting shakier and shakier, indeed was almost falling apart. But the last king of Babylon, Nabonidus (555–539 B.C.), made the most enormous efforts to salvage the situation by spending most of his time in western Arabia establishing military colonies along the line of the famous 'incense route' between the oasis of Teima and the city of Yathrib (modern Medina). Building and architectural traditions would certainly have been carried with him, for to build even military forts for military colonies you need masons and craftsmen whether they are military or not, and it is with craftsmen that cultural traditions travel fastest and surest.

When a tradition, however, lives for a century or more out of its original national environment it is bound to change and produce bastards of its kind. The early architectural style of Petra (Fig. 5), particularly as used in the monumental-carved façades, was just such a bastard, being a direct descendant from the work of the Neo-Babylonian craftsmen who went to western Arabia with King Nabonidus up to 539 B.C., but who never returned.

It was perhaps because of all this military activity on the part of the Neo-Babylonians in their attempts to secure the trade routes in north-western Arabia, that the local nomadic tribes felt it was time to move on. For a long time they had made a good living by plundering the caravans that passed, but with the

Fig. 5 The 'Streets of Façades' area in the Outer Siq.

tightening up on Babylonian security, life was becoming a bit difficult. Certain of their number had already gone north to new pastures and were finding the depopulated old kingdom of Edom very agreeable after the parched and uninviting desert to which they were used. There was no one to stop them from going, for Babylon, in its turn, had fallen and the Persian hordes under Cyrus had not yet extended their interests and activities across the whole of the Middle East. These nomadic people, about whose origins there is still considerable debate, were called the Nabateans.

III

From the evidence we have at the moment it seems that the arrival of the Nabateans was a protracted affair and that far from driving out the remaining Edomites, they integrated with them. At the end of the century so many Nabateans had arrived that the positions became reversed and it was the Edomites who were integrating with the Nabateans. In this context, the recently (1968) found Late Edomite pottery excavated at Tawilan may be taken as something of an indication. Its character is so remarkably akin to Nabatean pottery that it seems quite possible that it is the forerunner of that extremely beautiful ware. If one accepts this to be so, it would mean that the new arrivals were taught this craft by the Edomites.

When discussing the relations between the Nabateans and the Edomites it is well to remember this distinction between settled and nomadic peoples. The Edomites had been settled for a great many years and therefore their attitudes to life would have been markedly different from those of the nomadic Nabateans. The slowness with which the Nabateans arrived and the small numbers they came in in the early stages would have been an important consideration when it came to establishing a friendly rapport with the understandably suspicious and embittered Edomites. By the turn of the century the Edomites would have had time to get used to the newcomers, and in fact might well have started teaching them a few of the things which led them ultimately to adopt a sedentary life. It is quite possible that the new, Edomite-style, outlook and behaviour of the first- and second-generation Petran Nabatean would have surprised those who came later and were still imbued with all the old nomadic concepts. Settlement of people is a lengthy business, for old habits die hard: it is for this reason that it is believed that nothing Nabatean in Petra dates from much before 300 B.C.

The fact that both the Edomites and the Nabateans claimed descent from Ishmael would have provided at least some common ground for integration. One of Esau's three wives was a woman called Bashemath, who had a sister called Nabaioth, both being daughters of Ishmael: the Edomites claimed descent from Bashemath and the Nabateans from Nabaioth.

Before their arrival in Edom, and possibly for a long time afterwards, the Nabateans had lived as shepherds, augmenting their living with frequent bouts of caravan raiding. They were, however, a quite remarkably adaptable people as their subsequent history shows: this was an asset, but as nothing compared with their genius for trade and administration. It was they who first realised that it would be much less arduous and dangerous as well as a lot more lucrative to police the trade routes which passed through their lands. A safe passage is something a merchant will pay well for, especially if there is a chance of good business as well.

The Edomites never actually inhabited the exposed central area of Petra as far as we know. The Nabateans, however, saw the possibilities of the wadi-side site (Colour Plate 3b, facing page 128) and in the fullness of time laid out a city which had a population of something in the region of 30,000.

Being of nomadic origin, it is extremely unlikely that they embarked upon the building of a city immediately they arrived. Sherds from Greek vases dating from about 300 B.C. have, however, been found in Petra on the south rubbish-dump near the Faroun Pillar, and similarly dated material has been found in the excavations of the wadi-side of the Colonnade Street. The latter were found in association with roughly constructed walls. Both these instances indicate that at least some form of urban development was taking place by the year 300 B.C. The chronological record of the city's development is still to come and its preparation will depend on the results of years of archaeological excavation and examination of the site. Most of the visible remains are believed to date from the Roman period though, as with all towns, the ancient is worked in with the new creating a fabric of the utmost complexity, richness and fascination. It may well be, therefore, that much of the Roman fabric was integrated very carefully into the existing Nabatean work where it was considered that the latter was worth keeping.

An account written by the classical author Diodorus Siculus suggests that there was no city worth a mention on the site during the early occupation by the Nabateans. He did not write, however, from first-hand knowledge but from what appears to have been Seleucid records. He refers to Petra (by that name) as 'a rock . . . extremely strong but without walls'. This undoubtedly refers to Umm el Biyara for a Nabatean settlement—including possibly a temple—has been found on the top of that awe-inspiring mountain. It is more likely that the Nabateans had some semi-nomadic type of settlement in the valley—near the stream seems logical—and used the massif of Umm el Biyara as a refuge and base camp.

Siculus's account continues with the story of an attack mounted by the Greek ruler of Syria, Antigonus, in 312 B.C. It was part of his campaign to suppress the

Nabateans and spike the guns of Ptolemaic Egypt. His Commander-in-Chief, Athanaeus, crept in under the cover of darkness, arriving just after midnight. He found that the male population had gone off to a 'fair'—probably the usual impromptu market occasioned by the arrival of a caravan at the mouth of the Siq—leaving the rock undefended by all except a few old men and some women and children. The Greek troops, or some of them, for there were as many as 4,000 infantry and 600 cavalry, stormed and occupied the site. Hurriedly they grabbed all the booty they could find—amounting to some 500 talents of silver as well as quantities of frankincense and myrrh—and departed. One of the defenders must have got away in the general confusion for within the hour the menfolk had returned and were taking stock of the situation. This would not have taken very long for they were soon in hot pursuit of the invaders. The Greeks probably did not expect a reprisal until later in the morning, so had been somewhat nonchalant in the setting of their guards. The Nabateans swept in on them, massacring all but fifty of the cavalry who managed to escape. The Nabateans then withdrew with all their property regained.

Once back at the Rock, they sent a slightly apologetic letter to Antigonus explaining the whole incident. Antigonus pretended to accept the explanation and sent back the most felicitous reply, blaming the whole affair on the dead Athanaeus who he said had acted without orders. No doubt this was a bare-faced lie for there can be certainty that Antigonus had his eye on the profits of the trade passing through Petra and had instigated the attack himself. After a discreet lapse of time, during which he hoped that the Nabateans would drop their guard, he sent another army under the command of his son, Demetrius, to storm the Nabateans. They, however, still having much of the bedouin in them, were suspicious of the wily Greek king and when Demetrius arrived he found the stronghold—the Rock—stoutly defended by a small force. The remainder of the Nabateans had, on hearing of the advancing army, packed up all their belongings and departed into the secrecy and safety of the mountainous desert. Demetrius's attempts to storm the Rock were futile and in the end he allowed himself to be bought off with 'such gifts as are most precious among them . . .'

Some interesting points arise from this story. The first and most important is that the Nabateans evidently did not trust anybody—least of all a Greek—and that above all they wanted peace. The business of running an emporium could not prosper in wartime, hence the pacifying note to Antigonus when their natural inclination must have been to send an infuriated note of protest. The mention of frankincense and myrrh indicates that Petra was already established as a trading centre with 'warehouse' facilities for the storage of goods awaiting transit. The fact that they were able to pack up their valuables and carry them off into the desert at a moment's notice points to the Nabateans being still partly settled and yet clinging to many of the ways of the nomad: a fully urbanised and sedentary population would never have been able to do this. This in turn indicates that such housing as did exist could only have been of the most simple kind: here the poorly constructed walls excavated by the wadi-side of the Colonnade Street seem appropriate although we cannot be sure that they did actually feature at the time of the incident.

Siculus's further comment that they had a law ' . . . neither to sow corn nor to plant any fruit bearing tree nor to use wine nor to build houses . . .' points once again to a strong nomadic streak in them. It must be remembered though that he was writing at something more than second-hand, and that much of his information was decidedly out of date.

By 150 B.C. Hellenistic culture was sweeping the Near and Middle East and was being received with great enthusiasm. New ideas were pouring in to feed cultures which had grown thin through overwork. This new blood was taken into the existing culture, and not in place of it; so much is evident all over the Near East but nowhere is it more true than in the art of Petra. As Peter Parr has pointed out 'the oriental tradition in art is something which never wholly disappeared from the Near East . . .';* in Petra this ancient tradition, which stemmed fundamentally from Assyria and Babylon, was tremendously strong. The new Hellenistic culture was only accepted by the Nabateans cautiously and in a manner characteristic of a suspicious and conservative bedouin. However, it eventually gave a new dimension to their art and architecture.

The two great Hellenistic powers of Ptolemaic Egypt and Seleucid Syria were constantly at war contesting the inheritance of Alexander the Great. Trade in both countries suffered and in consequence the merchants moved to the safer and calmer waters of the Nabatean sphere. The war enabled the Nabateans to extend their influence, as well as their kingdom, far to the north. Indeed, by the reign of Aretas III Philhellen (84–56 B.C.) Damascus had been included in this kingdom of traders. Their power was obviously causing the Romans some anxiety for, in 63 B.C., Pompey sent an expeditionary force against them under the command of Scaurus. The idea was to take Petra by storm and smash the nerve centre of the nation. According to Josephus, things did not turn out quite like that, for the army went hungry to such an extent that Scaurus was forced to sue for peace. Once again the Nabateans did exactly what they had done with Demetrius, they bought off Scaurus with costly presents and they 'ceased to make war any longer . . .'

The reign of Malchus I (56–30 B.C.) was disastrous from an international political point of view. This certainly did not stop the city of Petra from

* P. E. Q., January 1960.

continuing to rise in dignity and magnificence and from becoming richer. Prosperity was on the flood-tide and trade, the life-blood of their success, had never been better. The machinations and intrigues of kings and emperors were of little concern to the merchants just so long as they did not interfere with the smooth running of business.

Obodas II (30–9 B.C.), who seems to have been an ineffectual sort of character completely under the thumb of his chief 'minister' who was referred to as 'Brother', had to face an expeditionary force sent against him by Augustus. His minister, Syllaeus, emerges from the incident as one of the slipperiest characters ever to walk the hot streets of Petra. As soon as he heard that Augustus was mounting this expedition, he scurried off with a body of soldiers and offered to guide the Roman force safely through the desert to Petra. He insisted that there was no through road to the city and that it was necessary to follow a particular route. How the Romans came to fall for this is a mystery, for the route they took led through the most arid and desolate land Syllaeus could find. The result was that many soldiers died and those who came through were in no condition to fight. The general concerned was no doubt bought off in suitable Nabatean style to compensate for the loss of his army. Once again the Nabateans pulled their city through unscathed.

It is interesting to speculate whether the passionate love of freedom and obdurateness which so characterises certain moods of the Nabateans was not in part an inheritance from the Edomites. The whole question of cultural and temperamental inheritance in this part of the world and at this time is a vexed question which requires a lot of work.

The remaining recorded history of the Nabateans as an independent state is a succession of political intrigues which take place on the wide international stage rather than in Petra itself. Though these events are interesting as part of the history of the Near East, they are of little relevance here where we are setting out to chronicle the history of Petra. Roman conquest and government had opened the political horizons of the world far wider than they had ever been before and events in history gravitated round the great figures of the day who usually acted in the big theatres. Occasionally the action shifted for a moment to this isolated spot and then to that, but it always moved back into the main arena very quickly: great men do not like to be parted from their applause for too long. The result was that the history of remote cities like Petra is recorded only in their stones.

The long line of Nabatean kings came to an end in A.D. 106, when Petra was made a Roman province. Rome did not, however, take over a culturally backward or impoverished people: all the evidence we have points to quite the opposite being the case. However, before looking at the Roman period of Petra it is worth considering for a moment the civilisation they inherited and what it had achieved.

Of all the products of the Nabateans their pottery is the most singular and outstanding (Fig. 6). This is of a fineness and thinness that one usually only finds in porcelain and must have been produced in prodigious quantities, for small pieces of it lie scattered liberally all over the site of Petra. It was all thrown on the wheel and turned, possibly being rubbed down afterwards to the satin-textured finish which makes it such a joy to handle. It was usually of a soft terracotta cum peach colour with formalised leaf patterns delicately painted in a colour which varies from a light reddish brown, through pale coffee to almost black depending on the strength of the

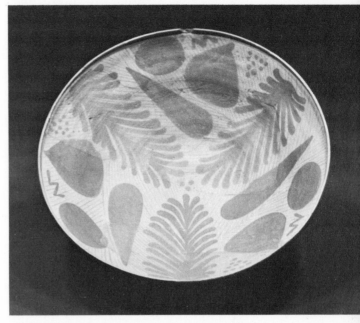

Fig. 6 Nabatean pottery which is notable for its thinness and the skill of its manufacture.

solution of manganese used. It was executed free-hand which gave it a gay spontaneity which is most appealing (Figs. 7 and 8). The usual shape was a shallow bowl which is a notoriously difficult shape to throw on the wheel: how the Nabateans came to do such work remains a mystery.

It is possible to suggest that Nabatean pottery was not made by the Nabateans at all but by a craftsman guild composed of those Edomites who remained in Petra and became full citizens of the Nabatean state.

The only other classical writer of any note, apart from Pliny and possibly Herodotus, ever to write about Petra was Strabo. Here again it is a case of the author having had his information at second-hand, for Strabo never visited Petra. He had his information off Athenodorus who was tutor to Augustus, and who had spent some time at the capital of the Nabateans during the first century B.C. Strabo's notes are worth quoting extensively. . . .

> The Nabateans are temperate and industrious so that the public penalty is imposed on those who diminish their substance, but to them that increase it honours are given, and, having few slaves, they are served for the most part by relations or by each other, or they serve themselves, and the custom extends even to the kings. They form 'companies' of thirteen men each and two musicians to each company. The king in his great house holds many companies. No one drinks more than eleven cups in one and then another golden beaker-full. Thus the king is a democratic one, so that in addition to serving himself serves others. He often also submits his accounts to the people, and sometimes also the conduct of his own personal life is enquired into. Their dwellings are extensive constructions of stone, and their cities are unwalled on account of peace. Most of it abounds in fruit except the

olive: they use oil of sesame. Their sheep are white haired, their oxen large; their country does not produce horses, camels render service in their place. Even the kings go out without tunics but in girdles and slippers only, but they do go out in purple.... They think dead bodies no better than manure; as Heraclitus says, corpses are more to be thrown away than dung heaps. Wherefore they bury even their kings beside their privies. They honour the sun, setting up an altar in the house, making libations on it daily and using frankincense.... The capital of the Nabateans is the so-called Petra, for it lies on ground in general even and level, but guarded all around by rock, outside precipitous and abrupt but inside having abundant springs for drawing water and for gardening ...

Not everything in this account is corroborated by what systematic excavation during the last few years has revealed. There are also one or two very strange contentions in it which make one wonder whether Athenodorus fully understood what it was that he was being told. Coming as he did from a completely Western civilisation he probably had difficulty in appreciating the point of many aspects of a culture which leaned heavily on an Oriental tradition.

The habit of eating in 'companies' is an interesting innovation which appears not to have been restricted to festive affairs. The numbers thirteen and eleven probably have considerable religious significance: many of the gods of the ancient world had sacred numbers or were associated in one way or another with one or a group of numbers.

The 'democracy', even of the king, is another notable feature for which it is difficult to account. If a closer link with Mesopotamia could be established than the obvious architectural one, it might reveal a connection between the 'democracy' of the Nabatean kings and the 'Primitive Democracy' (as suggested by Dr H. Frankfort) of the early Assyrians. Neither would have been true democracies as we know the meaning of the word today, but rather ceremonial fictions whose origins had been lost in the mists of time, but which were kept up as religious or regal observances. A parallel in our own day of such an observance is the Maundy Ceremony at which Her Majesty's attendants wear white sashes representing the towels with which the Sovereign is symbolically washing the feet of the poor in imitation of Our Lord. It must be several centuries since any British monarch has actually washed the feet of the poor as an act of humility on Maundy Thursday, but the sashes are still worn as tokens of this. So the 'democracy' of the Nabateans may have been a token perpetuation of a practice which had been long outmoded but which it was felt had religious significance and meaning.

Dr Margaret Murray has produced a theory in which there might well be quite a degree of probability. 'Evidently the king, in early times at any rate, was little more than a sheikh, hence the simplicity of his life and his democratic manners, for he not only waited on himself at table but sometimes waited on his guests. This would be quite in accordance with modern usage. . . . In fact he was not unlike the modern sheikhs, whose power depends largely on their ability to deal with strangers and to protect their tribe from others.'* This would certainly be true of the early period of the Nabatean occupation when they were still thoroughly bedouin, and in later years the customs of bedouin democracy may have been continued as part of state and religious ceremonials. This would have been done to perpetuate the spiritual union between the king and his people in a way which people like the Nabateans would understand and appreciate.

Strabo tells us that their houses were 'extensive constructions of stone' and this is confirmed by the recent excavations of the Katute area, on the south side of the city (Fig. 9). This excavation, conducted by Mr Peter Parr, brought to light the foundations of a large complex of buildings of a stately character, dating from around the time of the birth of Christ, which had been constructed—and reconstructed—in stone. This site will be discussed more fully later on but the excavations did reveal an appreciable quantity of Nabatean remains which verify Strabo's statement.

The internal appearance of Nabatean houses would have varied appreciably according to the social status of the occupants: it is highly likely that social status would have been synonymous with wealth. Fragments of a very strong plaster, which was frequently painted in bright colours, have come down to us, including

* *Petra, the rock city of Edom.*

Fig. 9 The fine stone walls of the Nabateans at the Katute excavations.

some good examples in the Petra Museum. These indicate that it was used extensively both internally and externally. A fair amount of architectural plaster-work still adheres to the outside of the Kasr el Bint (Fig. 10) but any colouring there might once have been has long since been bleached out. Perhaps the best remaining pieces of interior-painted plaster are to be found in the 'Painted House' in the el Barid Siq and on the central pillar of the staircase in the Baths complex beside the Temenos Gate. Rugs made from goat hair or wool would have been, in all probability, a major item of furnishing though it is unlikely that there would have been much in the way of tables and chairs, etc. The small rooms of the ordinary house would have been rather dark and smelly due to the smallness of the windows — a protection against both heat and cold — and the constant use of oil lamps which tended to emit the most choking fumes.

It is difficult to accommodate Strabo's statement that the city had no walls, for the Katute site actually straddles the old wall on the south side of the city; indeed, the course of all the city walls has been traced. It seems, therefore, that if Strabo is reporting fact, he must certainly have been out of date. The fact that his informant, Athenodorus, was blind would have put a certain limit to his ability to check observations.

The most perplexing thing in this extract is Strabo's reference to the Naba-tean's attitude to dead bodies and what to do with them. Funerary rites and rituals of the dead must have played an

Fig. 10 Ornamental plasterwork on the exterior of the Kasr el Bint. The Nabateans developed this means of decoration because the soft local sandstone was unsuitable for delicate carving.

important part in the life and religion of these people. The countless carved
tombs and their attendant triclinea are more than sufficient evidence of that. It
comes therefore as something of a surprise to have Strabo reporting that the
Nabatean kings were buried beside their privies. As Mr Lankester Harding has
observed, if this was so, then their privies 'must have been singularly magnificent
ones'.* To the best of our knowledge, no such royal conveniences have survived,
so it is difficult to say. And yet Strabo is very emphatic about this, brooking no
misunderstanding if translation of words into modern idiomatic language is to
be trusted. Mr G. R. H. Wright has suggested that the discrepancy does not lie
in any textual emendation whereby the sound of certain words could have been
mistaken for the sound of another word, e.g. the Aramaic and Syriac word for
tomb is 'Kophra', the Greek word for dunghill is 'Kopron'. As he has written,
'Strabo's phraseology may require and admit of textual interpretation but it is
difficult to believe that such a statement lacked all correspondence with reality'.†
His theory suggests that as Athenodorus's stay in Petra probably coincided with
the high-tide of reaction against the 'westernness' of Hellenism known as the
'Oriental Reaction', he could have been confronted with the importation of
Parthian funerary practices as part of a much wider appreciation and application
of Achaemenid, or Persian, social and religious ideas. All questions relating to
Iranian funerary rites remain highly controversial but there was a strong
tradition among the upper classes at that time, perpetuated by the present-day
Parsees, for 'Ritual Exposure' of their dead. Since the emphasis in the Strabo
account is on the disposal of bodies of kings, it seems probable that such a
practice was an aristocratic one: Petra would have been uninhabitable if all
classes and conditions of men went in for the practice. Mr Wright further suggests
that many of the smaller High Places which are frequently encountered in Petra,
are in fact not places of worship in the strict sense of the word—though 'Ritual
Exposure' would have constituted in some way an act of worship—but are
'Exposure Platforms' in the Persian—possibly Sassanian—manner. It is an
intriguing theory and as it stands is probably the most original and thought-
provoking argument put up so far.

The question does arise, however, of what the common folk did with their
dead. If they in fact buried them as we believe, then there must be extensive
cemeteries outside the city waiting to be found. The opening remark of Strabo's
account, however, strikes very true. As merchants and traders one can well
believe that they were industrious, though the penalty for making a loss seems
to suggest an almost obsessive regard for, and attachment to, money. Very early
on they adopted the Hellenistic idea of coins in place of the more cumbersome

* *Antiquities of Jordan.*   † P. E. Q., July 1969.

barter system. The advantages of this monetary system became immediately obvious and the kings began to strike their own coins: locally minted coins are not known until the first century B.C. The designs show a strong reliance on Greek prototypes though local symbols were used: the dress of the humans depicted on these coins is in the full Greek tradition, so gives us little in the way of a guide to their sartorial leanings. Small copper coins of Petra are found frequently but only very rarely do the silver pieces turn up, which indicates that the desertion of Petra was a gradual process in which the merchants and the other sectors of the population had plenty of time to remove all their belongings before moving on to wherever it was they settled.

This could also be the reason why so little in the way of Nabatean script has been found in Petra, either ostraca or papyri. The longest inscription we have to date is a papyrus found in a cave at Muraba'at on the shores of the Dead Sea. Apart from this, little remains and one must assume that the written records of the Nabateans were removed when their keepers left the city for good. There is a notable Nabatean inscription carved on one of the tombs (Fig. 11) and frequently graffiti scribbled with a hard point—probably metal—into the soft sandstone rocks.

The language is, however, most important for from it Kufic was derived and from that ultimately came modern Arabic. Nabatean seems to have been a variant of Aramaic with a strong Arab influence in it—not altogether surprising when one remembers that the Nabateans originated in Arabia. What is even more to the point is that Aramaic was the tongue of the

Fig. 11 The inscription on the façade of the Turkamaniya Tomb; the best preserved example of Nabatean script in Petra.

Aramaens who moved into Mesopotamia during the twelfth century B.C. and later established themselves in opposition to Assyria. One of the tribes of the Aramaeans was called the Kaldu who ultimately overran Babylonia and found the Chaldean (Kaldu) dynasty, otherwise known as the Neo-Babylonian Empire. As we have already seen, the last Chaldean king of Babylon, Nabonidus, spent the remaining years of his reign at Teima in north-western Arabia where he is certain to have come into contact with the pre-eminent local tribe, the Nabateans. The extent to which an indigenous written language existed in Arabia before his arrival is outside the scope of this book but the highly developed instrumentation of Aramaic script is bound to have had a decisive influence on the Arab language of the early Nabateans. At some stage the Arab speech was replaced as the basic language. The original Arab lingo would have persisted in influencing the Aramaic, thus accounting for the marked and pronounced Arab influence in the Nabatean script.

It is a pity that such inscriptions as we have give us little clue as to the nature of Nabatean religion, particularly as many of the graffiti are of a devotional nature. All that is offered are a few tantalising hints and an occasional deity's name. The details of ritual cannot at present be ascertained with any certainty but during the excavations alongside the Colonnade Street some objects were revealed in the early levels which provide interesting pointers. Small incense-burners of both stone and clay similar to others from Mesopotamia, southern Arabia and southern Palestine, were found along with cubes and obelisks repre-senting deities of the type common in Petra. But the unique find was a collection of crude, stone, portable 'face-idols' comparable to types found in the Hadramaut and the Yemen. It has long been suggested that before the Nabateans moved into the north-western quarter of Arabia, they were present in the south: these finds at the Colonnade Street certainly stimulate further enquiry but point rather confusingly in two directions, north-east to Mesopotamia with its immensely complex religious ritual and theology, and south to the Yemen about whose theology we know even less than that in Petra.

We can be sure that the Nabateans had two principal gods in their pantheon, to which would have been added a whole range of personal gods and spirits—'djins'—rather in the same way that Christians have created the concept of 'guardian angels' and 'patron saints'. The two chief deities were Dusares and Al Uzza.

The Nabateans probably adopted Dusares from the Edomites, for his name is derived from Dhu-esh-Shera which means 'He (Lord) of Shera': this denotes a localised deity, for even today the mountains about Petra are called the Shara range. Shara is also the same word as Seir by which the district was known in the Old Testament. Incidentally, it is to be noted that Jehovah, god of the Hebrews, was, like Dusares, said to be He of Seir—and to inhabit a rock called Beth El, the House of God. Dusares was symbolised by a block of stone, frequently squared in some way. In order to understand the religions of nearly all the peoples of the ancient Near and Middle East it is necessary to appreciate the crucial position that 'rock' or 'stone' held in their theology.

Unlike the Egyptians and the Mesopotamians, the early Israelites, and pre-sumably the peoples on the 'other side of the Jordan' as well, were too inartistic to make their idols as representations of the human figure and form. In the case of the Israelites this developed into an abhorrence of idols in general, a feeling which their bondage in Egypt intensified. They would have been sure to associate the brilliantly portrayed human and animal deities of the Pharaohs with their oppression and the denial of their own god. Their inability to portray their god would lead them to believe that such portrayal was taboo. The Nabateans, on inheriting the localised god of Petra, would have likewise inherited—at least in the early period—the Edomite inhibitions regarding portrayal. A block of stone, however, was perfectly acceptable for it represented the likeness of nothing in heaven above or in the earth beneath.

The block of stone fixation became widely accepted: frequent Biblical references are made to it, denoting that the symbolism was commonly understood, e.g. 'The Lord *is* my rock, and my fortress, and my deliverer; The God of my rock; in him will I trust:' (Second Samuel 22, 2:3). The block of stone, however, had a triple character, being not only the representation of the deity but also the abode of the deity as expressed in the Beth El concept. How this god-block idea was affected by their later contact with the Hellenistic world and later still with the Roman, is not known with any certainty but they were definitely creating human-form images in later times if the bold, rather childish and yet indisputably Hellenistic sculptures found at the Nabatean temple at Khirbet Tannur, just south of Kerak in Jordan, are anything to go by.

The Rock concept was known in Arabia in the time of the Prophet Mohammed, for when he entered Mecca in triumph he found the temple there surrounded by 360 different tribal idols, which he promptly overthrew. They were in the form and character of blocks of stone or pillars. Pre-Moslem Arab religions had an extensive pantheon consisting mostly of tribal and local deities as demonstrated by the temple at Mecca.

And yet the block of stone served another, third, purpose which made things very convenient when it came to conduct of ritual. It was also the throne or seat of the deity and thus could be regarded as the altar: indeed this is the origin of the concept of the altar. By these three-part means the whole religious paraphernalia was integrated and melded into one theistic attribute.

Although Dusares was originally a localised deity, he shed that limited capacity when the Nabateans began expanding their frontiers, for he is in evidence in districts and regions far removed from his home territory. Under the influence of Hellenistic culture he began to assume human guise and was equated, by the Greeks, with their god Dionysos. But in Petra, as far as we know at present, he remained in the form now familiar to us, the block of stone: this indicates a strong streak of conservatism in the Nabatean capital. According to the Greek lexicographer, Suidas, who is believed to have lived in the latter part of the tenth century A.D., 'the sacred image was a black stone . . .' of 4 × 2 × 1 dimensions, set in a shrine which was richly adorned with votive offerings. The actual size of the god-block does not seem to have mattered provided the mystical proportions were observed. This means that the 'sacred image' could be small and transportable, thus accounting for the otherwise unexplained socket on the altar on the High Place in Petra. Evidence of the cult of Dusares has been found as far away as Alexandria in Egypt, so one would expect his representation to vary appreciably, which is what happened even to the surprising extent of ignoring the mystical ratio so important to the early believers. Pillars and tapering obelisks are the most common alternative to the squared block, indeed the first real monument of any consequence the visitor to Petra sees is the so-called Obelisk Tomb in the Bab el Siq (Fig. 12).

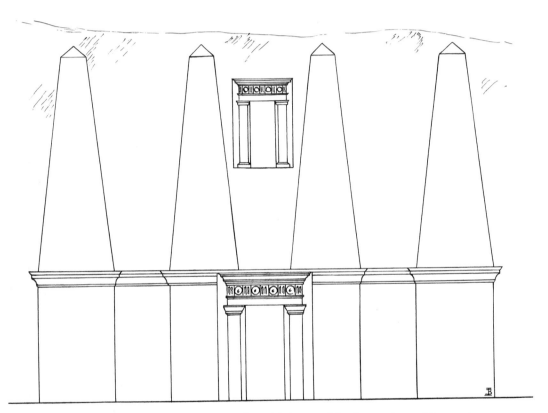

Fig. 12 Elevation of the Obelisk Tomb (restored) which is one of the first major architectural monuments encountered by today's visitors to Petra.

The rites of Dusares always seem to have been those which attracted the attention of the ancient authors most. So much so that the secondary deity, the goddess Al Uzza, has had to play a very muted second fiddle. It is a thought, however, that Dusares was a royal or aristocratic deity, worshipped by the royal house and the court in stately public view. Inscriptions frequently refer to 'the god of our Lord', which could be interpreted to mean 'the god of our King'. It would have been these classes only that could have afforded the sumptuous death palaces we see today: this would cross-relate with Mr Wright's theory on the Strabo comment and account for the apparently sacral, if not actually sacred, nature of the King. At least one Nabatean king, Obodas, was deified though we cannot be sure that others were not also: Obodas was buried at the town which still bears his name Oboda (Avdat).

If Dusares was the patrician deity, Al Uzza would have been the deity of the people. She was originally called Allat which became changed to Al Uzza when she arrived in Petra. The meaning of the two epithets is interesting, Allat meaning 'The Goddess' while Al Uzza meant 'The Mighty One'. The Arab author, Ibn al Kelbi, recounts her worship in Arabia, so she probably travelled to Petra with the Nabateans. Thus from being a purely local goddess, whose limited territorial appeal would have earned her the style and title of 'The Goddess', she became the guardian goddess of a whole race on the move into imperial pastures—sponsoring their achievements (and few deities could feel so well pleased with the results of their sponsorship as Al Uzza, fighting their battles and promoting their causes in the acrimonious clamour of the ancient pantheon with singular success) and thus earning for herself the greater accolade of 'The Mighty One'.

Al Uzza was the deity of springs and of water as befits a fertility goddess, and as such she would have been reverenced in Petra with particular devotion. Dusares seems also to have been a fertility god—it must never be forgotten that the Nabateans were, besides being traders, an agricultural people who pushed the fields of production further into the desert than practically any other people by means of their superb irrigation skills—and naturally was closely associated with the life-giving waters, but his exact patronage is not clearly defined. Being a male deity, the phallus could have featured in his festival rites so that the forces and power of re-creation and virility could be demonstrated. The Greeks mistook and misinterpreted the probable copulative 'orgies', which were not an uncommon feature of fertility cults, as being the same thing as the inebriated, and equally copulative, 'orgies' which attended the festival rites of Dionysos. As the Nabateans, during their early phase in Petra, are reported as eschewing wine, the parallel with Dionysos does not stand particularly close inspection: under Hellenistic influence later on, it is quite possible that the Dusares fertility rites did degenerate into the pornographic pop concerts which came to debase the once-glorious cult of Dionysos.

Of the other deities of the Nabateans we know very little, sometimes no more than their names. Qaush, Habalu and She'a-alqum are but three to be recorded, the last being the patron deity of caravans, comparable perhaps with the

Christian St Christopher. Rostovtzeff has suggested that the Khasneh in the Siq of Petra (Fig. 13) was the temple of the patron deity of the City of Petra, Manat or Manathu. She appears to have been a local goddess or 'genius' of the city: a sort of Fortuna. He suggested that she was an 'Hellenistic equivalent of the Iranian Hvareno and the Semitic Gad'. Her name appears on coins but like Dusares, Al Uzza and the other gods, she is represented by the eternal and all-personality god-block.

It was quite natural that the Nabatean deities should have a very close approximation with water, for this was the one single factor which made the city possible. Not only did their trade depend on it but also their agriculture was made possible by it. This they developed to a high degree and the remains of the walls of terrace fields can still be seen scattered across the desert surrounding all the known Nabatean settlements. Even the most improbable parts of the desert, where nothing but the wire grass and shiah herb now grows, have these crumbling reminders still holding back the remnants of soil from final erosion. None of this would have been possible had they not been skilled in irrigation.

The Edomites had started the process of water conservation in Petra but it was

the Nabateans who took such great pains to develop this into an elaborate system of control and regulation. Their water engineering was in fact their most impressive achievement: their architecture is remarkable, their pottery exceptionally fine, but their techniques of collecting, distributing and conserving water display outstanding ingenuity, skill and imagination which even the Romans could not better.

They had to contend with the problem that, at the height of its prosperity, the city area by itself probably housed between 18,000 to 20,000 persons. With the various suburbs such as the Wadi Siyagh, el Sabrah, el Barid, el Madras, etc., the total would have been as great as 30,000. The springs in the valley were quite inadequate to meet the need by themselves, but up the hill, outside the Siq, above the village of Elji, is the abundant and perpetual spring of Ain Mousa—Moses Spring. Other springs in the area also augment the generous supply. By means of conduits and lengthy stretches of earthenware piping (Fig. 14), the Nabateans brought the precious

Fig. 13 The Khasneh, the most celebrated monument of Petra, from the great gorge known as the Siq.

1. The Obelisk Tomb in the Bab el Siq

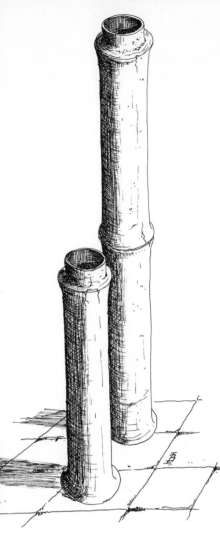

waters of Ain Mousa through the Siq and round the great flank of the mountain el Kubtha, right into the heart of the city area—perhaps to feed the Nymphaeum, the ruins of which stand on the Colonnade Street (see Map 3, page 120).

The winter rains were quite capable of turning the Siq into a raging torrent. A freak flood, after a violent storm, some years ago caught a party of unsuspecting tourists in the Siq and swept them to their deaths. Happily this can never happen again due to the barrage dam which the Government has built across the mouth of the Siq and which diverts the water through a tunnel (Fig. 15) specially cut through the side of the mountain for that purpose—by the Nabateans. It is believed that this was done just before the Roman annexation and that their dam was constructed in much the same way as the present one.

It is amazing that a race so expert in rock excavation should have been so unskilled in building. Nabatean buildings erected before the

Fig. 14 Earthenware pipes, designed by the Nabateans.

annexation are astonishingly poorly built. Mrs Crystal-M. Bennett has suggested to the author that the 'Unfinished Tomb' (Fig. 16) could possibly provide a clue to the reason why this was so. Here it becomes obvious that the Nabateans carved down from the top. The whole intellectual concept of excavation is one of mass and volume in the truly Oriental archaic tradition—the pyramids of Egypt and the ziggurats of Mesopotamia are obvious examples. Enclosure and space are the hallmarks of Western constructional—and philosophical—thought. The problem of roofing in stone even the most modest space in a constructed building must have been

Fig. 15 The Bab el Siq tunnel was cut to divert the flood-waters of the Wadi Mousa from the Siq.

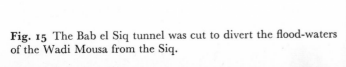

a nightmare for the Nabateans, for this would have presented problems of thrust and support if the roof and walls were to stay standing up. In a cave, the roof and the walls support themselves independently of each other: there are no problems

Fig. 16 The Unfinished Tomb.

of stress and strain and this was a philosophy they could readily understand. To reduce this argument, however, and reformulate it in constructional terms is impossible. So it is plausible that the Nabateans were incapable of discovering for themselves the theory—however much they might practise—of large-scale, monumental construction. This was a facility they learned later, probably through their contact with Hellenism, for the Kasr el Bint (Fig. 91), which is Nabatean and not Roman, is a masterly exercise in construction on a monumental scale.

The Nabatean city, before the annexation, would have had the look of any prosperous Arab town up to a decade ago before modern building techniques ruined an urban tradition which had lasted for thousands of years (Fig. 17). Houses would have been of a single storey, huddled together along narrow, twisting gravel-trod lanes, each built round its own semi-porticoed courtyard. Roofs would have been flat and the windows regular and small. The temple and markets provided the only large-scale spaces in this human ant-hill but even these would have had a somewhat stark appearance without much structural ornament. The harsh straight lines would have been relieved by the use of bright colours on the plastered walls and cornices. Only those buildings of stately proportions would have had any pretentions to architecture and even these would have had an Arab simplicity and strength wholly different from the Western tradition.

It was the inexorable expansion of the Roman Empire rather than anything the Nabateans had done that ultimately brought about their downfall. No state, however great its past or present, remained independent once the Romans had arrived.

The annexation was long delayed, perhaps by the diplomatic skill of the Nabateans, but under their last king, Rabbel II (A.D. 71–106), the final blow was struck and his reign ended when a Roman Governor of Syria, Cornelius Palma, was ordered by the Emperor Trajan to annexe the kingdom and incorporate it into the Province of Arabia. This may have been part of a deal with the Romans by which they guaranteed the total independence of the Nabatean kingdom so long as Rabbel lived, in return for which he made over the state to the Romans on his death. There is no evidence of a fight to the last by harassed Nabateans: the Roman occupation seems to have taken place almost as a matter of course. On 22 March, A.D. 106, Petra ceased to be either a national or provincial capital, for the city of Bozrah, in Syria, was made the capital of the Province into which the Decapolis was also incorporated.

IV

The idea that, as soon as the Romans took over, the city experienced a sharp decline in its cultural life and fortunes is rapidly becoming discredited. Indeed, there is much to indicate that the Roman administration gave a new stimulus to the cultural life of the city as well as increased civic consciousness which, in

Fig. 17 The Arab system of courtyard housing probably shows what average Nabatean housing looked like.

consequence, led the city to experience something of a renaissance which lasted at least until the end of the reign of the Emperor Septimus Severus.

Roman administrators abroad were careful not to trample unnecessarily upon the feelings and susceptibilities of the nations they conquered. They realised that with the enormously extended lines of communication which the size of their Empire demanded, it was vitally important that their presence in foreign lands should be as welcome and beneficial as possible. All the marvels of Roman 'technology' were made available to the conquered races which enabled them to enjoy a better mode of life. Even though they, the Romans, were determined to have their own way, they were wise enough to realise that there were better ways of getting it than by dog-in-the-manger attitudes. Alongside a perfectly genuine do-gooder instinct on a materialistic level, the Romans trained their highly efficient propaganda machine on their new subjects and convinced all but the most obdurate that Roman rule brought greater benefits than it did disadvantages.

Local traditions and cultural background were respected and taken as points of departure for new improvements. In Petra these included the creation of the Colonnade Street (Fig. 18) out of the street running beside the Wadi Mousa which, with the best will in the world, must have been a pretty unpretentious affair before. Even this was done in such a way and in such a style that the local inhabitants would have recognised it as an advance *of* their own native architecture rather than an advance *on* it. The parallel with the Colonnade Street at Jerash is unlikely to have disturbed them, indeed they could have taken the comparison as rather flattering. It has been suggested that the Romans went so far as to completely reorganise the whole of the city layout, but the truth of this will only be ascertained by future excavations.

In short, the Romans recognised that in the East particularly, there was a well established cultural tradition and way of life which went along rather different lines from their own, and which they disturbed at their peril. In fact this tradition — the Oriental tradition — never wholly disappeared from the Near East, and in Petra its presence was felt very strongly. Instead, the administration, under its Governor, skilfully adapted its own way of life and culture, which owed so much to the Hellenistic ideal in any case, to suit these particular people. To some extent this is confirmed by the fact that a Roman official of high rank, Sextus Florentinus, was provided with a rock-cut tomb (Fig. 159) in the true Nabatean fashion.

Perhaps it was in order to demonstrate their good intentions, and their belief in the future, that the Romans embarked on the lavish programme of reconstruction, embellishment and civic planning of the city soon after the annexation. Such civic transformations could have been one way of reassuring the Nabatean citizens about the future of their city.

The Roman presence was to have a profound effect on the structure of the Near East. Previously the area had consisted of a set of constantly warring small nations, each with its own contained economy. The economic *status quo* worked so long as the states remained separate entities. When the area was compounded into one larger economic unit within the vast frame of the whole Empire, local advantages ceased to have any relevance. That the trade routes could be changed so as to serve the greater good of the Empire as a whole instead of the interests

Fig. 18 A reconstruction of the Colonnade Street, a Roman 'improvement', looking towards the Temenos Gate which closed the vista at the western end.

of one member nation only, was evident and was taken by a good many Nabateans as the writing on the wall for Petra. That some read the message this way is indisputable, for the Katute excavations showed that with the coming of the Romans, the size of the city's limits contracted: the once prosperous and stately

Katute building was not occupied properly after this period. Merchants, loyal in the final analysis only to their own pockets, moved away to the new pastures of wealth opening up in the growing trade cities of Jerash and Palmyra.

The Roman effort must have been one of continually trying to stem the tide of a gradual decline for the city of Petra. It must have been a sustained effort for inscriptions in Petra mention the names of the Emperors Maximian and Diocletian, thus indicating that the city was still worthy of consideration as late as the early fourth centry A.D. Mr Peter Parr has confirmed that 'as late as the middle of the fifth century, Petra was still a centre of some importance . . . and it is possible that some sort of settled town life went on for at least another hundred years.'* This, however, takes us prematurely into the Byzantine period, but it does show that the disappearance of the all-important trade was an extremely slow and protracted affair.

Even so, Petra was no longer the hub of any wheel and is mentioned by the classical authors less and less. The occasional splutters of Imperial celebration which seem to have punctuated the decline were all too often the result of Roman propaganda and were not the effect of deep-seated 'national' causes. Historically, therefore, they were meaningless and contributed nothing to the future of the city. Such an event could have been a visit by the Emperor Hadrian in A.D. 130., but it should be remembered that the city was still of importance in the world of trade at this time and could possibly have expected, almost as a right, a visit if the Emperor happened to be in the area. It is easy to write off such visits as being either a prestige and morale-boosting gesture, or on the other hand as a well-deserved acknowledgement of prosperity. The fact remains that the Romans must have thought the exercise was worth the trouble.

In A.D. 199, the African-born Emperor Septimus Severus and his Syrian wife toured the eastern Provinces, which may have included the Province of Arabia. If this were the case, he could well have visited Petra (even though Bozrah was the Provincial capital). Much commemorative civic building usually accompanied such jamborees and it is possible that Petra profited from the tour: one is reminded of the huge schemes of civic grandeur which were triggered off in Leptis Magna when Severus visited the city of his birth. The tragedy there was that the city had even then passed its zenith and was on the downward slope, making the construction of such display too late to have much meaning. The staggering scale of civic pride, and the hideous cost, in Leptis Magna did not reflect the state of the fortunes of the city and as such were sheer ostentation. The Roman world never learned when it was running out of fuel and went on merrily burning the lamps of extravagance and excess until the skies were thick with the fumes of folly. Petra and Leptis Magna present very different cases, but when

* P. E. Q., January 1970.

looking at the sculptures of Petra and of Leptis Magna one is struck by something more than the basic common heritage of their character; there is a desperate feeling of 'pomp and glory' which lacks the final calm of real self-assurance. They exude the message that they were commissioned for, and inspired by, a great occasion, proud panoplies put up in an euphoric, shimmering memory of a blindingly splendid event. A happy and unashamed but somehow frenzied nostalgia permeates the very marble of their substance.

The troops of the Fourth (Martia) Legion, stationed not far away at Adhruh, would have found it a very grand place, full of fine buildings testifying to the glory of Rome, panache and ceremonies—and really rather dull. Their job of policing the trade routes and maintaining internal security had been inherited from the Nabateans who had performed this task successfully for over 250 years. The prosperity of the trade depended greatly on the safety of the route over which it travelled. The Nabatean military forces and customs officials must have felt rather at a loose end when they suddenly found that they were no longer required, which was bound to have had a depressing effect overall.

There is no clear stylistic demarcation line between the pre-Roman and the Roman periods in Petra. Roman political influence had been increasing strongly over a long period before the annexation, but it seems unlikely that they had much cultural impact until they had actually taken over the administration of Petra. The Colonnade Street as presently laid out, and some of its attendant stately buildings such as the Nymphaeum, etc. are of Roman date.

All sculptural work of this period in Petra is marked by a greater degree of refinement than one encounters in other Nabatean settlements such as the temple precinct at Khirbet Tannur, where the orientalism of the work is blatant. As Mr Parr points out, this is 'the art of a capital city, a metropolis, influenced by and catering for the tastes of a much more sophisticated clientele than must have existed in the purely religious centres such as Tannur.'* Many of the works indicate that as late even as the early third century there was in Petra a society sufficiently sophisticated and cultured—and prosperous—to appreciate imported foreign works of art which possessed a cultivated style and execution.

The difference between the two approaches to construction in stone is clearly demonstrated by the way they each built up their pillars. The tall Roman pillars of the Colonnade Street (Fig. 19) have a slender, and yet robust, grace and are made up of relatively few cylindrical sections. Even though they are widely spaced the Romans felt that they were quite safe carrying a considerable weight. They had confidence in a slender vertical shaft of stone provided it was balanced properly. On the hill above the Colonnade Street, to the south, there lie the as

* P. E. Q., January 1958

yet unexcavated ruins of what is surely a Nabatean temple. Here the pillars are built up of a number of thin, flat stone discs (Fig. 20), one piled up upon the other: the resulting effect would have been a squat, dumpy pillar which looked—and was—enormously strong. The fact that it was unnecessarily strong and that its method of construction was also unnecessarily laborious seems to have escaped the Nabateans; a slender column would have served just as well.

Fig. 19 The Colonnade Street today.

The Nabateans seem to have suffered from rather the same spacial timidity that plagued the early Egyptians, who filled their halls with closely spaced pillars of titanic proportions. By this means they could be sure that the roof would stay up: well were such halls termed hypostylate.

Life would have gone on very much as usual except that the natural tempo would have probably slowed down gradually as more and more merchants departed. With the withdrawal of the Legions, however, it must have been obvious that Petra had no future. The only unifying force left in the land was Christianity which had been adopted as the paramount religion in A.D. 333 with the conversion of the Emperor.

V

The establishment of the 'Empire in the East', or the Byzantine Empire, by the Emperor Theodosius in A.D. 395 would have meant little to the remaining inhabitants of the city, except that the area would have come in for its fair share of hermits and fanatical anchorites. The barren hills which surround the city could have fired the ecstasy of even the most masochistic recluse. Petra became the seat of a bishopric in the fourth century. This was later elevated to the dignity of a metropolitan. In common with the whole of the Near East, churches sprang up in all the most unlikely places: a Greek inscription dated to A.D. 446 in the Urn Tomb informs us that the interior was converted into a church and there are a number of

Fig. 20 The fallen columns of the 'Manathu' Temple show clearly that the Nabateans constructed their pillars with thin discs of stone as opposed to the Roman method of a few cylinders.

crosses scratched on the walls of the Deir which could be taken as denoting consecration marks.

The pattern of civilised life under Byzantine rule was virtually the same all over the Near East and, therefore, even though we have singularly few records of Petra at this period, we can fit together a reasonably accurate picture of the city's swan song. This is borne out by the results of excavation. The city boundaries contracted still further, once dignified and gracious buildings in the centre of town degenerated into hovels, their fine rooms being subdivided into squalid small compartments. This was shown particularly clearly by the excavations along the Colonnade Street where the Roman period shops had later, Byzantine, walls intruding into the original shape, so much so that it is difficult sometimes to determine exactly what the original plan was like.

One gets the feeling that the authorities had at last given up the unequal struggle of trying to pretend that their city mattered at all in the councils and history of the world. The vitality of people was being sapped by squalor and the continual bickering between the Christian churches did not help matters. Without even vain hope, a sort of torpor settled across Petra; life became an existence valued for its own precarious self and not for any prospect of achievement. Control by the central authority became looser and looser, to such an extent that Petra virtually returned to being independent again.

The absence of inscriptions, or texts of any kind, in the Nabatean tongue after the late fourth century is pregnant with possibilities. Was it a case that Greek or Latin had superseded the native language in the speech of the Nabateans? The survival of the Nabatean tongue, through Kufic, and its emergence in modern Arabic would lead one to believe that this was not so; in any case a language is not just discarded like that and a new, alien, one adopted in its place. It is worth considering the possibility that the whole of the true Nabatean population moved out long before the final desertion leaving behind only the polyglot, alien population which is an inevitable parasite of any wealthy trading nation with international ramifications and connections. The Nabateans to a man were traders of one sort or another so it would be natural for them to move to where business could be found. Jerash and Palmyra have already been mentioned as possible destinations and there can be little doubt that expatriate Nabatean merchants were seen there.

The Emperor Heraclius (A.D. 610–41) had to contend with increasing Persian activity in the area and in the end succeeded in beating off what amounted to a minor invasion. The situation was, however, too far gone for any real good to come of his brave actions; the Empires of the classical world had worn themselves out and the Eastern peoples lay exhausted awaiting a strong leader with new ideals and infectious ambition to pick them up.

VI

The first Moslem expansion (A.D. 636) brought the curtain down on ancient Petra. The lands of transjordan were still kept in some sort of cultivation along Nabatean lines. In many parts of the world this terrace farming is referred to as Arab farming (Fig. 45): it is an interesting reflection, however, that this style of land conservation and agriculture was derived from the Nabateans who probably learned it from the Edomites.

Of Petra, the records of the world are silent after the fanatical hordes of Islam had moved in. Jordan as a whole was maintained on the bread-line throughout the Omayyad period, for as Mr Lankester Harding has pointed out, 'so long as the Omayyad court was at Damascus, Jordan was on the direct road to Mecca and so was looked after and kept secure. But with the shift of the Abbasid court to Baghdad, Jordan was no longer of any importance and was left entirely to its own devices, security broke down, and the country lapsed into a state of abject poverty.'*

The condition in which the ruins were found when serious archaeological excavation started in the early 1930s showed very clearly that it was a natural catastrophe which had wrought the final destruction of the city. It is tempting to think that the violent earthquake which destroyed Jerash and caused extensive damage throughout Jordan and Palestine in the middle of the eighth century was responsible for the final disaster in Petra. The tumbling masonry fell into a bed of soft, virgin sand and river mud which had collected across the site over 180 to 200 years. From this it is possible to hint at a date of about the middle of the sixth century for the final collapse of civil life and the departure of the remaining survivors.

The Crusaders came and built a small fort on the top of el Habis, the remains of which can still be seen. This would have been more in the nature of an outpost of the great fortress at Shobak than a full-scale castle in its own right. Like the Byzantines before them, they probably pilfered the stone with which to build it, from the derelict city below. It would be fascinating to know how much of the city was still standing when they were there, but no one in the garrison has left a record. It could not have been really much fun up there in a silent, awe-inspiring and utterly hostile landscape, so one can sympathise with them that they had no inclination to wax eloquent on the glories of the view, or on the prospect over the strange, crumbling and deserted city.

* P. E. Q., January 1957.

THE 'KINGS' OF EDOM

Time of Moses	Rekem
Before Saul	Bela, the son of Beor
	Jobab, the son of Zerah
	Husham of the Land of Temani
	Hadad, the son of Bedad
	Samlah of Masrekah
	Saul of Rohoboth by the River
	Baal-hanan, the son of Achbor
	Hadar of Paul
Time of Solomon	Hadad?

747 B.C.	Qaush-malak	reigning at the same time as Tiglath-Pileser IV of Assyria
705 B.C.	Malikram	reigning at the same time as Sennacherib of Assyria
681 B.C.	Qaush-gaber	reigning at the same time as Esarhaddon of Assyria
688 B.C.	Nathu	reigning at the same time as Ashurbanipal of Assyria

The dates against the last four names are those of a particular incident which occurred in the relevant reign, to which it has been possible to give a date by cross-checking other historical sources. They do not, therefore, indicate the start or finish of a reign, but rather an approximate date during it.

NABATEAN KING LIST

312 B.C.	First mention of the Nabateans in the war with Antigonus of Seleucid Syria
c. 168 B.C.	Aretas I (known as the 'tyrant of the Arabs' and 'King of the Nabatu')
	Rabbel I
c. 100 B.C.	Aretas II (concerned with the siege of Gaza)
c. 93 B.C.	Obodas I (defeated Alexander Jannaeus)
84–56 B.C.	Aretas III Philhellen
56–30 B.C.	Malchus I
30–9 B.C.	Obodas II
8 B.C.–A.D. 40	Aretas IV Philopatris
A.D. 40–70	Malchus II (lost control of Damascus)
A.D. 71–106	Rabbel II (last king of the Nabateans)

This King list with its dates is based on information given in 'Pétra et la Nabatène' by the Abbé Starcky, published in 1966 in *Supplément au Dictionnaire de la Bible*, Vol. VII.

CHAPTER THREE

John L. Burckhardt and Others

IF the Nabateans were a courageous and adaptable people, it was fitting that their metropolis should have been rediscovered after a thousand years of obscurity by a man who enjoyed in good measure just these qualities.

John Burckhardt (Fig. 21) was the son of a Swiss Colonel of the French Army who gave him a Christian education at Neuchâtel, Leipzig and Göttingen. The remainder of John's short life was spent exploring the Near East successfully disguised as a Moslem. This was no charade or romantic frolic toying with fate like Hester Stanhope's journeys, but a period of preparation, undertaken in great earnest, for an adventure which never came off.

John was evidently popular at Göttingen where his talents and knowledge, even at the age of twenty, commanded the respect and admiration of both his fellow students and his superiors. Even then he must have been displaying those marks of strong character which resounded across the pages of his panegyric, zealous in work, disinterested, honourable, generous, open-handed, affectionate in family and a staunch friend. One can imagine that there was also a slight lack of a sense of humour. His departure from Göttingen in 1806 must have been a loss to all his friends, but they sent him on his way to London armed with a letter from the naturalist, Blumenbach, to Sir Joseph Banks. Sir Joseph was a man of influence and wealth whose latest obsession was the Association for Promoting the Discovery of the Interior Parts of Africa.

John seems to have hit it off very well with Sir Joseph for he was soon volunteering to carry out exploration work for the Association. This would have been a perfect mutual agreement, for the social life of London, even the intellectual or 'advancement of knowledge' fringe, would hardly have satisfied John's tireless energy. On the other hand the Association, brimming over with a zealous spirit of enquiry, found in the young Swiss an ideal tool to further their laudable causes. The offer was accepted. Then came an unexplained pause of three years, for it was not until the end of 1809 that he finally received his marching orders. Before sailing for Malta in March the following year, he spent some time in London and Cambridge attending lectures on chemistry, astronomy and medicine and in taking a 'crash course' in Arabic. At the same time he started hardening himself up in anticipation of the rigours ahead, by going for long walks bareheaded, sleeping on the ground and eating nothing but vegetables. All this was taken very seriously and pursued with admirable Teutonic application.

Fig. 21 J. L. Burckhardt, the rediscoverer of Petra, from the Frontispiece to his *Travels in Syria*.

He spent seven weeks in Malta improving his Arabic and gathering together the necessary paraphernalia to enable him to pass himself off as a Moslem trader

from India. It was in this guise that he proposed to visit Syria to further his study
of the Mohammedan way of life. His period on the island seems to have been
uneventful and he duly set off for Antioch. The journey, however, was not to
prove quite so uneventful, for he was put ashore in Karamania, near Tarsus, and
only after many trying adventures did he reach his immediate destination. Here
he was not received with open arms; indeed, the man-handling he received
would have set a man of lesser determination back on the road for home.

Not so John, who promptly joined a camel caravan and journeyed on to
Aleppo. His Arabic was evidently by no means perfect for he was frequently
questioned about his curious accent. This he blamed on the fact that Hindustani
was his mother-tongue and Arabic did not come naturally; on being asked for
a sample of Hindustani he would launch into a great spiel of guttural Swiss–
German which seemed to satisfy even his most critical hearers, sage heads nodded
in recognition of the mother-tongue of the great subcontinent.

He spent over two years in Aleppo perfecting his Arabic and studying Islamic
and Koramic law in which he became so fluent that questions of doctrine and
exegesis were brought to him for elucidation and interpretation. Not all this time
was spent, however, in learned discussions with the elders of the mosques, for
during the turn of 1810–11 he made a journey into the interior and visited the
majestic ruins of Palmyra and Baalbeck and the great trading city of Damascus.
His reputation would have stood him in good stead in the cities and towns, which
is more than can be said for his guides and servants while he was in the desert.
Twice they deserted him, leaving him to an untimely and unrecorded death. His
remarkable resolution and toughness, to say nothing of an admirable desire not
to die quite so young, carried him through and he returned to the safety of
Aleppo.

The object of his commission from the Association was to discover the 'Interior
Parts of Africa', so, having equipped himself to his satisfaction in the Moslem
mode of life, he set off in 1812 for Cairo from where he proposed to launch his
first expedition into those 'Interior Parts'.

He first went to Tripoli, Syria, and then set out southwards down the dusty,
hilly road across the Biblical lands. He was not particularly taken with
Philadelphia, present-day Amman, but recorded in his Journal all that he did
and saw there.

As the high, rolling hills of Moab tipped over into those of ancient Edom, he
began to hear the local people telling of a wondrous ancient city buried away in
the heart of a seemingly impenetrable mountain. His curiosity was aroused and
he cast about to find a pretext for visiting it. He could not openly declare a desire
to do so, for this would have been immediately interpreted as spying. The fear
and suspicion engendered by centuries of isolation from any civilising force had

made these desert men suspicious of any motive they could not understand. Greed was the only thing they recognised in strangers and this they could deal with. Knowing, however, that the tomb of Aaron was in the vicinity of the ancient ruins, he let it be known that he had made a vow to sacrifice to the Prophet Aaron. None of his companions would dare to object to so laudable an intention, and so as they descended from the bleached hills there was nothing they could do but grumble silently.

The bare, open hillsides lay tensed in the heat, rolling their bald eyes at a blazing sun set in a fiercely blue August sky. Down in the valley the silvery green of olive and oleander stood motionless while the rich dark green leaves of the fig-trees cast stygian shadows in which dark pools of stifling treachery enticed the unwary into their fly-ridden seclusion. The men of the 'Lyathene' tribe were encamped on the hillside above Ain Mousa, the Spring of Moses, and towards them, through the hypnotic glare, strode John and his companion, dragging a reluctant goat behind them. On arrival it was pointed out that the goat could be sacrificed there and then, for the tomb of Aaron was visible high up on the summit away to the west (Fig. 45). The irritable guide had already pointed this out to John but, Ibrahim ibn Abdallah, the name used by John—and which today is carried on his tombstone in the Moslem cemetery in Cairo—had vowed to make the immolation at the very tomb itself.

Having allayed at last their fears and suspicions, John was allowed to pass. With his guide he went down through the village of Elji and the deserted ruins of Badabde which had until recently housed a community of Greek Christians now moved north to the more hospitable clime of Kerak.

They followed the dry water course of the Wadi Mousa (Fig. 22) which led through the echoing Siq coming to the silent, deserted Treasury (Frontispiece), el Khasneh. Here he stopped and nearly aroused the suspicions of his guide by going and having a look inside. Such monuments were the work of the great magician, the Pharaoh, and were of no concern to a devout believer. All the while John was making notes in his Journal which he kept concealed under his voluminous garb. He dared not bring it out, for its disclosure would have meant certain death as a spy. Somehow he even managed to draw a plan of the Khasneh with near correct proportions.

The party went on down the Outer Siq, visiting the cave with fourteen graves which must have taken them slightly out of their route. They then proceeded across the central valley to the Kasr el Bint before turning south towards the ridges of el Barra (see Map 3, on pages 120–21). The guide was by now getting more and more irritated at this diversion from their route and urged John to make his sacrifice as soon as possible. As the lower slopes of the Gebel Haroun were approaching, John began to feel 'exceedingly fatigued' and decided that he

2. The Siq at its narrowest part

Fig. 22 The Bab el Siq, with its 'djin' blocks or square carved towers.

had gone far enough. He proposed, because it was getting dark, to make his sacrifice at the foot of the mountain instead of at the shrine on the top. Heaving a huge sigh of relief the guide was only too pleased to assist in the ritual and then hurried his master back across the darkening hills, through the now inky Siq and back up the hill to Elji.

For the men of the 'Lyathene' tribe, 22 August 1812 was just another day with little to distinguish it from the rest of time and nothing to remember it by. But for Western scholars of the antique it was an important day in a momentous year, for John Burckhardt, being a man of considerable, even prodigious, learning and remarkable intelligence had realised what he had seen: '. . . it appears very probable that the ruins in the Wadi Mousa are those of ancient Petra.'

The city he saw was the same sand-covered, crumbling ruin we see today (Fig. 23). Across it the bedouin had tramped their unmomentous ways for a thousand unrecorded years. Its isolation had been due not only to its remote position but also to the local tribesmen who actively discouraged visitors. Travel in the Near East at this time was a perilous undertaking and there were none of the amenities which exist today. The learning which had kept alight, however feebly, the lamps of classical thought which had sustained Petra for so long, had moved to the West, and was now pitted against the 'new' thought of Islam. This conflict caused an isolation of the most hostile kind. Such words as 'infidel' were used by both sides and are indicative of the depth of the division.

To cross such a barrier was to take one's life in one's hands. One had either to be stupid, neurotic or enormously brave. The first can't be helped, the second won't be helped, the last help themselves. And they help themselves by making meticulous preparation before they embark on an adventure. But yet, for all his long and careful preparation for the part he was to play, John's exploits took him

Fig. 23 The 'Triumphal Arch' by Léon de Laborde which now no longer exists.

into an area for which there is no possibility to plan; such is adventure. It was his personal strength of character, his natural courage in adversity, which carried him through instant crises and long-term perils.

He arrived in Cairo in September where he immediately started laying plans for the great adventure into those 'Interior Parts of Africa'. The object was to explore for the source of the River Niger. In the meantime he journeyed into Upper Egypt, Abyssinia (which probably means the south Sudan) before crossing the Red Sea to Jeddah. With the aid of the Viceroy of Egypt, Mohammed Aly, who was furthering his Wah haby campaign locally, he visited Mecca in 1814 where he was introduced to the Kady, the chief religious judge. The impression he made on the wise old man was very favourable for he was regarded not only as a most devout Moslem but also an exceedingly learned one. Thus he became the first Christian to enter the sacred city, in which he spent three months. Had his identity—and Journal—been discovered the penalty would certainly have been death. January 1815 saw him in Medina on a pilgrimage to the Prophet's Tomb where he was struck again with fever. It was not until April that he returned once more to Cairo to continue with the preparations for the great Niger expedition into the Fezzan. The delays in setting up this expedition must have been exasperating to a man of action like John.

The organisation of the expedition was still not complete in 1816 and one begins to suspect that it was to a great extent in the hands of 'professional organisers'. In a fury of irritation John took himself off to Suez and into Sinai on another solo ramble. This was to be his last great journey for, back once more in Egypt, he contracted dysentery and died on 17 October 1817, after only eleven days' illness. At his own request he was buried in the Mohammedan cemetery in Cairo under the name he had used throughout all his travels, Pilgrim Ibrahim ibn Abdallah.

For John Burckhardt the assumed role of a Moslem was not play-acting, for even though he never renounced his Christian faith he came to respect and understand the faith and world of Islam. No affront was meant by his 'illicit' entry into Mecca and Medina nor were his discussions of Koranic law with the Kady and others undertaken lightly or with frivolous intent; he discussed and interpreted with sincerity and great understanding. He, like Lawrence of Arabia almost exactly one hundred years later, was one of those very few, indeed rare, individuals who have managed to bridge the yawning cultural and intellectual gap which divides the world of Islam from that of the West.

His Journals were written under the most dangerous and secret conditions, but it was only in 1822, five years after his untimely death, that his account of the journey from Damascus to Cairo was published under the title *Travels in Syria*. His *Travels in Nubia* was published with an obituary in 1819, and in 1829 *Travels in Arabia* completed the cycle of his writings.

Knowledge of Burckhardt's discovery of Petra had spread long before the publication of his Journals, for in May 1818 two commanders of the Royal Navy, the Hon. C. L. Irby and Mr J. Mangles, spent some days sightseeing in the ancient city. They would have spent longer but were perpetually in fear of their lives. It may have been for this reason that they dressed as 'Arabs', though the early nineteenth-century romantic notion of how an Arab should look would have hardly been much of a disguise. They approached from the west and north by way of the huge Crusader castle of Shobak and eventually came down to the village of Elji where they experienced endless troubles with the local population. Visitors in the back-woods of the Near East were still a great rarity and those who did venture forth were really quite intrepid. The habit of gazing at a façade for the pleasure of gazing at it would have been inexplicable to the bedouin who must have been sure that such visitors were either spying or looking for treasure.

The naval gentlemen spent two days on an intensive expedition through the ruined city, visiting the Theatre (Fig. 24), Corinthian and Palace Tombs as well as the Kasr el Bint. They do not seem to have had much of an opinion of the Nabatean classical style, though the qualifications of Mr Banks who, with a

Fig. 24 Léon de Laborde's 'View from the top of the Theatre'.

certain Mr Legh, accompanied them to assist in the matter of judgement, are
debatable. They found it '. . . loaded with ornaments in the Roman manner, but
in a bad taste, with an infinity of broken lines and unnecessary angles and projections, and multiplied pediments and half pediments, and pedestals set upon
columns that support nothing (Fig. 37b). It has more the air of a fantastical
scene in a theatre than an architectural work in stone; and for unmeaning richness, and littleness of conception, Mr Banks seems to think, might have been the
work of Boromini* himself, whose style it exactly resembles, and carries to the
extreme.'

They may not have been particularly impressed by the architectural style but
the scenery absolutely bowled them over. This was the age of the Romantics, so
it is not surprising that their rhapsodic writings allude to the greatest of all the
Romantic landscape painters. 'Salvador Rosa never conceived so savage and
suitable a quarter for Banditti . . .', while '. . . nature in her most savage and
romantic form' was presented by the summits of the hills; 'whilst their bases are
worked out in all the symmetry and regularity of art, with colonnades, and
pediments, and ranges of corridors, adhering to the perpendicular surface' (see
Fig. 25).

It seems that the Wadi Mousa was still in flood when they were there for they

* Boromini was the first great master and innovator of the Italian Baroque, a style then
held in very low regard.

Fig. 25 'The Ravine', the name given by the Royal Academician, David Roberts, to the Outer Siq.

speak of it flowing rapidly. On their last day they ascended the Gebel Haroun (Fig. 26), finding the going very hard in places. From the summit they saw the top of the Deir and later tried unsuccessfully to find a way up to it from the central valley. All in all these two naval officers seem to have seen a considerable amount even though they found the weather exceedingly cold for the end of May. They did not confine themselves to the handful of showplaces but went off exploring and, in fact, saw considerably more than the average visitor today who enjoys all the ease and safety which their time in history denied them.

The next visitors were Monsieur le Marquis, Léon de Laborde (Fig. 27), and the engraver Linant who came in 1826. De Laborde (1807–69) came from a family justly noted both for its colossal wealth and for its cultural and academic leanings. He himself was to become Director-General of the Archives of France, a Deputy and a Member of the Académie Française. His sister, Valentine, however, served in her own fashion at the altar of culture by becoming, for eighteen years, the mistress of Prosper Mérimée, the author of *Carmen*, confidante of Napoleon and Inspector-General of the Monuments of France. His visit to Petra resulted in a fine series of etchings which, for all their 'picturesque' qualities — and defects — capture in a delightful, almost naïve, way the scenic spirit. Unlike most of the early visitors, de Laborde noted and commented on the Assyrian monuments. However, having indulged in some fulsome criticism of the classical ones, he resorted to quoting the Biblical curse on Edom and observed how totally it had been fulfilled.

O, thou that dwellest in the clefts of the rock, that holdest the height of the hill, though thou shouldest make thy nest as high as the eagle, I will bring

Fig. 27 Léon de Laborde in Arab costume.

thee down from thence, saith the Lord. Also, Edom shall be a desolation; everyone that goes by shall be astonished.

They all seemed to forget, very conveniently, that for many a year after this curse, which was little more than a piece of nationalistic spite, Petra continued to enjoy prosperity. The Romantic Age could well be termed the 'Retreat from

Fig. 26 The Gebel Haroun, on the top of which is the reputed tomb of the prophet Aaron.

Reason Age', for the visitors to Petra were not so much 'astonished' by the sheer scenic wonders which time had wrought, as by the devastation which the Lord was supposed to have brought down.

Ten years later the Reverend Edward Robinson, an American Biblical scholar and virtual founder of Biblical archaeology, spent a day in Petra and was taken aback by finding a ruined city as well as a whole host of carved façades. The other writers had said almost nothing about the city site and had given the impression that there were only carved façades to be seen. Robinson noted, also, the Assyrian monuments and recognised the style. It was, however, the Theatre which seems to have fascinated him most, for he commented: 'Strange contrast where a taste for the frivolities of the day was at the same time gratified by the magnificence of the tombs; amusement in a cemetery; a theatre in the midst of sepulchres.'

His visit was part of an extended tour of the Holy Land where, Bible in hand, he successfully identified a large number of sites that had hitherto been only names. The fact that he was able to demonstrate that place-names in the Bible were actual sites gave birth to the desire for a more scholarly and 'scientific' investigation of the Holy Land than had previously been the case. It was not, however, until thirty years later that the first of the great learned societies came into being with the avowed intention and object of serious study of Palestine and its neighbouring Biblical states. This was the Palestine Exploration Fund, founded in 1865 in London. It was followed five years later by the American Palestine Exploration Society. Then came the German Orient Company, the British School of Archaeology, the American School of Archaeology, the French Biblical School and School of Archaeology, and many others. These societies and schools, or their successors, are still one of the main front-line forces in Biblical archaeology and research. Their strength and effectiveness is a fine and lasting tribute to Robinson whose early activities were the inspiration which brought them into being.

The Royal Academician, David Roberts, came in 1829 and made some beautiful drawings (Fig. 28). Given the short time at his disposal the accuracy of his work is remarkable; this is not to say that he did not get some things wrong for he certainly did. As a colourist he was always rather weak but as a draughtsman he was in a class all of his own; by comparison, Linant's work was thick and overworked. The text by Kinnear which accompanied his folio publication contributed nothing to our knowledge of the place.

The great Henry Layard, discoverer of Nineveh and one of the father founders of archaeology as a science, came in 1840 and thought 'The most striking feature at Petra is the immense number of excavations in the mountain sides (Fig. 29). It is astonishing that a people should, with infinite labour, have carved the living

Fig. 28 The 'Eastern end of the Valley', drawn by David Roberts.

rock into temples, theatres, public and private buildings and tombs, and having thus constructed a city on the borders of the desert, in a waterless, inhospitable region, destitute of all that is necessary for the sustenance of man—a fit dwelling place for the wild and savage robber tribes that now seek shelter in its mountains.'

It is surprising that so observant and discriminating a man as Layard should have succumbed to the popular belief that the whole city was excavated into 'the living rock' when it is abundantly obvious that a fabricated city of considerable dimensions was at his feet. However, he expresses what many a visitor has felt about the 'astonishing' and 'infinite labour' that must have been put into the production of the thousand façades which are worth looking at. Perhaps to refined Western sensibilities which have put caves behind them as a reasonable proposition for dwelling in, the notion of being a troglodyte must be both disturbing and inexplicable.

Layard was robbed by the locals and seems, in consequence, to have shared the popular view of the people of Elji and the area about. For some reason this village has acquired an evil reputation which persisted right up to after the First World War. Layard went on to discover the lost capital of Asurbanipal of Assyria; Petra was not his 'scene' and his comments, though interesting as those of a great explorer and the founder of Assyriology, contribute little to the study of Nabatean culture and civilisation. He thought the architecture 'debased, of a bad period and corrupt style, and wanting in both elegance and grandeur'. He was, however, prepared to concede that the ruins were unlike anything else to be found in the ancient world. In this he was very nearly true, for only at Medain Saleh (ancient Hegra), to the south in Saudi Arabia, is there anything comparable to the conglomeration of carved façades such as in Petra.

PETRA March 1st 1839.

Fig. 29 'The Urn Tomb' by David Roberts captures in a remarkable way the huge scale of the so-called 'Royal Tombs'.

After Layard there was a steady, biannual trickle of dauntless travellers arriving in Petra, some of whom wrote of their experiences and ventured into print. Some of these accounts are trite and actually misleading because of their inaccuracies or their gross exaggerations. For instance, one writer refers to the

Siq, the gorge by which one enters Petra from the east, as being three miles long and 1,000 feet deep. It is in fact a little over a mile long and at its deepest is never more than 400 feet. Some, however, are useful records and can now tell us of things long since vanished; the arch over the entrance to the Siq is an example. One of the most remarkable descriptions was that by Harriet Martineau who described the Wadi Mousa in spate, a thing not seen now—certainly not in May. The year was 1847 and she was returning to camp after having toured the northern area of the city.

I knew that the tents lay south-west, on the other side of the water-course. So off we went, as straight as an arrow—across gullies, over hills, through ankle-deep water, for it was no time for picking and choosing our footing. One of my companions was lame that day; but on he must go, over stone-heaps and through pools. We found a way down into the water-course, walked many yards along it, knowing now where we were, and got out of it not far from our platform. Within three minutes, before I had half put off my wet clothes, I heard a shout: the torrent had come down. Down it came, almost breast-high, rushing and swirling among the thickets and great stones in the water-course, giving us a river in a moment, where we had never dreamed of hoping to see one! As soon as I could, I ran out to the verge of the platform; and I shall never forget the sight. It was worth any inconvenience and disappointment. We forgot the dripping wet tent, from which little rills ran upon our bedsteads: we forgot the lost hours of this last day, and our damp wardrobes, and all our discomforts. There was the muddy torrent—or rather, the junction of two torrents, which divided the channel between them for some way—the one which had come from the Sik, and past the theatre, being muddy, and the other, from the north-east being clear. On came the double stream, bowing and waving the tamarisks and oleanders—the late quarters of the Arabs who were now looking on from the opposite bank. Just before sunset, I went to look again. The white waterfalls were still tumbling from the steeps; and the whole scene was lighted up by a yellow glow from the west, where the sky was clearing. The torrent was still dashing along, making eddies among the stones; and beyond it, under a wall of rock, was a group of Arabs round a fire, whose smoke curled up above the trees. At night, I went once more; and that was the finest of all. The torrent was too deep within its banks to be touched by the moon, which was now shining brightly. The waters could scarcely be seen, except in one spot where they caught a gleam from an Arab fire. But at this hour, its rush seemed louder than ever . . .'*

* *Eastern Life: Past and Present* (1848).

Edward Lear's drawings of Petra are lovely and intensely interesting. Not that he painted the contortions of rock which Julian Huxley has described as being 'like human constructions which had begun to melt and lose their sharpness of outline'. He just presented broad, expansive views which catch the image of the land so well. It was the riotous colouring which bewitched his cook, Giorgio, who in an ecstasy of delight yelped: 'Oh, Signore, we have come into a world where everything is made of chocolate, ham, curry-powder and salmon.' Not exactly a recipe but a 'deliciously' novel description of the colours of Petra.

Doughty paid a short, harassed visit in 1876. His intense dislike of the place is by now legend and is best summarised in his own words. 'Strange and horrible as a pit in the inhuman deadness of nature is this site of the Nabateans' metropolis. The eye recoils from that mountainous close of iron cliffs, in which the ghastly waste monuments of a sumptuous barbaric art are from the first glance an eyesore.' There would seem to be little chance of redemption before such an indictment, but the author of so noble a work as *Arabia Deserta* was capable of being moved even by works which he did not like. After all, it was much more the setting of the place that he loathed, even though he does not seem to have thought very highly of the façades. But when he first saw the Khasneh as he approached from the Outer Siq, he was enchanted and his lines of admiration have a simple, telling acceptance about them that comes only in response to simple, telling beauty. Next 'is that most perfect of the monuments, Khasna Faraoun, whose sculptured columns and cornices are pure lines of a chrystalline beauty without blemish, where-upon the golden sun looks from above, and Nature has painted that sand rock ruddy with iron rust.'

The first published work, however, which made any serious attempt to sort things out was *The Jordan Valley and Petra* by Drs Libbey and Hoskins, published in 1905. It was they who first noticed and recognised the High Place behind el Habis. But their work is all too often disturbed by what nowadays seem fatuous and naïve descriptions. A particularly irritating one is their description of the narrow upper end of the Wadi al Jarra in which the Khasneh stands, which they call the 'Fairy Dell'. This smacks of 'butter-cups and daisies' and polite children's tales: the wadi, even in spring when it is surely most attractive with its wild desert flowers and lush greens, is not remotely like a fairy anything.

It was Professor Alois Musil who undertook the first really scientific exploration of Petra, in 1896. His work *Arabia Petraea* was not, however, published until 1907, by which time Brünnow and Domaszewski had published their massive survey and critical analysis. Although Musil was undoubtedly the first to undertake such researches he confined himself curiously enough to the classical monuments with which he deals quite extensively. To compensate for ignoring the Nabatean monuments, he paid particular attention to the 'cult' sites, i.e. High Places, etc.,

which he explored and described thoroughly. By the time he was ready to pub-
lish, he had the advantage of Brünnow's work and this he used, particularly in
the matter of nomenclature.

The German scholars, Brünnow and Domaszewski, and later Dalman, were
like Musil in that their text was not narrative or given to an occasional humorous
aside. For all these scholars, the work in hand was a scientific operation which
required its own serious language and factual mode of expression: not the
faintest glimmer of humanity comes through their writing. They drew a whole
series of maps, accurate enough to be useful, on which they marked over 800 of
the more important and recordable monuments. Each was given a number and
a brief description: each was classified as to style and conjectured use.

Sir Alexander Kennedy was unable to accept Brünnow's nomenclature for the
various styles and propounded one of his own devising. Regrettably, the author
of this book has not found it possible to accept Sir Alexander's schedule and the
next chapter draws on a completely new nomenclature.

Dalman came to Petra with a particular interest in the religious sites, or places
of worship. His opus is remarkable in its analytical prowess but is slightly marred
by his persistent attempts to belittle the work of Brünnow and Domaszewski,
almost it would seem out of spite. Although he published in German he did write
an article on the Khasneh for the Palestine Exploration Fund's Annual in 1911.

It is, however, with the early visitors that we are here most concerned. Their
picturesque accounts abound with splendid passages written in a style of English
not heard today.

> The solitude (of the Siq) is disturbed by the incessant screaming of eagles,
> hawks, owls and ravens, soaring above in considerable numbers, apparently
> amazed at strangers invading their lonely habitation. At every step the
> scenery discovers new and more remarkable features; a stronger light begins
> to break through the sombre perspective (Fig. 61), until at length the ruins
> of the city burst on the view of the astonished traveller in their full grandeur,
> shut in on every side by barren, craggy precipices, from which numerous
> recesses and narrow valleys branch out in all direction . . .
> The ruins of the city itself open on the view with singular effect, after wind-
> ing two or three miles through the dark ravine. Tombs present themselves
> not only in every avenue within it, and on every precipice that surrounds it,
> but even intermixed almost promiscuously with its public and domestic
> edifices; so that Petra has been truly denominated one vast necropolis.
> The immense number of these stupendous ruins corroborate the accounts
> given, both by sacred and profane writers, of the kings of Petra, their courtly
> grandeur. . . . Great must have been the opulence of a capital that could
> dedicate such monuments to the memory of its rulers.

These extracts, taken from Crighton's *History of Arabia and its People*, epitomise all the writings which went before, and from which the information is largely derived. But almost inevitably the curse of Edom is quoted with what Sir Alexander Kennedy has called 'a most unchristian rejoicing—one may, in fact, say, a pious chortling'.

> These magnificent remains can now be regarded only as the grave of Idumaea, in which its former wealth and splendour lie interred. The state of desolation into which it has long fallen is not only the work of time, but the fulfilment of prophesy, which foretold that wisdom and understanding should perish out of Mount Seir; that Edom should be a wilderness, its cities a perpetual waste, the abode of every unclean beast. 'Thorns shall come up in her palaces, nettles and brambles in the fortresses thereof; the cormorant and the bittern shall possess it, and it shall be an habitation of dragons, and a court of owls. The wild beasts of the desert shall also meet with the wild beasts of the island, and the satyr shall cry to his fellow; there shall the vultures also be gathered, every one with her mate; there shall the screech owl make her nest, and lay, and find for herself a place of rest' (Isaiah 34, 13: 14). Nowhere is there a more striking and visible demonstration of the truth of these Divine predictions than among the fallen columns and deserted palaces of Petra. The dwellers in the clefts of the rock are brought low; the princes of Edom are as nothing; its eighteen cities are swept away, or reduced to empty chambers and naked walls; and the territory of the descendants of Esau affords as miraculous a proof of the inspiration of Scripture history as the fate of the Children of Israel.

For these early travellers, a visit to Petra was one of the great experiences; the hazards and perils, at the hands of both nature and of humans, added greatly to the thrill. The amazing thing is that, even though it is now quite simple and safe to visit this long lost city, the same sense of excited enchantment still pervades the expedition, and visitors still sense all the same thrills and climaxes about which our forbears wrote.

CHAPTER FOUR

Great and Sublime Ideas

'ARCHITECTURE ... applies itself, like music (and I believe we may add poetry) directly to the imagination, without the intervention of any kind of imitation. . . . In the hands of a man of genius it is capable of inspiring sentiment, and of filling the mind with great and sublime ideas.' The explanation for this fact, noted by Sir Joshua Reynolds in 1786, may be that architecture, like music, reflects the intellectual and spiritual character of the epoch which created it. This is exactly true of the architecture of Petra. Although it is not possible yet to date with certainty, there are clearly distinguishable periods which demonstrate a continual development. This development from the earliest façades can be traced, and the style thus appears to be the result of a conscious working towards an ideal of beauty rather than a haphazard arrangement of ideas. The designers, probably architect-engineers, displayed a growing assurance and self-confidence as they experimented with more advanced architectural ideas, all the time slowly absorbing new concepts from alien cultures.

PERIODS OF ARCHITECTURAL DEVELOPMENT IN PETRA

1	Rectilinear		
2	Assyrian	Phase I	single-band multiple crow-step
		Phase II	double-band multiple crow-step
3	Cavetto	Phase I	single-divide crow-step unadorned
		Phase II	single-divide crow-step with pilasters
4	Double Cornice	Phase I	single-divide crow-step with pilasters
		Intermediate	single-divide crow-step with pilasters and four caps in sub-attic
		Phase II	single-divide crow-step with four pilasters and caps in sub-attic
5	Nabatean Classical		
6	Roman Classical		

At present there is little architecture of the living to be seen, in fact only the Kasr el Bint and the Temenos Gate (Fig. 23), and one has to fall back on the carved façades which are largely sepulchral in association.

These façades and their decoration can be divided into six main groups, three of which may be further subdivided to express particular phases of development. There is an additional group dealing with the arch-headed monuments which stands apart from the main development which was primarily concerned with straight lines. As with all other architectures, one period does not suddenly stop and the next one begin, they merge gradually, some characteristics being retained after the full concept of which they were a part had been abandoned.

The author has not found it possible to agree completely with either Brünnow's or Kennedy's nomenclature for these groups or periods, so the names given here are, in part, new. An attempt has, however, been made to simplify them and make them easily understood and unambiguous.

I

Rectilinear

This is probably the earliest form of decoration to be found on the monuments of Petra. In its simplest form it is a single groove cut above a doorway (Fig. 30a, b). There are one or two examples of this, although in most cases the feature has become very badly eroded. A later development doubled up the line, with sometimes a crude outline pediment. Often there is no actual façade, and the features appear by themselves over a doorway in the rock face; as architectural façades began to appear it was natural that rectilinear ornament should be incorporated into the design. Examples of both incised and relief ornament are found all over Petra. Two of the finest are beside the Lion Tomb just off the Wadi al Deir. The earlier of the two is a more complicated design than at first appears (Fig. 31). A groove just over the width of the door supports a band of stone upon which rests another wide band. This second band is divided from a third by another, longer groove, the whole composition being completed by an outline pediment. It has been suggested that these sunken pediments and grooves might originally have housed memorial plaques, but there is no evidence on this façade of dowell holes or other means of holding the applied

Fig. 31 The Rectilinear tomb beside the Lion Tomb. Note the diagonal hatching of the stone, a feature which was to persist in a refined form in all major Nabatean carved monuments.

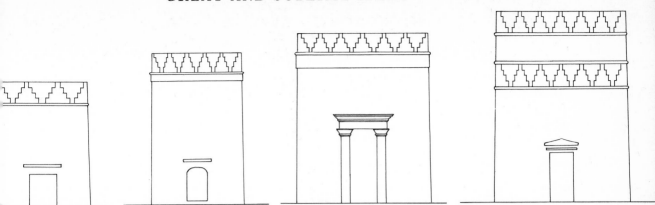

Figs. 30*a, b, c, d* Assyrian-type façades.

surface in place. The smooth surface of the rock around the 'façade' shows an early, and not particularly competent, attempt at the diagonal dressing of stone which is such a feature of Nabatean work. From the inexpertness of the treatment it is possible to suggest that this is very early Nabatean work executed when they were still experimenting with the new-found, or inherited, skill of working stone. It fairly disposes of the notion that all rectilinear ornament is pre-Nabatean.

The monument to the right displays embryo pilasters, which shows the Nabateans groping towards an 'architectural' expression; interestingly enough it was not, however, with pilasters that they finally produced their first architectural statements. This 'façade' shows, therefore, that the Rectilinear style of decoration persisted for a long time, in fact right up to the time when the influence of Hellenism was beginning to be felt.

Sir Alexander Kennedy thought that there was a possibility that this form derived from Egypt, or possibly Mesopotamia. This may be true, but the fact is that it is a very rudimentary form and one related to the visual impact of beams of constructed buildings. All primitive constructions in wood used straight lines, and the methods often produced pleasing patterns; these were reproduced in later buildings in different materials long after the primitive form had been submerged in later techniques. Greek architecture is the perfect example of this.

II

Assyrian

The Assyrian monuments account for over half of the façades in Petra, and can be divided into two distinct phases. Phase I was the first architectural expression of the Nabateans and is possibly a reproduction in carved stone of the mud-brick structures of Mesopotamia. The dominant characteristic is a band of multiple crow-steps which cap the composition. In only one instance in Petra does this serve as anything more than mere ornament (Fig. 33c) but this monument properly falls into a later period and is in any case unique and, therefore, not representative. The crow-steps always start and end with half-stacks and there are always four steps to each side; the number of stacks is variable. The proper Assyrian version of this motif has only three steps; even so, there can be little doubt that it was from that Mesopotamian civilisation the Nabateans acquired the basic idea. A superb example of this is shown on Panel 124867 of the Lion Hunt Reliefs from the North Palace at Nineveh, now in the British Museum. These bands of crow-step ornament rest on a curved 'tenia' or bold round string-course. The 'Streets of Façades' in the Outer Siq abound with monuments of this type which occur in many other places as well.

Phase I is distinguished by having only a single row or band of multiple crow-step ornament (Fig. 30a, b, c). The monuments are, by and large, very simple, modest in scale and often retain a Rectilinear groove over the door. It is a style of architecture, or rather a type of decoration, on which any development is very limited; little variation is possible. A flat apron string-course below the tenia was sometimes added (Fig. 30b) and this certainly did add a little solidity to the effect.

The fact that, even at this early stage, an attempt was occasionally being made at incorporating a 'classical' feature such as a pilastered door frame (Fig. 30c) indicates that the Phase I was still operative about 300 B.C. It would be extremely dangerous to try and date these monuments on comparative styles, but as Hellenism did not start until the time of Alexander the Great, and it can be safely assumed that the 'classical' or Hellenistic features did not appear in remote Petra until well after his death, we have at least a date before which these façades are unlikely to have appeared. The 'classical' vocabulary is very much what one would expect from someone who was trying to remember what he had seen elsewhere. The detailing is amateur and clumsy and shows little or no understanding of proportions: these are consistent faults through the Nabatean Classical style, even though this fault did eventually evolve from being a second-hand copy into an individual set of rules upon which it is perhaps more appropriate to judge the style. In the beginning, however, the total lack of understanding of what classical detailing meant is comparable with early English Jacobean work in wood and stone. It was a fashionable innovation applied with out any appreciation of the rules. As with Jacobean, it developed into a vernacular style quite independent of the mother character.

The next stage of development, Phase II, was to add another band of crow-steps above the original one (Fig. 30d), with a wide, plain sub-attic storey between the two. The tenia was retained on both bands but only the lower one had it above and below the ornament; the upper band had it only below. The apron string-course does not seem to have been regularly applied. This phase must have been a fairly quick development on Phase I, for Rectilinear ornament of a more sophisticated kind appears on some of the façades. It is likely that the two ran concurrently for some while but Phase II extended right into the time when the 'classical' features were becoming a bit more correct, implying a greater degree of contact with Hellenism. Minor variations occur in the treatment of the multiple crow-step such as in Fig. 32a, where the tops of the stacks were tied together by an imitation string-course.

III

Cavetto

A major break in the architectural tradition came with the introduction of the cavetto cornice (Fig. 32b). Above this a band of multiple crow-steps would have looked lost and rather ridiculous, so at the same time another major innovation was made in the form of the single-divide crow-step of monumental proportions.

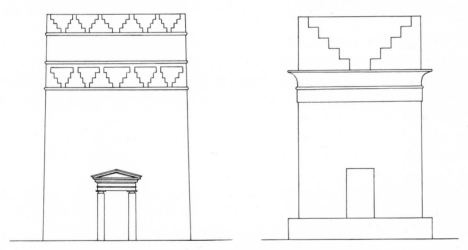

Figs. 32a and b Assyrian and Cavetto type façades.

There is obviously at work here a strong cultural influence which was not present before, for the break with the older form is so great. Egypt is a strong contender as the source of inspiration, for the cavetto cornice is a persistent feature of Egyptian architecture over many hundreds of years. Why, however, should it suddenly start making its influence felt when it had already gone out of fashion in its own homeland, as it surely did with the coming of the Ptolemies? The same feature, however, is also much in evidence in Persian work of this period and it is possible that the idea came from that direction. The Nabateans had always kept their lines of intellectual communication open towards the East, and continued to derive a certain spiritual comfort from that direction even though they might increasingly embrace the Hellenism of the West. Their reliance on this spiritual comfort is evident by the retention of the Assyrian crow-step idea, albeit in a new, dramatic form, in the bold, sweeping change which the Cavetto period denotes.

The familiar tenia is retained and the apron string-course reappears; the earlier examples show a massive strength and economy of form which is very assertive and powerful. The whole scale, however, becomes obviously much larger as the period goes on.

Phase II sees yet another major innovation into the scheme with the introduction of feigned classical pilasters on either side of the façade, supporting the apron string-course which now becomes an entablature (Fig. 32c). The designer must have been well aware of this metamorphosis in the function of the apron string-course, for the earliest examples of it are set on a narrow architrave which still preserved the identity of the apron. The capitals to the pilasters look like blocked-out versions waiting to be finished. This character persists right into the period of Roman Classical architecture and becomes one of the dominant features of the Nabatean style.

Even at this late stage there are occurrences of the Rectilinear groove over the door even though the usual ornament is a classical composition of increasing lineal complexity. We can see here (Fig. 32d) an early expression of that love of horizontal lines which became almost a disfiguring fetish of the Nabatean designers.

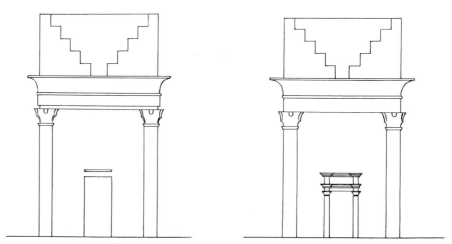

Figs. 32c and *d* Cavetto type façades.

Eventually the architrave disappears and the apron string-course gives way to a deeper, fully confident entablature below the outward-sweeping curve of the cavetto cornice. The powerful, single-divide crow-step commands the attic storey.

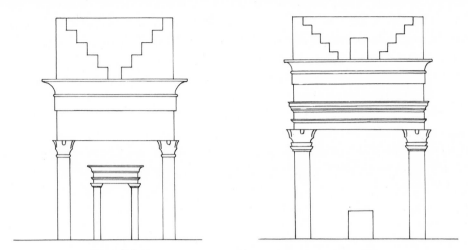

Figs. 33a and b Cavetto and Double Cornice type façades.

The 'classical' doorways shown in Figs. 32d and 33a hint at the development which was to take the style into its next recognisable period. Again it relies greatly on the Nabatean love of horizontal lines divided by flat, unornamented surfaces. Fig. 33a additionally shows a rare but crucial example of a transitional façade where the entablature has reverted back to being an apron string-course and has been hoisted up above a sub-attic resting upon the pilasters. This sub-attic cries out for some kind of relief and for some means to connect the 'floating' cavetto section with the pilaster part below.

IV

Double Cornice

The answer came with the Double Cornice Period which only achieved a complete resolution, however, in the Intermediate Phase.

Phase I saw the introduction of an additional cornice across the sub-attic, below the cavetto cornice (Fig. 33b). The cornice is always in the classical idiom; there are no examples in Petra of a double cavetto cornice, and the cavetto cornice is always the upper of the two, acting as the base for the single-divide crow-step. Right through Phase I the apron string-course persists below the tenia of the cavetto and above the sub-attic. The distance between the two cornices, i.e. the depth of the sub-attic, never seems to vary much, unlike the spacing of the entablature of the classical cornice. This is, however, always boldly treated, with the frieze divided from the architrave by a heavily moulded tenia. The capitals of the pilasters now rest on the double cushions, which henceforth become a constant feature right into the Roman Classical period.

Fig. 33c is a curious and highly ornate hybrid with a finely observed Hellenistic doorframe, accoutred with a pediment and acroterions, round the space where the door was obviously intended. There is, however, no door and this sculptured tabernacle becomes a piece of surface ornament. It is debatable whether it was ever intended to have a door. The capitals too have been carved with stiff floral scroll work, and the multiple crow-step which uniquely surmounts the cavetto cornice is the only example of it being used as an actual battlement instead of as a 'blind' band of relief carving. This monument stands at an important point in the Outer Siq where originally everyone coming down that way must have seen it. Is that, perhaps, of some significance?

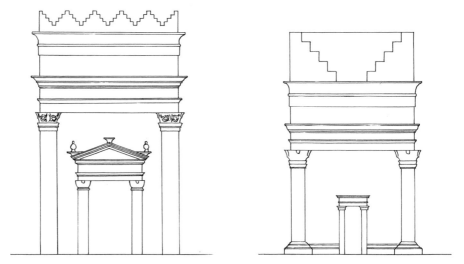

Figs. 33c and d Double Cornice type façades.

Only minor variations on this basic formula seem to have been made, such as the provision of a sculptured base for the composition (Fig. 33d), or a capping for the crow-step (Fig. 34a) and the beginning of extremely elaborate doorframes. These doorways seem to be an extension of the horizontal line obsession, for they gradually become more and more complex and congested—and not, surprisingly, rarer. A low-pitched pediment now appears to be *de rigueur*, properly adorned with the flat, cavetto-shaped acroterions.

The Intermediate Phase saw the joining up of the cavetto and the classical cornices by means of capitals on bases placed in the sub-attic (Fig. 34b). The two outer ones were placed, logically, over the flanking pilasters but the inner pair eventually led to the idea of a four-pilaster façade. The implications of this were important and one can see how it came about. To have had only two capitals bases, one on either side, would have given the impression of sagging in the middle which the designer rightly wanted to avoid. This arrangement was all right so long as the doorframe continued to occupy, indeed fill, the whole area between the two outer pilasters. If the doorway, however, was made too small the main impact of the façade would be lost. The designer's mind was, anyhow, now preoccupied with the new idea of four pilasters on the façade and this musing over the new possibilities was to spell the death of the inflated, double doorway. If there were to be two more pilasters accommodated on the façade there simply would not be room for such doorways except on the most colossal façades.

Phase II of the Double Cornice Period saw the introduction not only of the four-pilaster façade but also a development of the treatment of the outer pilasters

Figs. 34*a* and *b* Double Cornice type façades.

(Fig. 34*c*). Gone has the double doorway and in its place there is a simple, almost stark, composition. The flanking pilasters are now in the form of a round quarter column in the angle of a square half-column, with the extraordinary feature of both parts enjoying one and the same capital. This characteristic carried on into the rather tame period of Nabatean classical and the later Roman Classical.

In a way it was a pity that this native tradition could not have led to further developments. This final phase of the native imagination possessed a nobility and simplicity which makes it the best of all the design periods. The number of façades of this type are not many; the Turkamaniya Tomb (Fig. 34*d*) is a fine, though mutilated example. They represent the culmination of the native imagination working on basically native ideas before they tried bravely, but disastrously, to grapple with the implications of the classical language of

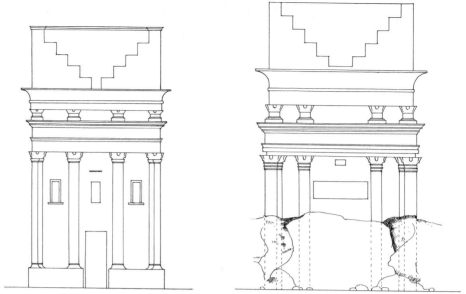

Figs. 34c and d Double Cornice type façades.

architecture. To this they brought, unfortunately, the worst of their native ideas.

The Double Cornice Period shows just how much of the classical tradition the Nabateans could digest and adapt to the advantage of their tradition. Beyond that point they threw up all the bad ideas they had had which imitated those of the classical tradition that they could not assimilate.

The period does, however, demonstrate a growing desire to incorporate new forms with which their interests abroad had brought them into contact. There can be little doubt that they were impressed by Hellenistic art and that of the rising star of Rome, which was at that time sweeping the Near East, but all the same, being so conservative, they were very reluctant to abandon their native tradition and architectural forms. Hand in hand went a desire to be in the forefront of architectural fashion and a feeling that at all costs they must not lose their national identity. The compromise which resulted gave rise to the unique character of Nabatean architecture.

Hellenism was eventually to swamp the local tradition and to lead to a period of almost architectural chaos which was only sorted out by the Romans. It is strange that this chaos should have been occasioned by the creation of one of the most beautiful monuments in Petra. The fact that it owed little to the native tradition, however, was to have a disastrous effect, for imitations became inevitable, or worse, attempts would be made to try to relate the local classicism, with its obsession for horizontal lines, to the classicism of the West. Worst of all was the combining of these bastards into one composition. Nevertheless, from this disturbed and floundering period emerged one of the most powerful and serene architectural statements in the whole of Petra, the Deir (Fig. 35).

Fig. 35 The upper part of the Deir façade, a monument in which carved elaboration was abandoned in favour of bold elementa architectural forms.

V

Nabatean Classical

There are only seven monuments in this period and each is of great individuality, denoting an amazing eclecticism and instability in the sphere of architecture. The reason for so small a number of carved façades of this period could be that most architectural activity and inventiveness was being concentrated in the building of the city rather than in carved sepulchral works. The Kasr el Bint (Fig. 91) is an important case in point and as excavations continue, it is probable that the list of Nabatean Classical monuments will increase.

The Palace Tomb (Fig. 36) stands alone and did not exert any great influence on subsequent façades; in any case it was such an enormous undertaking that there could only have been a few occasions when such a work was required. The alternating projecting and recessed bays of the first and second storeys find their inspiration and origins in the broken planes of the Khasneh, while the sculptural details are Nabatean in character. Parallels for many individual features can be found in other monuments, which indicates that the architect borrowed freely from many sources.

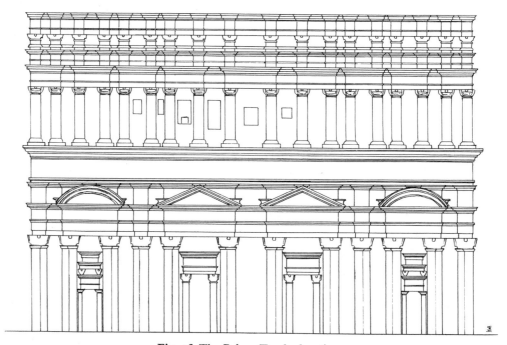

Fig. 36 The Palace Tomb elevation.

The Corinthian Tomb, Bab el Siq Triclinium, Renaissance Tomb, Tomb with a Broken Pediment, and the Deir are schematically related and are treated here as a group. The Sextus Florentinus Tomb, although Roman, also falls into this bracket.

The monument which started all this off was the Khasneh (Frontispiece). There was no build-up to the creation of this uniquely beautiful monument and as all its characteristics are totally foreign to the native tradition, one must believe that it was designed by an architect from outside the Nabatean orbit. Why, though, was such a monument created? We do not know the answer, nor do we know its date. It is such an odd, unprecedented piece of work that some clue may be found in the history of the Nabateans. At present one can only make intelligent guesses but what follows seems reasonable to the author.

Aretas III Philhellen reigned from 84 to 56 B.C., and lived while the Nabateans enjoyed their period of greatest territorial expansion and its attendant prosperity: it was during his reign that Damascus came into the Nabatean empire. This expansion would have not only made them a 'world power' but also brought them into direct contact with first-class Western art. It would not have taken Aretas or his envoys long to appreciate that their capital city was backward and that their version of Hellenistic architecture was naïve. They must also have been acutely conscious that if they were to cut any sort of figure in the world of fashion they would have to do something rather drastic to Petra. Even with the best intent their native designers could never produce rivals to the wonders of the Hellenistic Near East, so it is conceivable that Greek artists, possibly from Damascus, were invited to work in Petra.

The Khasneh, which they produced, must have had a high voltage effect on the Nabateans and the local artists must have felt impelled to match it or, at least, show that the classical spirit could be equally well expressed in the native tradition. The first thing for advanced thinkers of the day to do was to advocate the abandonment of the old-fashioned crow-steps and the further development of the sculptural details, such as doorways, which they had been designing before. For some reason the Nabateans seemed to think that the essence of classical architecture lay in the cornice, a long, moulded, horizontal line, and this they drove into a nightmarish 'infinity of broken lines and unnecessary angles and projections, and multiplied pediments, and pedestals set upon columns that support nothing'* (Fig. 37b).

The first stage of this hectic development was, however, almost a measure of desperation for, somehow, they had to match the 'pure lines of crystalline beauty' of the Khasneh. The only thing to do was to repeat the upper part of the Khasneh elevation and incorporate it into a programme of native classicism. The result was the Corinthian Tomb (Fig. 37a). It is as bad a piece of architecture as one might

* Irby and Mangles (1832).

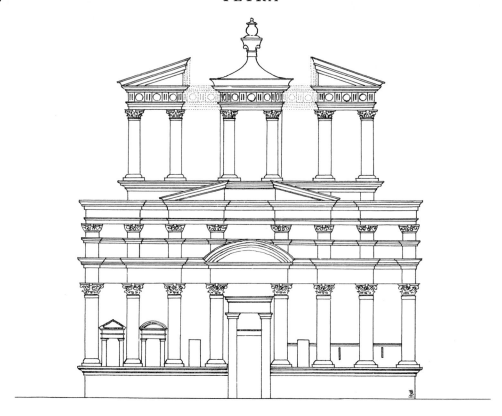

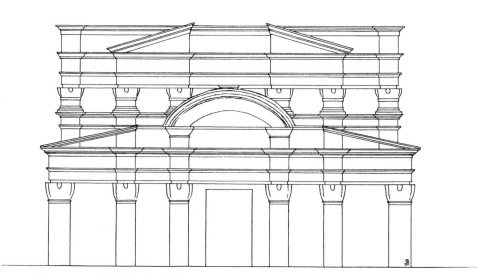

Figs. 37*a* and *b* The Corinthian Tomb and Bab el Siq Triclinium elevations.

expect from this unhappy union, but it is not without interest in that it shows that the designers were aware of the problems facing them. The main one was that of the relative scales, for the tripartite upper part would dominate oppressively the lower façade of Nabatean Classicism. They surmounted this by extending the lower façade by one bay in each direction, thus providing a firm, wide base on which to set the admired tripartite upper part.

The overall effect is confused and much overworked, and a few foreign eyebrows must have been raised even if tongues refrained from comment. If this was the tomb of Aretas III Philhellen, one can be sure that the king was well pleased and flattered that his mausoleum should incorporate a replica of his most celebrated brainchild. What comes out most clearly, however, is that the architect did not really understand the language he was using: it is a creditable piece of experimental work but whereas others, more fluent in the classical repertory, succeeded in experimenting with the rules without actually breaking them, he did not. The great mistake was in trying to combine in the same composition two totally different traditions even though they both might be wearing the same style of clothes.

The Corinthian Tomb gave rise to three other façades and, indirectly, to one more. The Bab el Siq Triclinium is a straight copy of the lower part, less the two additional bays (Fig. 37b). Having worked out what they considered to be a satisfactory formula, the Nabateans decided to let their innovation stand on its own. It was probably given its prominent position in the Bab el Siq as much for advertisement of the Nabatean Classical as for anything else.

The fact that there are only a handful of monuments of this type surely denotes that even the patricians were not following the royal lead in patronising, maybe for political reasons, the new classical style, and were probably sticking to the Double Cornice II: a few reactionaries might even have gone back to the Assyrian types. Perhaps Fig. 33c is a case in point.

People must have begun to realise how inept the Bab el Siq Triclinium looked and one can almost imagine a row in the Town Planning Committee with someone asking how it was ever allowed to get there.

On the other side of Petra, in the Wadi Farasa, two façades appeared which looked back to previous periods but which were yet distinctly classical. The Renaissance Tomb (Fig. 38a) is one of the most attractive things in Petra besides being a work of great ingenuity and artistic skill. Within a tall framework, which relies for inspiration on the Double Cornice I Period, is the familiar double doorway motif. This has, however, undergone a transformation, for above the 'standard' size inner door frame sweeps a monumental segmental arch which rests on boldly moulded pilasters and entablatures. This arch is very much like the central segmental pediment in both the Corinthian Tomb and the Bab el Siq

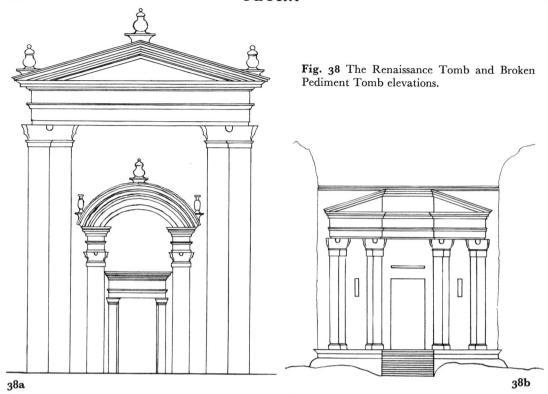

Fig. 38 The Renaissance Tomb and Broken Pediment Tomb elevations.

38a

38b

Triclinium. The composition fills the space between the pilasters but never crowds it; the handling of the relationships between mouldings and flat surfaces is masterly and shows great sensitivity. The lesson of this façade is that such ornament as there is, is functional and reasonable and not applied just for its own sake.

The Tomb with the Broken Pediment (Fig. 38*b*) employs the broken pediment of the Corinthian Tomb and the Bab el Siq Triclinium as its main decorative feature. There is still a suggestion of the obsession with horizontal lines in the detailing of the façade but the composition achieves such simplicity that the result is an effect of great strength. An unusual feature is the use of two-part Nabatean pilasters for the two central as well as the two flanking pilasters.

It is only a short step in design from the Renaissance Tomb to the Sextus Florentinus Tomb (Fig. 39) which, although Roman, is very much in the Nabatean Classical style. It was also inspired by the Double Cornice Period, this time Phase II, even though the terms used are classical throughout. Above the grand double doorway is a segmental pediment springing from the centre of the first cornice. An Imperial eagle sits on the top while the low-pitched pediment over its head pulls the whole design together. The main entablature rests on capitals/bases which extend down to the first cornice forming a second tier of

Fig. 39 The Sextus Florentinus Tomb elevation.

pilasters. It is a brilliant resolution of all the conflicting characteristics of the Nabatean Classical style. Though small in scale, the design is so compact and co-ordinated that it has a monumental quality which many a larger façade does not possess.

For their final word on architecture, the Nabateans returned to the basic formula of the Khasneh. Like the Sextus Florentinus Tomb, it might actually fall into the Roman period but its date is immaterial for the style is Nabatean Classical. The Nabateans never seem to have favoured sculptural detail, probably because the local sandstone was too soft to carve well, and in the Deir we see how they stripped the Khasneh of all its Western decoration and presented the structural form in a powerful and moving way (Fig. 40). Gone, too, is the in antis portico, for the lower half is a solid wall pierced only by the central doorway. The architect had learned from the Corinthian Tomb that, although the over-elaboration of lines was a mistake, the solid base gave a much greater impression of strength and substance than any portico. The spacing of the pilasters

is approximately the same though the capitals are wholly Nabatean in character. The main, indeed fundamental, difference lies in the addition of one bay to either end of the façade. In the Corinthian Tomb this was confined to the lower storey, but in the Deir the tripartite upper storey is flanked by single projecting pilasters which guard, like angels' wings, the spirit of the composition.

In the design of the Deir, Hellenism has been brought to heel and made to serve the Nabatean tradition.

VI

Roman Classical

The remainder of the 'classical' monuments in Petra are probably Roman in inspiration; their date is still a question-mark. The Romans, however, were cautious not to press their ideas too quickly on to their subject peoples. It may be for this reason that the two-part pilasters, as well as other Nabatean architectural characteristics, persisted right to the end of creative work in Petra. The 'horned' and 'cushioned' capitals are another good example. Even so demonstrably Western a façade as the Roman Soldier Tomb (Fig. 41) has the flanking pilasters and capitals of the Nabatean type.

The native tradition as a whole became submerged under the standardised work of the Roman designers, so that only faint glimmers of individuality now appear. The list of Roman Classical monuments is not long nor by and large is it particularly impressive. The largest single undertaking would have been the

Theatre but of this we know very little. It is believed that after A.D. 106 the city was considerably altered, and it may well have been that like Nabatean classical work, the best Roman architecture was for the living and has yet to be found. We already have the Temenos Gate and part of the Colonnade Street but these are not enough to start making assertions on.

Accepting regional differences, Roman architecture is the same all over the Roman world, from Corstopitum near Hadrian's Wall to Dura in eastern Syria. For this reason it is not necessary to deal at any

Fig. 41 The Roman Soldier Tomb. The carving in the central niche has sometimes been identified as of a Roman soldier; the tomb is certainly of the Roman period of Petra's history.

Fig. 40 The Deir or Monastry, the largest of the rock-cut monuments of Petra; note the size of the man standing in the central doorway.

length with the monuments of this period, for they speak for themselves in a familiar language; such comment as may be necessary occurs in the next chapter.

*   *   *

The round- or arch-headed monuments present a particular problem for they do not seem to fit in with any of the other phases. Those in the 'Streets of Façades' (Fig. 42) are probably much older than those below Umm el Biyara (Fig. 43) which have the appearance of being related to high-pitched segmental pediments rather than to proper arches. It has been suggested that these find their origins in Syria, in which case the influence is again Hellenistic through the Seleucid dynasty which ruled until 64 B.C. These monuments are curious intrusions in a culture which was obsessed by the straight line.

Nothing has been said of the Kasr el Bint for the simple reason that it is still undergoing critical examination and it would be premature to start forming conclusions.

The carved architecture shows that Petra was subject to many of the cultural ideas which were current in the Near East after the time of Alexander the Great. What the particular influences are and where they originated has not yet been fully determined. Two traditions stand out clearly, the Assyrian and the Hellenistic; both were adopted, modified and then assimilated into the Nabatean tradition. This tradition was not so much a school of architecture as a cultural

Fig. 42 An arch-topped tomb near the Theatre.

Fig. 43 A group of two arch-topped tombs below Umm el Biyara.

force, a seed bed of great fertility, deeply rooted in the almost pathological love of independence and national identity of the Nabatean people. Roman architecture had an entirely different relationship to that tradition for it never became wholly absorbed into it. After the fourth century there are no more records of the Nabateans in Petra and many people believe that by that time they had left for the new centres of trade which were springing up elsewhere. With their going passed the native genius which by adaptation and compromise had brought their world into being.

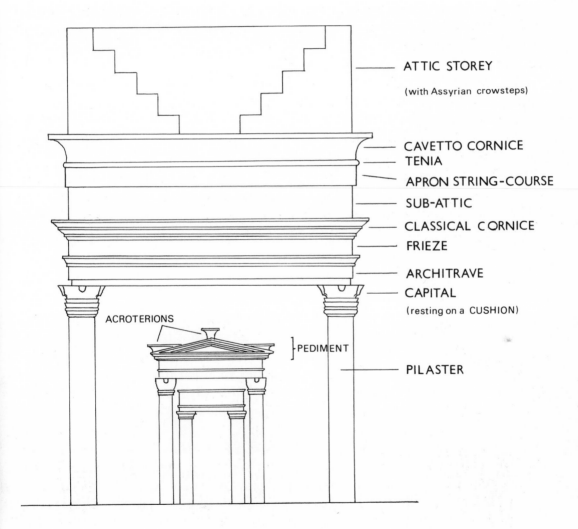

ATTIC STOREY

(with Assyrian crowsteps)

CAVETTO CORNICE
TENIA
APRON STRING-COURSE

SUB-ATTIC

CLASSICAL CORNICE

FRIEZE

ARCHITRAVE

CAPITAL

(resting on a CUSHION)

ACROTERIONS

PEDIMENT

PILASTER

CORNICE, FRIEZE & ARCHITRAVE together constitute an ENTABLATURE

Fig. 44 Guide to architectural terms.

CHAPTER FIVE

Petra Today

I

Tawilan, Bab el Siq, the Siq, the Khasneh, Outer Siq, Theatre

THE road to Petra curls into the hills soon after the turning off the Aqaba road to the south of Ma'an. It crosses a bare, featureless landscape with wide and shimmering distances. Rock-strewn wastes of russet dust dip and fold hiding the dried-up beds of wadis. In winter, icy winds drive demented curtains of sleet across this forgotten land and the rocks wink at you as you pass, like glistening black eyes in the grey, sullen light of noon. In summer, a shrill silence and tireless heat hang poised in the motionless air. The bleached land slips away from ochre into violet and the distant horizons vibrate with cobalt energy.

Higher and higher the narrow road climbs, snaking its way up and round wadis, along swelling ridges with the contours of the terrain becoming bolder and more expansive as the summit of the Shara range is approached.

Beyond a shallow cutting the land falls away sharply from the left, revealing a distant panorama of vast dimensions (Fig. 45). The best time to see it is at dawn before the sun has touched the distant peaks and the whole wide valley below is suffused with an ethereal light. The middle distance bounds about in blue shadows until it forms into deep wadis with terraced fields curling round the contours. The village of Elji lies quietly in a fold a thousand feet below to the right, its white walls and box-like shapes sunk in trees and patches of vegetation, striking a contrasting note to the pale, rounded harmonics of the hills. Beyond this, and lower still, rear the barrier walls of rock that hide Petra from the world. Like a tossing sea of softly tinted purple waves they merge ineffably with the pale, honey-coloured, dream-like Gebel Haroun upon the top of which stands the reputed tomb of Aaron. The tiny speck of white which is the shrine is too far away to see. Beyond this crag-bound mountain lies the pale blue haze that hangs in the Wadi Arabah, with Sinai and the Negev in the distance.

Later in the day when the sun is up, it is still a staggering view and always gives the visitor a thrill of anticipation. But the magic by then has gone and the clear brilliance has been dissipated, leaving the barrier ranges sharply painted in clear colour and shadow.

Fig. 45 The panorama westward from above the village of Elji. The Government Rest House stands out squarely against the rounded contours of the ridge of white limestone which guards the entrance to the Siq. The Gebel Haroun towers in the distance—on the far side of Petra.

The road sweeps down across the steep hillside in a series of long graceful curves—punctuated by one or two alarmingly sharp bends at which local drivers spurn any idea of slowing down—until it reaches less precipitous country and the ungainly mass of the village of Elji comes into view.

Petra lies snugly in a valley between the two barrier ranges, open to the north and south. The popular belief that there is only one way into the city is quite untrue, for there are many. Modern visitors, unlike the caravaners of old, nearly always arrive by the Ma'an road and enter Petra through the famous gorge called el Siq, having driven through the village of Elji.

Before descending into the village, however, there are two places which should be seen: the partly excavated site of the Edomite community at Tawilan, and Ain Mousa or Moses' Spring.

Excavations conducted by Mrs Crystal-M. Bennett in 1967 and 1968 confirmed a generally held belief that the Edomite community at TAWILAN was considerably larger than its contemporary on the top of Umm el Biyara, the great rock massif overlooking the central area of Petra. A great number of sherds had been noticed scattered about the site in addition to surface indications of walls. Biblical scholars had been interested in the site because it was thought that it might equate with the city of Teman which is mentioned in the Bible.

Tawilan is on a very exposed site, 4,500 feet above sea-level and about half an hour's walk from Ain Mousa across a stony, windswept hillside (Fig. 3). It is a place of wide views, bright, almost glaring light, huge skies and has the feeling of being on the roof of the world. To the east the Gebel Heidan roams largely across the horizon while to the north are the sweeping curves of the Gebels Unagreh and Shabaraheh. Incessant high winds rise out of the overheated basin below and stream up across these open hillsides, causing severe erosion. This has meant that in many cases only the footings or foundations of buildings are left for inspection. It is a site, none the less, of great beauty with superb views down the precipitous slopes towards the tumbling walls of rock that enfold the ancient city of Petra.

Initially five trenches were put down to find out the meaning of some very evident buried features. The two on an outer wall, which gives the appearance of enclosing the site of about thirty dunams or approximately seven and a half acres, were soon abandoned when it was realised that this wall was no more than a field boundary of post-Nabatean date and had nothing to do with the Edomites. It had been suggested that the remains might be of a defensive wall but, like Umm el Biyara, the site was so ideal for defence that no such measure would have been necessary. One of the outer trenches did, however, strike an enormous pit filled with Iron Age II (Edomite) pottery dating back to the beginning of the community. The limits of this pit were never reached.

Trenches were put down on an inner wall and what looked like the stumps of two towers. These revealed the complex of domestic buildings dating from the end of the ninth century B.C. to the sixth, if not later: individual buildings proved to be so large that it was not possible to reveal a complete one. A scarab bearing possibly the symbol of the Edomite god, Kaush, a crescent moon with its points upwards, surmounted by a star (Fig. 4), was found in a large structure with three central pillars and a plaster floor (Fig. 46). We still know very little of Edomite religion, except for the name of the principal deity, which makes this scarab an important 'find'; this is the first time that such a symbol has come to light in this region. It was hoped that the pillared building might turn out to be a temple but this was not to be and it must remain as a substantial structure of unknown use. The quality of the masonry, as in all structures on this site, is very poor.

Storage pits, both lined and unlined, stone mortars, grinders, pestles, iron sickles and knives were also found, attesting to considerable agricultural activity. It was, however, the fine Edomite pottery of Tawilan which proved to be the most important and significant discovery. Masses of it were found with some complete pieces wonderfully intact after over two and a half thousand years. It had been thought that Edomite ware was much cruder and coarser, but here was found beautifully smooth, well-fired and made work of a thinness which seems to anticipate the much later Nabatean ware.

The so-called 'watch tower' with which the southern trench was concerned has provisionally been dated to the Arabic period. It stood on a wildly confused pattern of walls of the Iron Age among which many skeletons were found. They were all aligned east/west with their heads turned to the south—towards Mecca. For this reason they were taken at first to be Moslem graves dug into the much earlier

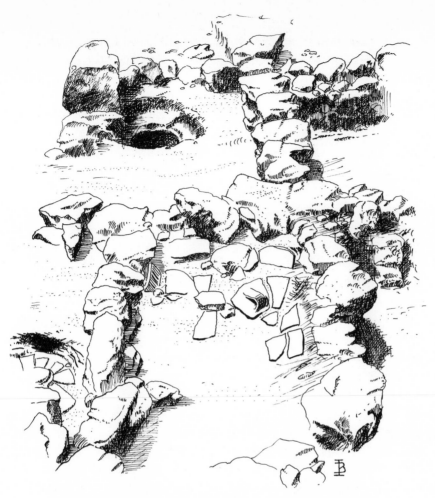

Fig. 46 Tawilan excavations; remains of walls of unidentified 'buildings', with sherds shown still *in situ*.

Iron Age levels, they are, however, now shown to be earlier — probably Nabatean.

On the natural terraces above and below Tawilan, indications have been found of occupation going back to 4,000 B.C.

AIN MOUSA is on the roadside below Tawilan. There is so much controversy about the route taken by the Israelites in their wanderings that it is pointless to argue here the case regarding the claims of Ain Mousa to be the place where Moses struck the rock. This is certainly the local legend but in the light of present-day knowledge it seems unfounded for if it was the spot then the Israelites were certainly off course.

The spring has been walled up so that one can no longer actually see it. The bright, clear water now bubbles out from under a stone wall and along a pebbly channel before slipping beneath the spreading black shadows of a voluminous fig tree and disappearing off downhill to Elji and beyond. There always seems to be

a small congregation of donkeys, asses and mules—even an occasional proud
horse—standing nonchalantly about, oblivious or scornful of the heat while in
the presence of so much life-giving water (Fig. 47). Men sit on walls and chew
while goats converse in tones of neurotic petulance. A dog scuttles past, a tail or
two swishes persistent flies from blinking eyes, an occasional hoof goes 'clop' on
the metalled road in an irrational, unconnected way, and the men keep on chewing. It has been like this for centuries, with only the slowly changing patterns of
dress and transport to mark the passing of the years.

The village of ELJI, in which Irby and Mangles had so much bother, lies some
distance down the road, a higgledy-piggledy collection of white and not-so-white
walled, flat-roofed houses of the familiar box-like appearance. It is an alive,
tumbling and excitable place which leaves an impression of a sleepy time-bomb
that has forgotten to go off. Two horrid blind corners on a steep hill, at which the
taxi drivers rush with gay abandon, are overlooked by a minaret and a sort of
Beau Geste police station. Children run about the street shouting while men
stand about doing nothing—chewing perhaps—in dark doorways. And then you
are out again on the open road as it makes the final descent amid clumps of trees
and red terraced fields to the long straight which leads to the comfortable eyesore
that is the GOVERNMENT REST HOUSE.

To the right is the Tourist Office where one hires—and then waits for—the
horse which will take one on the nerve-racking journey down the Siq into the
fastness of Petra. Behind this is a vast tarmac area like a car park with a row of
mounting blocks for the use of those not accustomed to getting on to horses. Some
of the nags are such sorry beasts that even if one were the Horseman of the Year it
might be kinder to mount them from the blocks rather than subject them to the
imbalances of a conventional mounting.

Overlooking the car park, on the far side, is a long, low wall of large dressed
blocks. This is the remains of a Nabatean reservoir which is known locally as

AL BIRKA; there is nothing to see here but it is the first encounter one has with the remarkable water engineering of the Nabateans.

The Government Rest House is an instance of a building whose appearance is totally unsympathetic to its surroundings; perhaps the lateral additions at present being built will soften its abruptness. Unfortunately it can be seen for miles. The 'candy floss' trees and the flowers of the garden, added to the simple comfort and the delightful hospitality, quickly make one forget the unfortunate height of the building. Internally it is most interesting for it is built over, and incorporates as its dining-room a notable Nabatean tomb known as AL KHAN.

The façade of this tomb is carved back deeply into the rock providing the central feature with a natural courtyard. The main façade has the single divide Assyrian crow-step ornament with which visitors to Petra will become very familiar. The walls of the court have been carved out themselves to make two pillared colonnades, one on each side. The one on the left is severely damaged but the right-hand colonnade forms a prominent feature of the hall/lounge of the hotel with an angular spiral staircase climbing up in one corner. The façade which in this context becomes the west wall of the hall, is rather worn but one certainly gets a very clear impression of the wild size and scale of Nabatean work.

The white rocks of this area, which is called the BAB EL SIQ or Gate to the Siq, look rather like great saucer domes piled one upon the other in a haphazard way (Fig. 22). Below them, and to the left of the Rest House, there is a path which follows the course of the Wadi Mousa. The area is suffused with a curious white light akin to glare but softer tones of buff and putty begin to creep into the colouring and here and there is a hint of the lovely soft gold which is so much a part of Petra. As yet there is no sign of the 'rose-red' which most people expect. Clumps of oleander, bright with pink, white and red flowers if the season is right, stand motionless in the sunshine. The only thing to be heard as the hills imperceptibly close in about you, is the rattle of stones under foot.

*   *   *

The first of the monuments of Petra to be encountered is a group of carved stone 'towers' known variously as 'sahrij' blocks, pylons and DJIN BLOCKS (Fig. 48). The first of these names derives from the Arabic for a subterranean water channel, cistern, reservoir or water tank. This use of the word probably came about because these 'towers' were mistaken by the local Arabs as defunct water tanks. The name 'djin' is another Arabic word, meaning ghosts, spirits, kelpies, etc., and is the one used in this book for this sort of monument. In the Bab el Siq there is a group of three such monuments with an additional one much further on. Altogether there are approximately twenty-five such monuments in

Fig. 47 Ain Mousa, one of the traditional places where Moses is
◀ supposed to have struck the rock and brought forth water.

Petra. Their use is still controversial but there is a general opinion that they were tombs. One, however, in the triple group has a chamber in it. The others might have had a constructed superstructure containing a burial-chamber.

One is very simply a block of stone, some 20 feet high, carved well out from the hillside so that it stands isolated from the others. The one next to it is of an interesting shape because it appears to be rather truncated and has a finely moulded base, a feature not so apparent in the others. There is also a curious knob on the top. It was carved close to the side of the cliff from which it is cut so that the vertical wall of rock seems to form a backdrop to it. The upper part was probably built up with harder stone and could have contained a chamber. There is unfortunately nothing left of this upper storey or of any of the masonry. The third 'djin' block is the most interesting of the three and is probably the latest in date. There are still clear indications of engaged pilasters on each of the four well-worn sides. These give a strong vertical emphasis which is capped by bold horizontal lines reminiscent of Hellenistic architecture: this block is in fact the most architectural of the three. Above the pilasters deep grooves were cut into the stone, probably to house a set of cornices of harder or more brightly coloured stone. The effect would certainly have been more ornamental.

Behind and above these 'djin' blocks is a so-called SNAKE MONUMENT which looks, as its name implies, like a snake coiled up on top of a small pinnacle of rock. It is badly worn and difficult to recognise. There is in Petra so much erosion of the rock into suggestive shapes that the imaginative mind is in danger of attributing planned causes to accidental phenomena.

From now on the northern bank of the Wadi is ringed with a succession of caves and niches.

The OBELISK TOMB stands high up on the left bank with the classical Bab el Siq Triclinium below it (Colour Plate 1, facing page 48, and Fig. 49). It is doubtful whether the two are related for they are not vertically aligned, nor are they on exactly the same axis. The tomb, judging from stylistic considerations, is probably the earlier. The upper part of the tomb is dominated by four massive, rather squat obelisks which originally would have been about 23 feet high, set upon a long, unadorned plinth. Between the two middle obelisks is a niche, with a classical surround,

Fig. 48 'Djin' blocks in the Outer Siq, the purpose of which is unknown.

which contains some form of image which is now very eroded. The plinth is recessed in the centre and houses a handsome classical portal. This gives into a single chamber measuring approximately 20 feet by 16 feet, with two graves on each of the flanking walls and one in the back wall (Fig. 50).

This tomb is unique in Petra and its stylistic origins probably lie in Egypt: were it not for the classical features such an attribution would be obvious. If, however, one remembers that the obelisk was an extension of the god-block idea, the monument can be recognised as having four deity images on it. Translate the obelisks into seated colossuses of the Egyptian tradition like the statues on the Temple of Rameses II at Abu Simbel, which has just such a niche containing a statue between the central pair, and you have an approximation of the Obelisk Tomb. The most important festivals of Dusares appear to have been held at Elusa and at Alexandria. As Alexandria was the fount of Ptolemaic

Fig. 49 The Obelisk Tomb and the Bab el Siq Triclinium. They should be viewed as separate entities for they are not the upper and lower parts of a single monument.

Egypt—Hellenistic Egypt—it could account for the classical features on an otherwise Egyptian-inspired tomb. For this to be reasonably so, it would mean that the tomb could not have been created before approximately 250 B.C. and then only for someone, or by someone, who was really familiar with architectural thought in Ptolemaic Egypt.

The BAB EL SIQ TRICLINIUM, which lies almost immediately below the

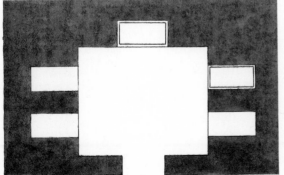

Obelisk Tomb, is a much more complex yet pedestrian design. It is a thoroughly Nabatean Classical work incorporating, it could be suggested, some features common to other tombs in and around Petra. The broken pediment on the upper half is very reminiscent of the 'Tomb with a Broken Pediment' in

Fig. 50 Ground plan of the Obelisk Tomb.

the Wadi Farasa, while the segmental pediment below smacks of the 'Renaissance Tomb', also in the Wadi Farasa. There is a strong affinity between this whole design and that of the lower part of the Corinthian Tomb. It looks uncomfortably cramped in its position and it remains a question why so limiting and inauspicious a site was chosen for it.

The central chamber, with its 7-foot wide benches on the traditional three sides, measures some 24 feet by 21 feet, and is totally unadorned (Fig. 51).

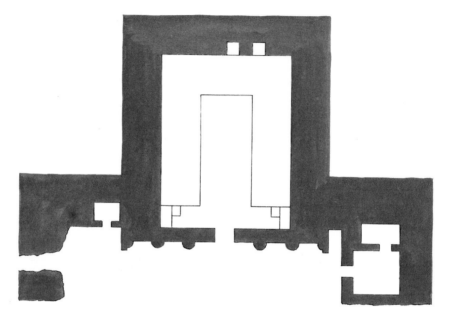

Fig. 51 Ground plan of the Bab el Siq Triclinium.

Beyond the Obelisk Tomb and the Bab el Siq Triclinium, the Wadi Mousa appears to be heading for a dead end. Tawny walls of rock fold in on all sides with no indication of a way out. Unexpectedly the Wadi turns to the right and seems to run uphill along the line of the rock barrier. On the left is a dam built across an opening in the wall of rock. This is the ENTRANCE TO THE SIQ of Petra.

Opposite the dam there is a set of small obelisks carved in low relief into the rock with an inscription to each (Fig. 52). One inscription is of particular importance for it is in remembrance of a man who 'lived at Rekem but died in Jerash, and was buried there'. Rekem is the ancient Semitic name for Petra and this inscription is the first to be found using this name.

A short stretch of masonry walling near these carvings is all that remains of the original revetting of the Wadi. The DAM is quite modern, built to prevent a recurrence of a tragic accident in which some tourists were killed by a flash

Fig. 52 The 'Rekem' carvings at the entrance to the Siq, which have been so important in modern historical researches (*see* Preface).

flood which swept down through the Siq. It replaces one built by the Nabateans to divert the waters of the Wadi Mousa from the Siq. Bachmann's reconstruction of this dam places the approach road on the raised level above the walling (Fig. 53). The top of the dam was reached by means of a bridge thrown over the Wadi. When this complex was being built it was necessary to bury the row of obelisks under the approach road. This accounts for their remarkable state of preservation. From the style of writing these inscriptions can be dated to the beginning of the first century A.D., and as they were obviously covered by the approach road fairly soon after execution, we can give a date during the reigns of Malchus II (A.D. 40–70) and Rabbel II (A.D. 71–106) to the original dam. The top of the present dam is reached by a ramp on the left; this feature was never a part of the earlier structure.

The water diverted by the dam passed along an excavated channel close under the left-hand cliff until it disappeared down a TUNNEL specially dug for that purpose (Fig. 15). Thereafter it circumnavigated the whole mountain, el Kubtha, coming eventually into the central city area of Petra. The tunnel is worth spending a few minutes looking at for it is an important example of the Nabatean brilliance in water engineering. It would probably have been made at the same time as the original dam.

Above, and somewhat to the right, of the tunnel there is another 'djin' block with an Assyrian frieze of multiple crow-step decoration round its top (Fig. 54).

Fig. 53 A reconstruction, after Bachmann, of the Barrage and Bridge with its approach road, which was built across the entrance to the Siq in late Nabatean times.

It is interesting that these 'djin' blocks all occur near places of flowing water. It may be, therefore, that the name given to them by the Arabs, 'sahrij', is accidentally not too wide of the mark: they were never 'water tanks' but may have had some ritual significance in the worship of water as a fertility gift of the gods.

Carved into the rock on the other side of the tunnel is a square panel from which a very imperial eagle looks blandly away from you. The EAGLE

Fig. 54 The tunnel by which the Nabateans diverted the waters of the Wadi Mousa from the Siq, overlooked by an isolated 'djin' block.

MONUMENT is probably a votive niche and of Roman date (Fig. 55). It is not all that large and is difficult to spot.

As a suburb, EL MADRAS is a microcosm of Petra. It is situated high up on the top of the mountain to the left of the Siq and is approached by a long flight of steps. There are monuments of nearly all types to be found here in close proximity. The main importance of this suburb, however, lies in the fact that it still retains the name by which it was known to the Nabateans. An inscription mentions Dusares as being the god of el Madras. The translation of the word 'madras' is most likely to be 'with rugged prominences', but with the often disconcerting ambiguity of Arabic, it could mean 'school' or 'oil press'.

The entrance to the Siq is now disappointingly undramatic. Early travellers all referred to entering a deep and narrow gorge, but the construction of the dam has changed that. The present arrangement is, however, much more true to the ancient one with walls of rock about 30 feet high on either side.

Just inside the entrance, on either side, there are the blurred and battered remains of a niche with bold flanking pilasters (Fig. 56). Above the left-hand one two courses of masonry still mark the springing of a MONUMENTAL •ARCH which originally spanned the

Fig. 55 The Eagle Monument.

gorge (Fig. 57). Everyone, from Burckhardt onwards, mentions this arch and it was still standing as late as 1894 though in a fairly precarious state (Fig. 58). According to Mr Gray Hill, the arch fell down in 1896. Some writers have tried to prove that it was an aqueduct or viaduct, but there is no sign of either water channel or of a road leading to or from it and it is most likely to have been ornamental.

A WATER CHANNEL has been cut into the foot of the cliff on the left-hand side and passes directly beneath the base of the abutment of the arch and continues for the whole way through the Siq (Fig. 59). The flat, vertical surface of the rock was first cut into and then the base of this excavation was carved to form a neat, wide channel. Its descent is consistent with the fall of the ground as it goes down steeply into the gorge. The angle at which the original paved road descended from the top of the dam would have been very much the same as at present.

As the channel cuts through the base of the arch abutments and follows the fall of the slope of the inner ramp, it is logical that both the ramp and the abutments are earlier than the water channel. As the fall of the inner ramp is dependent on the dam it follows that the water channel was made after the construction of the dam also. From this

Fig. 56 The much worn abutments of the Triumphal Arch which originally spanned the Siq; the spring courses of which can be seen on the top.

one may suppose that the creation of the arch was all part and parcel of the development of the entrance to the Siq and the water works. This indicates a post date somewhere in the latter half of the first century A.D. for the creation of the water system of which this channel is a part.

*   *   *

The sides of the water channel have been completely worn away in many places but so much of its course is wonderfully intact that it is quite easy to trace its passage through the Siq.

After its initial confined nature, the SIQ opens out for a short distance and then plunges again into the narrow defile. The mile-long length of this remarkable entry to the city is consistently downhill and the further one goes the deeper and narrower it becomes. Tight little wadis, thick with tumbled boulders and lush with green vegetation, occasionally creep in from either side, sometimes a flight of worn steps leading tantalisingly to nowhere. Votive niches appear at irregular intervals — there are said to be nearly thirty — carved into the walls. There is a fine Hellenistic one with a pediment, containing a god-block, surmounted by a row of six more god-blocks (Fig. 60). Whether this indicates six different deities or six people paying their devotion to one deity, is not certain.

Fig. 57 A reconstruction of the Triumphal Arch in the Siq. It is not known whether the niche housed a statue as shown here, nor is there any record of the detail of the arch and its superstructure.

59   60

There is another niche which shows the weathered figure of the goddess (? Al Uzza) standing between two leopards over a Greek inscription mentioning the name of the dedicator 'Sabinos Alexandros': this must at least imply a Greek trader in Petra. Those with keen eyes will notice occasional Nabatean and Greek graffiti scratched on the face of the rock, recording that 'so-and-so passed this way' or 'peace be to so-and-so'.

The towering walls of rock glow with bands of colour ranging from pearly white to softest yellow, gold to madder, red, carmine, and mauve. The floor of the ravine is strewn with small white stones which rattle in the stillness of this strange, echoing world. One moment the sunlight is streaming down across a smiling, curving, pirouetting wall of rock with nubbed pinnacles sharing secrets with the sky (Fig. 61). The next, all is in shadow and the colours glower sullenly while they writhe convulsively in their scramble to get back into the light.

There are moments when the chasm opens out and the vivid green of trees and oleander adds a brilliant touch of capricious gaiety to the scene. But all too soon the walls of rock press in again, higher than before. At the narrowest part the walls overhang the path so that it is not possible to see the sky above.

The Siq is the result of a natural fault which ran right through the mountain. In the darkness of time, huge, subterranean forces started pushing upwards with violent energy, trying to lift the mountain up. It cracked down the fault and split apart. Rock stratas can even now be seen to stop abruptly on one face of

Fig. 58 Léon de Laborde's view of the Arch.

61   62

Figs. 61 and **62** The Siq.

the chasm and pick up again on the other immediately opposite. The Attuf
Ridge on the western side of this mountain fractured away creating the Outer
Siq at the same time. The seismic upheaval has created one of the most justly
celebrated gorges in the world. The waters of the Wadi Mousa found their way
into this crack and carried in the rubble and sediment which make the path we
walk on. Not only is the colouring superb but the twisting path reveals constantly
new and exciting geological spectacles (Fig. 62). The contrasts between light and
shade are startling. Man's only contribution is a wretched telephone wire which
zigzags from side to side the whole way through.

Towards the end, the Siq becomes very narrow, deep and dark. The walls
close right in creating a twilight gloom (Colour plate 2 facing page 64). The
echo of crunching, rolling, scuttling stones is thrown back immediately and with
oppressive insistence. Then a thin, vertical strip of contorting daylight is seen

63 64

Fig. 63 The first glimpse of the Khasneh from inside the Siq. **Fig. 64** The Khasneh, or Treasury. The position of this very classical façade is highly dramatic, confronting the visitor as he emerges from the narrow and gloomy Siq.

ahead. Framed by the black walls of the Siq is part of a classical façade (Fig. 63).

As one comes out of the cool gloom of the chasm into the brilliant sunshine which floods the Wadi al Jarra, one is confronted by possibly the most beautiful and certainly the most famous monument of Petra, the KHASNEH or TREASURY (Frontispiece and Figs. 13 and 64).

The hard, dramatic colours of the Siq do not prepare one for the glowing richness of the Khasneh, which is in the only part of Petra that can be called 'rose-red', and then only in the shadows when direct sunlight is picking out the famous façade in sharp, dazzling golden shades of peach. It is worth trying to arrange one's arrival so as to see the façade with the sunlight on it, but even when it is in the shade the effect is always exciting.

In his prize-winning Newdigate poem (see page 1), John William Burgon, later to become Dean of Chichester, besides pirating from Samuel Rogers the

famous line 'half as old as time', managed to fire the imagination and romantic
interest of the Western world when he so skilfully caught the spirit of Petra. His
lines are often misquoted, but 'A rose-red city etc. . . .' is known to most people.
But this quotation has also done something of a disservice to Petra, for it suggests
that the whole place is of this colour, like an over enthusiastically feminine
William Morris wallpaper. Nothing could be further from the truth; it is about
as misleading as Rostovtzeff's description of the colour as being like a 'piece of
reddish-mauve raw flesh'. When Burgon eventually visited Petra, sixteen years
after writing his poem, he told his sister that 'there is nothing rosy about Petra,
by any means'.

The monument is carved deeply into the rock (Fig. 64); in fact the cliff seems
to weigh rather heavily over the façade. It is perhaps because of this that it is
still so superbly intact. It is well protected from the wind that has played such
havoc with much else in Petra. The architectural detail is still wonderfully crisp
and fresh; Andrew Crichton declared 'there is scarcely a building in England
of forty years' standing so fresh and well preserved in its architectural decoration'.
Alas, though, vandals — or to be more accurate, fanatical iconoclasts — have
smashed the reliefs which once adorned it so that they are now featureless,
unrecognisable blemishes.

The German scholar, Dalman, was the first to measure the monument, which
he did with the aid of a long ladder and an agile Arab boy. Photographs in books
have always tended to make the Khasneh look much larger than in fact it is; it
is large enough by any standard but this blowing up of its size has led many
people to remark that it is smaller than they had expected. The façade is approximately 92 feet wide, just a fraction under that of the west front of Westminster
Abbey, and to the top of the urn which surmounts the tent roof of the central
kiosk it measures 130 feet. The urn itself is some 11 feet high.

It is this urn which has given the monument its name, the Treasury. The full
name is the Khasneh al Faroun, or Pharaoh's Treasury. With the collapse of
classical learning, the Near East withdrew into a long period of legend-forming
and legend-ridden illiteracy. The powerful new culture of Islam could not be
expected to dispel this darkness for its values were so totally different, indeed
alien, to those of the classical West that there could be no sympathy or understanding of each others' aspirations. The works of Petra became unintelligible.
To the bedouin who lived in tents and knew nothing of history, these monuments were miraculous creations of Pharaoh who had assumed the guise of the
greatest black magician of all time, very much what the Devil is in Western folk-
lore. The great white magician was Moses. But whereas Moses had control over
natural forces, Pharaoh (Faroun) demonstrated his power in remarkable
monuments made by human agency such as the Khasneh.

Fig. 65 Léon de Laborde's view of the Khasneh. In the foreground can be seen an Arab marksman shooting at the urn on the top of the monument in the hope of releasing its reputed treasure of gold. The practice is now forbidden by law.

The story relates that Pharaoh deposited his treasure in an urn and placed it out of human reach on the top of the central kiosk of this monument; why he spent so much time and effort detailing the rest of the façade is not explained. Over the years the bedouin have spent a lot of time and even more ammunition in firing at the urn in an attempt to break it open. It is riddled with bullet marks. The idea was that once broken the urn would shower the lucky marksman with gold, precious stones and baubles, making him rich beyond even the most avaricious avarice. The practice is now strictly forbidden but the engraving in Léon de Laborde's book shows a kneeling marksman aiming at the urn with a long-barrelled rifle (Fig. 65). The Wadi in which the Khasneh stands is not unnaturally called the Wadi of the Urn, the Wadi al Jarra.

Hidden treasure is supposed to be buried all over Petra and this led the tribes to be highly suspicious of the early visitors. One can imagine the reception of the early archaeologists like the Horsfields and Margaret Murray received, turning up with their tools and digging holes in the ground. But one can also imagine the chagrin and the bewilderment when they started getting excited over a few pieces of broken pot.

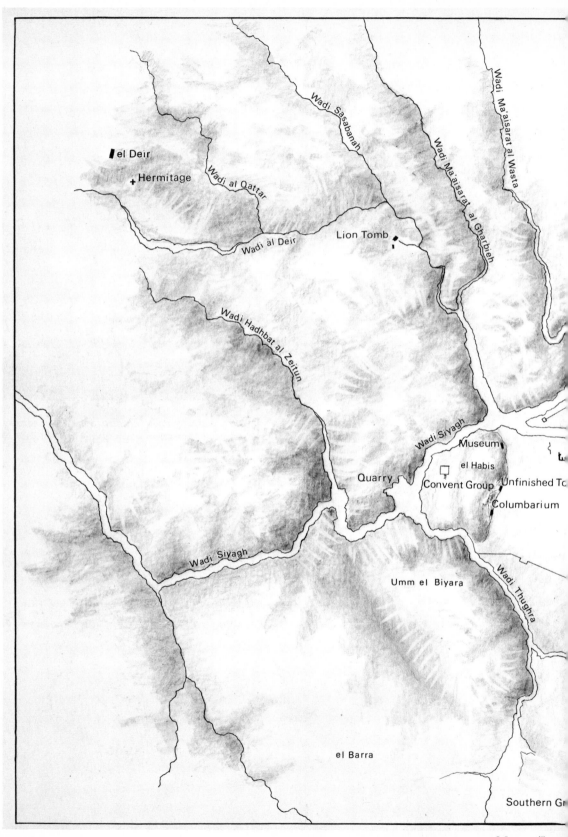

el Deir

+ Hermitage

Wadi al Qattar

Wadi Sasabanah

Wadi Maʿaisarat al Wasta

Wadi Maʿaisarat al Gharbieh

Wadi al Deir

Lion Tomb

Wadi Hadhbat al Zeitun

Wadi Siyagh

Museum

el Habis

Quarry

Convent Group

Unfinished To

Columbarium

Wadi Siyagh

Umm el Biyara

Wadi Thughra

el Barra

Southern Gr

Map 3. 'Loca

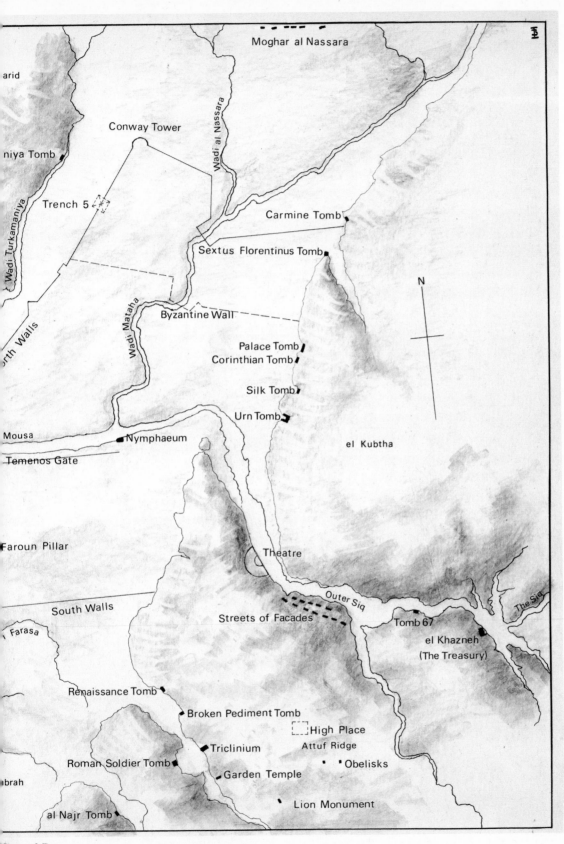

Moghar al Nassara

...arid

Conway Tower

...niya Tomb

Wadi al Nassara

Carmine Tomb

Trench 5

Sextus Florentinus Tomb

Wadi Turkamaniya

...rth Walls

Wadi Mataha

Byzantine Wall

N

Palace Tomb
Corinthian Tomb

Silk Tomb

Urn Tomb

...Mousa

Nymphaeum

el Kubtha

Temenos Gate

...Faroun Pillar

Theatre

South Walls

Outer Siq

The Siq

Streets of Facades

Tomb 67

...Farasa

el Khazneh
(The Treasury)

Renaissance Tomb

Broken Pediment Tomb

High Place

Triclinium

Attuf Ridge

Roman Soldier Tomb

Obelisks

Garden Temple

...abrah

Lion Monument

al Najr Tomb

Central Petra

It is not surprising that there has been endless discussion as to the date and original use of the Khasneh. There is no strong archaeological evidence, so all suggestions have to be based on style and related historical considerations. Domaszewski thought it was Hadrianic (Roman *c.* A.D. 131) while Dalman disagreed and placed it much earlier. The fact that the monument is a totally un-Nabatean work tends to confuse the issue. Corinthian capitals of this kind, elaborate architectural mouldings, statuary and decorative reliefs are all foreign even to the Nabatean Classical tradition and its conventions. One is forced to the conclusion that it is the work of imported artists and architects. It was suggested in the previous chapter that this happened during the reign of Aretas III Philhellen (84–56 B.C.) when foreign craftsmen capable of executing designs comparable with the Hellenistic wonders of the Near East were brought in. Certainly there is no precedent in Nabatean architecture for the undiluted Hellenism of the Khasneh.

The siting, therefore, becomes particularly relevant. The visitor coming down the last few yards of the Siq has a partial view of the monument, but as he enters the Wadi al Jarra (Fig. 66) he is confronted with a monument of the highest quality both in terms of execution and of design. It stands alone, uncluttered by other façades: a positive statement that you have arrived in a city of great opulence and importance.

The best vehicle for expressing this would have been a temple, and the tripartite plan of the Khasneh conforms to that of an Egyptian temple. There is an outer court represented by the spacious portico, an inner court formed by the single great chamber with a sanctuary immediately beyond. This sanctuary is approximately 10 feet square and is approached by three steps.

To whom this temple was dedicated we cannot tell but Rostovtzeff put forward the idea of Manathu, the patron deity of the city. As, however, it is usual to find the shrines of patron deities in the centre of the city they are supposed to protect, one must have reservations about this theory. The Khasneh is not properly in the city of Petra, only at the entrance to it. The patron deity of caravans and caravaners, She'a-alqum, about whom we know virtually

Fig. 66 The mouth of the Siq from inside the Khasneh.

nothing, might seem to be a more reasonable candidate. Dalman, however, favoured the mother-goddess Al Uzza, for she equated with the Egyptian goddess Isis whom he distinguished in the battered sculpture on the central kiosk. He considered it a 'Temple-Tomb' of one of the later Nabatean kings, although there is no evidence, such as loculi, to suggest that it was used as a tomb.

   Dalman's description of the façade is still the most concise and intelligible and is, therefore, quoted here in full:

> The architect designed the front of the vestibule like the front of a prostyle temple with four columns, entablature and pediments, but to get a broader and more imposing façade added to the portico one column on each side and extended the entablature accordingly, only letting it first recede, and then, beyond this addition, again project in the original line of the front. A façade of this kind would have been possible for an independent building at the side of a low hill; here it would have been dwarfed by the huge wall of rock towering over it. A second order was, therefore, indispensable above the first one, and the question was how to form it without destroying the impression of the temple façade, the nucleus of the whole building. The architect added first an unbroken attic, which really accentuates the independence of the lower order, but at the same time could serve as the base for another. The upper order might have consisted of a simple colonnade, but its weight would have pressed heavily upon the temple façade, and it seemed better to let the colonnade recede in the centre, in correspondence with the vestibule of the lower storey, and to put a small round temple (kiosk) in the middle of the open space. In order to unite the three pavilions, which now appeared in the front of the second storey, the two side pavilions received broken pediments, whose rising lines pointed exactly towards the top of the 'tent roof' of the central pavilion (kiosk). Thus a second temple rose over that in the lower storey. And if this last was in fact no real shrine but the entrance to a tomb, the round temple of the second storey had the full appearance of a sanctuary, being adorned in its front by the figure of the goddess Isis. . . . This combination of the front of a temple as a lower storey, with a colonnade encircling a round pavilion as upper storey, has been imitated at Petra in the so-called Temple of Ed Deir and the Corinthian Tomb. but is as far as we know without any parallel elsewhere. . . . It is against all classical custom, but suits the place, and its decorative effect is happy.*

Before leaving the consideration of the façade, it may be wondered whether the

*P.E.F. Annual, 1911.

Fig. 67 Ground plan of the Khasneh.

central kiosk, or pavilion as Dalman calls it, might not be by happy chance a Hellenistic mutation and interpretation of the 'djin' block idea. The terms of reference for the designer might have required that a 'djin' block appear prominently. It can, indeed, be said that the kiosk is a brilliant resolution of a very difficult architectural problem; it could also be the outcome of having to incorporate a given emblem into the design.

The central chamber (Fig. 67) is 40 feet square and is unadorned except for architectural surrounds to the flanking doorways to small rooms on either side. The two doorways under the colonnade (Fig. 68) lead into two small rooms, presumably for priests, and are sumptuously adorned. The sanctuary door is quite plain like the rest of the interior, but it may not always have been so. The Nabateans used extensively a hard plaster which they frequently painted. The walls and ceilings of the Khasneh demonstrate, however, very clearly a certain craft of the Nabateans which will be encountered in nearly all the other monuments. The stone surfaces were never rendered completely smooth but were dressed with rough, closely spaced grooves scored into the rock. This was done with almost mathematical precision and always diagonally across the surface. Why it should have been done in this way we do not know; it may have been to act as a key for the plaster and as it is so shallow it is not surprising that there is now no plaster left.

All the early drawings and photographs show the Khasneh with one of the pillars of the portico missing. We do not know when the missing member collapsed but it was reinstated by the Department of Antiquities in 1960 with Mr G. R. H. Wright directing the work. Its replacement has restored the classical balance of this fine monument and it has been done in such a way that does not attempt to deceive. Its treatment is sympathetic and appropriate. However, had this been a constructed monument, the collapse of a pillar in this position would have spelt disaster for the whole façade: as it is the remainder just stood firm.

There is still one other unsolved problem in the Wadi al Jarra with its clumps of soft green oleander. On the recessed walls to the sides of the Khasneh façade are two rows of vertical footholds rising up the full height of the monument. The purpose of these cannot be determined. Mr Parr has written of them that they 'are the work of the iconoclasts rather than the original builders. If cut by the latter to facilitate their work it might be expected that all of the tombs would possess them: but this is not so.'* However, these footholds occur also on the

walls of the quarries in the Wadi Siyagh and on the Attuf Ridge. No iconoclast would be interested in cutting footholds up a blank, unadorned wall that had no human or animal representations on it that he could smash.

The gorge from the Wadi al Jarra to the point where it opens out into the central valley of Petra is known as the OUTER SIQ. Why it is not called the Inner Siq one cannot understand. It is relatively narrow to begin with but is not so confined as the Siq proper. Shortly, however, it gets wider and the walls of rock begin to have monumental façades carved in them. Particularly there is a group of three, the dominant one being a fine, bold Double Cornice II type which, even though badly worn, is none the less of commanding presence (Fig. 69).

It is not only convenient but also practical to follow Brünnow's numbering of the monuments. Many of these

*P. E. Q., January 1968.

Fig. 68 One of the pair of elaborately carved doorways under the peristyle of the Khasneh; their indebtedness to late Hellenism is marked.

have famous names so one need not refer to the Khasneh as 'Monument No. 62' or to the Palace Tomb as 'Monument No. 765'. However, where no particularly appropriate name springs to mind, use has been made of the German's number.

NUMBER 67 has caught the notice of many observant travellers though not so frequently as the so-called Royal Tombs. It is one of the three large façades on the western wall of the Outer Siq and one comes upon it having seen only relatively few other monuments. One is, therefore, by no means surfeited with carved troglodyte wonders.

The Journal recording the doings of Irby and Mangles in 1818, mentions this tomb and comments that the 'attic' storey, between the crow-steps, has 'no visible access; there may possibly, however, be some stairs in the interior . . .' They found the lower doorway far too choked for them to be able to see whether this was so. There is, however, no internal staircase, access being only from the outside. Gilbert Kennedy and William Lancaster gained access in 1959 by jumping the space to the right – the same route by which, legend has it, an outlaw managed to avoid his pursuers.

This monument which is a Double Cornice I type, has been studied recently (1962) by Mr Parr and Mr Wright. At their instigation the famous Himalayan mountaineer, Joe Brown, was invited to Petra and by scrambling across hair-raising vertical façades, gained access to the attic chamber. This proved to be some 6 feet square and totally unadorned except for a small niche cut in the left-hand wall which is certainly not large enough for a burial. There can be little doubt that it was a burial-chamber, relying on its supposed 'inaccessibility' for protection against the ravages of animals and robbers. The doorway of this chamber is adorned with the traces of flanking Nabatean pilasters and an

architrave, above which can be seen the lines of a rather highly pitched pediment. The whole of this architectural feature is set within an almost square recess between single-divide 'flights' of crow-steps.

These crow-steps provide a point of interest in that the lowest steps on either side are cut through diagonally by a small hole starting in the tread of the step and appearing in the riser. This hole is then cut down vertically through the cavetto cornice upon which the attic storey stands. Mr Parr suggests that these holes have played some part in the lifting gear necessary for the lifting of the sarcophagus to be placed in the chamber.

By detailed inspection it has been possible to ascertain that at least part of this façade was covered by plaster, samples of which have been analysed by the Building Research Station at Watford. It was made of equal parts of crushed limestone and quartz sand without traces of burnt lime, providing a material of reasonable strength. It was suggested that any colouring there might have been was applied later as a thin slurry. There are other instances of exteriors in Petra where stucco decoration had been used, and this would have made the original appearance very different from that which we see today.

Beyond this there is a further group of large monuments, one of which is free-standing and has strong, finely chiselled 'classical' details and most dramatic colouring (Fig. 70). The multiple crow-step band which forms an actual battle-ment on the top, is unique in Petra on a monument of this type: elsewhere the single-divide is used. The whole monument is terribly eroded and looks as though the classical garb is struggling to get out of the rock but not quite succeeding. Much the same impression is given by the Corinthian Tomb. It is an example of the ghoulish effects which nature can produce. Further on down, the Outer Siq opens out appreciably and sunshine floods the bed of the wadi of gleaming white pebbles below high, golden brown cliffs. The path clings to the left-hand wall over-looking a large, open rectangular area. A little further on the lower part of the right-hand cliff closes in again on the path, thus forming a natural arena.

The level of the Outer Siq has obviously risen over the years, for the tops of Assyrian-type monuments appear on the right almost at ground level (Fig. 71). There is a whole row of them climbing up a long-buried hillside, getting taller as they emerge from the ground. The buried tombs afford a chance to get a good close-up of the bands of multiple crow-step ornament which is such a feature of the 'Streets of Façades' a little further on.

Fig. 69 Monuments carved into the wall of the first part of the Outer Siq.

Fig. 70 The Brünnow Tomb.

Fig. 71 A series of buried tombs in the Outer Siq indicates the extent to which this part of the gorge has filled up over the years. The line of the water pipes, set into the cliff above the tops of the tombs, can be seen clearly.

Above the buried tombs is what looks like a deep, lateral crack in the strata of the flat rock face. The lie to it just being a fault in the rock is given by the set of footholds which climb up from the floor of the wadi to the supposed crack. A natural fault it might well have been, but this was put to good use by the Nabateans who buried in it earthenware pipes to continue the water system first seen at the beginning of the Siq. At a point some distance down the Siq, the channel crosses the chasm and changes over to pipes. As the floor of the Siq went progressively downhill so the piping remained approximately level in the wall of rock and so, gradually, got higher up the cliff face; in fact it remains very nearly level except for the necessary gravitational incline. Some complete lengths of this piping are now in the Petra Museum (Fig. 14).

In the far corner of this open area a large Double Cornice I monument is set deeply into the wall of rock. The internal arrangement of this tomb is interesting, for on the floor there are fourteen irregularly disposed graves with three more in the back wall. On one side wall five obelisks have been delineated (Fig. 72); this is about the only instance of the obelisk being actually associated with burials. On the base of two of these obelisks are short inscriptions naming the son and grandson of one Iakun, but no date.

The main interest of the exterior is the way in which the water pipes were carried across the façade. This was done most discreetly by letting them into the architrave of the first cornice without disfiguring the architecture.

At the angle where the lower cliff reaches the path, there is an isolated 'djin' block.

Fig. 73 The 'Streets of Façades' area in the Outer Siq.

3*a*. The Colonnade Street

3*b*. The central area from the Nymphaeum

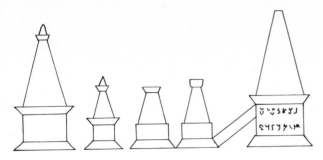

Fig. 72 Carvings on the wall in the Tomb of Fourteen Graves.

As though to compensate for having closed in again on the right, the Outer Siq suddenly opens out on the left to reveal one of the strangest conglomerations of monuments in Petra, the so-called STREETS OF FAÇADES (Figs. 5 and 73).

Whether or not these pink-grey fronts are of tombs or houses is still a matter of debate. Whichever is the case, they form the most remarkable collection of Assyrian I and II façades in Petra. There are long runs of them—streets—with other 'streets' across the face of the hill immediately above and below. Tucked away in the left-hand corner is a façade with an arched top, a small, simple design but one which is perplexing, for we cannot be sure that it is related, even stylistically, with the other monuments in this area. The round-topped façades are, in fact, one of the minor puzzles of Petra.

To reach them one has to go down a slight dip and then up on the other side in much the same way as one would have had to do with the buried tombs further back before they became inundated with silt and rubble. Most of them are Assyrian II monuments with the usual two bands of crow-step ornament round their top. It is not possible to date this area and these façades but it seems likely that they are among the earlier works of the Nabateans. Most of them have simple rectilinear carved slit ornament above the door, though one or two do boast a primitive classical pediment. It seems likely that the main development was put in hand over a relatively short period because the façades represent

only a slight development in style. To the right there are one or two later Double Cornice I types with the single-divide crow-steps and much more assured classical features. The lowest level of 'street' has been badly smashed and worn away, so much so that one or two of the façades have lost their tops. This could have been due to a monstrous fall of rock from the lumpy headlands above.

There is no way of telling at present whether this area is the site of the earliest settled Nabatean community. The configuration of the land as an easily protected position with difficult access for attack lends itself to this idea. The area has a 'contained' feeling about it which would have been highly attractive to settlers (Fig. 74).

The opposite, northern or right-hand, side of the Outer Siq has nearly as many monuments of the Assyrian I and II as well as many Cavetto and Double Cornice types, all on a higher level. The main 'Street of Façades' on the left is brought, however, to an abrupt halt by the Theatre (Fig. 75).

The THEATRE is probably Roman and may have been one of the lavish civic 'improvements' which the Romans inflicted on Petra soon after A.D. 106. Scant regard was shown for existing Nabatean monuments, as indeed was shown for Nabatean structures when the Colonnade Street was laid out. A 'street' at one time spread across the whole hillside now occupied by the upper auditorium. It started in a narrow cleft high up on the left where its beginnings can still be seen very clearly, and ended up in another narrow, constricted gully high up on the right. The great bulk of the 'street' was ruthlessly gouged away to accommodate the rear of the auditorium. The last few façades at each end now appear abruptly and then disappear into their respective gullies. The interiors of some of these houses which had their façades hacked away are left looking like gargantuan projection rooms in some science-fiction cinema (Fig. 76).

The Theatre is of a standard Roman, as opposed to Greek, pattern with a semi-circular orchestra measuring about 125 feet across its broadest point (Fig. 77). Before this is set a raised stage, above which would have towered a wall or *scaenae frons* now marked by two re-erected pillars. Classical theatre design demanded three entrances on to the stage through this, a centre and two flanking ones. The usual practice was to set these in shallow apses or exedras, the lines of which can be seen in the Petra Theatre. The rear of the *scaenae frons* would have

Fig. 74 The Outer Siq from the top of the auditorium of the Theatre.

Fig. 75 The Theatre from the Outer Siq. Compare with Fig. 78.

Fig. 76 To create the rear wall of the auditorium, the Romans carved away the majority of a street of façades, leaving some of the interiors of the vanished houses looking like gargantuan projection rooms.

presented a high wall to the Outer Siq, completely hiding the sweeping curves of the auditorium (Fig. 78). Whether this would have been as blank and unadorned as the fiercely slab-fronted rear wall of the reconstructed Roman theatre at Sabratha in Libya, is a matter of debate.

The auditorium held between 3,000–4,000 people. The thirty-three rows of seats are carved out of the rock, though the stone here is so soft that it has become badly worn causing the sharpness of edge to be lost in most places. The colour of the stone is a lifeless purple-grey and is probably the least attractive coloured area in the whole of Petra, for it makes everything look so flat and dried out. This particular stratum extends across the city area to the west and recurs at the foot of Umm el Biyara in the Wadi Thughra where it has worn away to make a powdery purple sand.

The stage has been partially restored, with its front put back completely. This was done by an American expedition under the direction of Dr Phillip C. Hammond of the Princeton Theological Seminary, in co-operation with the Department of Antiquities. In its original state it is likely that this front was faced with carved marble reliefs. The stage has not, however, been boarded over and in the cool shade of the voids, plants and spindly shrubs have taken root giving a most picturesque touch (Fig. 79).

Behind the stage there must have been dressing-rooms, etc., but there is now no trace of them. To the left and to the right entrances constructed of dressed stone with groined vaults covering passages and steps lead to the orchestra and the auditorium (Fig. 80). The stonework is now much eroded but it must be remembered that this was probably covered originally with ornamented and painted plaster, if not with marble.

A short distance beyond the Theatre the Outer Siq opens out into the wide central valley of Petra. There are a few more monuments carved into the face of the wadi, including a group of four 'djin' blocks, one of which has split diagonally from top to bottom causing it to slip into a rather drunken stance. The massive wall of el Kubtha, the mountain on the right, draws away from the path until it is set back at the top of a sharp slope. The left-hand

Fig. 77 The orchestra and stage of the Theatre conform to the established Roman pattern.

Fig. 78 A reconstruction of what the rear wall of the *scaenae frons* might have looked like from the Outer Siq. There is no evidence to suggest the height or appearance of this wall, but whatever was there would have cut the Theatre off from the Siq completely.

wall, the northern buttress of the Attuf Ridge, has gradually lost in height until it has dwindled away into a confused jumble of boulders and rocky outcrops. The

Fig. 79 The stage of the Theatre today.

Fig. 80 The partly excavated, partly constructed vault beneath the southern end of the auditorium.

sandy path continues northwards along the banks of the Wadi Mousa until it rounds the end of the Attuf buttress, and heads westwards for the beginning of the Colonnade Street. Visitors have the option of going straight on towards the Kasr el Bint and the city excavations, or of cutting up the slope on the right to the so-called Royal Tombs (Map 3, on pages 120–21). Here the former route is taken.

II

Central City Area: Colonnade Street, Temenos, Kasr el Bint

Bachmann indicated on his plan the visible ruins of a SMALL THEATRE at a point roughly where the course of the Wadi Mousa turns westwards. The author has been unable to locate them. Bachmann is, however, remarkably reliable and so it can be assumed that these ruins existed at the time of his survey. The Wadi Mousa may have changed its course slightly during the interim causing the remains to be swept away. Failing that they could have become buried by driven sand.

As one approaches the beginning of the COLONNADE STREET (Colour plate 3a, facing page 128)—or that part of the Street which has been excavated so far—it would be well to remember that the wide, open hillsides were, at the height of the city's prosperity, packed with buildings of one kind or another. The destruction of this metropolis will be seen to have been complete.

A row of ugly bollards cross the track, designed to prevent vehicles from going any further. In the sand round the southern end are deep tyre tracks.

The rich green foliage of the one and only tree in the middle of the central valley shades the ruins of the NYMPHAEUM (Colour plate 3b, facing page 128). A Nymphaeum was a public drinking fountain suitably dedicated in honour of the water nymphs who flitted so delectably about the woods. The Romans seem seldom to have been able to resist the temptation of constructing the most grandiose fountains with cascades frothing in all directions, and to find such an edifice on the Roman Colonnade Street of Petra comes as no surprise (Fig. 81). It is, however, a modest affair compared with the colossal Nymphaeum in Severan Leptis Magna and at Olympia, but is none the less not without pretentions. Only the foundations now remain. It is not certain how far the Colonnade Street extended eastwards beyond the Nymphaeum, and the encroachment of the Wadi Mousa will probably preclude us ever knowing. If Bachmann's small theatre did exist, it seems likely that the Colonnade Street would have extended as far as that at least. It is conceivable that it went right up to the foot of el Kubtha and the Royal Tombs.

The Nymphaeum marks the junction of the Wadi Mousa with the Wadi

Fig. 81 A reconstruction, based on Bachmann's plan, of the Nymphaeum, a public fountain, on the Colonnade Street.

Mataha (Map 4, facing this page). It was by the Wadi Mataha that the waters diverted by the dam at the entrance to the Siq eventually came into the heart of the city. The Nymphaeum was designed as a very flattened triangle to assist the confluence of the two streams and may have been one of the terminals of the water system which went through the Siq. It is not possible to assign an accurate date to the Nymphaeum but it was probably put in hand shortly after the Colonnade Street was laid out.

Opposite the Nymphaeum will be seen, deeply imbedded in the steeply rising

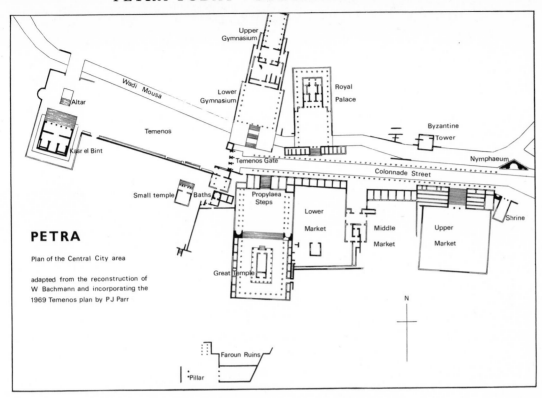

PETRA

Plan of the Central City area

adapted from the reconstruction of
W Bachmann and incorporating the
1969 Temenos plan by P J Parr

Map 4. Central City Area (After W. Bachmann)

hillside, the stumps of two pillars flanked by a wall, the right-hand one displaying a shallow niche. This feature is badly worn and could easily be passed by unnoticed. Bachmann called it the 'South Nymphaeum', but it is more likely to have been a small votive shrine or chapel. The site has not been excavated, only the front was exposed when the debris along the Colonnade Street was cleared.

Just beyond this a wide flight of steps up the steep bank has been opened up. This led to the UPPER MARKET and two fallen columns at the top attest to the grandeur of its approach. The hillside to the south has been carved out to accommodate the corners of both the Upper and Lower Markets, thus permitting their sites to be roughly level. The fronts of the markets facing the Colonnade Street were fitted up with small shops, the remains of which can be seen, but the markets themselves have not been excavated. Bachmann's plan showed three markets side by side along the length of the Colonnade Street. The lines of the Upper and Lower Markets are reasonably clear, but the Middle Market seems to have been an amorphous affair and it is possible that it was never actually a market as such. Rather it could have been a camel-stance conveniently situated between the two main markets.

It has been assumed that these notable and obviously important sites were markets, but future excavations may reveal that one was a Forum and another possibly a *Palaestra* or other fine adjunct to a classical city. The list of buildings possible to find in such a place is lengthy, for cities of the importance of Petra were as conscious of civic amenities as we are today. For the time being, however, it is convenient to regard these spaces as markets in view of the importance of trade to the Nabatean way of life.

Odd stretches and unrelated fragments of wall lie scattered all over the slopes above the Wadi Mousa. Bachmann tried to make sense of these in his map by devising hypothetical buildings in which the fragments could have served a useful function. His work has been the basis of the plan of the city in this book (Map 4), but Mr Parr's plan of the Temenos has been incorporated into it.

In 1960 the Department of Antiquities re-erected, completely or in part, a handful of the columns which originally lined both sides of the Colonnade Street (Fig. 19). It requires some imagination to visualise what it would have looked like in its heyday with the double colonnade blocking out the open-to-the-sky views which today lie on both sides (Fig. 18).

Some distance beyond the pillars the British School of Archaeology in Jerusalem examined an area in an effort to establish a 'grammar' of Nabatean pottery. It was also hoped to find evidence of the earliest Nabatean occupation of Petra, and where more promising a place than at the side of the wadi along what has surely always been the main arterial route within the city boundaries. At the same time as these aims were being pursued, it was intended to investigate in detail the architectural development of one, very restricted part of the city in an attempt to locate a key to its history. This site is known as TRENCH 3.

A magnificent stretch of paving had been exposed by the Department of Antiquities' expedition under the direction of Diana Kirkbride (Mrs Helbaek) in 1955–6, revealing into the bargain a series of rooms in a range of buildings near by. The 1958–9 expedition decided not to move the paving-slabs of the street itself, but instead an area between the actual street and the wadi side was chosen where the paving had already been robbed-out.

It was found that below the street there were a number of levels which could best be described as gravel tracks. It has been convincingly argued that the Colonnade Street we see today was a Roman period creation, probably put in hand shortly after the annexation in A.D. 106. This indicates that the strata of gravel which lie beneath the paving-stones are of the Nabatean period. Some of the material found in the examination of these levels is of a very early date including Hellenistic Black glazed sherds and Phoenician coins, notably of the third century B.C. From this we can deduce that there was a street on this site, albeit a dirt track, from soon after the Nabatean occupation. We know little or nothing of the pre-Roman layout of the city, but the information drawn from this site helps to start a picture. The original street would certainly not have looked like the grand Roman period construction, the remains of which we see today.

The wadi side buildings were probably two-storey constructions with the upper storey on the level of the street, the lower on the level of the wadi. A footpath ran beside this lower level with a narrow, cramped set of steps leading up at one point to a higher level. These steps were roofed over in a characteristically Nabatean way, with massive stone slabs such as one finds in the Nabatean buildings in the Hauran. Roman coins of the fourth century A.D. were found in the upper building, so one can say that in one guise or another these buildings enjoyed an extremely long life and usage. It is unfortunate that none of the structure above street level survives, but it is probable that the pre-Roman period structure was incorporated into the aggrandising of the street, and suitably embellished.

The cramped flight of steps is masked by the very necessary revetting of the wadi which was constructed by the Department of Antiquities in 1954 (Colour plate 3b, facing page 128). Its newness tends to jar rather in a setting of such antiquity: its completeness and freshness to startle in such a scene of ruin and time-worn fabric. It serves, however, to preserve what is left of the original revetting from further erosion. This revetment extends as far as the Temenos Gate and there are plans to continue it down the north side of the Temenos as far as el Habis. The sooner this can be done the better, for it will protect the Temenos from a very real danger.

A wide bridge probably crossed the wadi at the point of the excavations, carrying a staircase into a formal courtyard of what Bachmann referred to as the ROYAL PALACE. Little remains of this bridge and the plan which Bachmann devised is based, with great skill, on only a few fragments of the Palace that can be seen on the surface of the hill. It is hardly worth crossing the wadi to inspect these but the abutments of the bridge are worth noticing. No excavations have as yet taken place on this north bank of the wadi, even though surface evidence leads one to believe that important remains lie buried here.

A little further down the north bank, approximately opposite the Temenos Gate, are the scattered and unexcavated remains of yet another huge building complex which climbs the steep hill. This has been dubbed the UPPER and LOWER GYMNASIUM but why is not known; could the thought of gymnastics have been promoted by a notable piece of sculpture depicting a putto between two winged lions or griffins, which was found here and recorded by Domaszewski? This piece of sculpture is now in the Petra Museum in el Habis.

The start of the steps which crossed the wadi on a bridge below the

Gymnasiums has been revealed now that the area in front of the Temenos Gate has been cleared. The abutments of this bridge are much better preserved, and on the north bank there are clear indications of the structure. Again it is hardly worth crossing to inspect the ruins of the bridge or of the Gymnasiums. At present a track runs along the wadi side probably on the line of the north bank street in ancient times.

Just before the Temenos Gate is reached, a partly restored flight of steps climbs the steep bank on the left of the Colonnade Street (Fig. 82). At the top a level area leads to another short rise which bears a conspicuous row of collapsed pillars (Fig. 20). The centre of the steps is in the same axis as the centre of the fallen pillars—of a portico—and it is obvious that this is the site of a temple compound. Bachmann designated it the 'Great Temple' but this could lead very easily to it being confused with the Kasr el Bint. Nothing beyond the steps has been excavated but it looks as though full advantage was taken of a natural rise in the ground at this point to create a monumental approach to a temple of importance. One has seen just such arrangements before, at Jerash where the glorious Propylaea (a grand ceremonial entrance to a sacred precinct) has been remarkably well preserved, and again on a quite gigantic—and utterly vulgar— scale at Baalbeck. The PROPYLAEA leading into the sacred compound of a temple was a regular and established architectural format in the classical world— particularly the Hellenistic world.

All one can say at the moment is that the fallen pillars on the hillside mark the site of a temple of great importance. The whole arrangement does, however, lead one to speculate on the possibilities. The fallen pillars appear to be pre-Roman thus indicating a Nabatean temple, a Nabatean temple, what is more, right in the heart of the city. This is the place where one would expect to find the shrine of the patron deity of the city, if not the shrine of the chief deity of the people. Were it not for the evident importance— indeed supreme importance—of the Kasr el Bint, one would be strongly tempted to designate the temple on the hill as the prime sanctuary of Petra.

The position and scale of this temple leads the author to suspect that the site has been occupied by a temple complex, however large or small, from the time

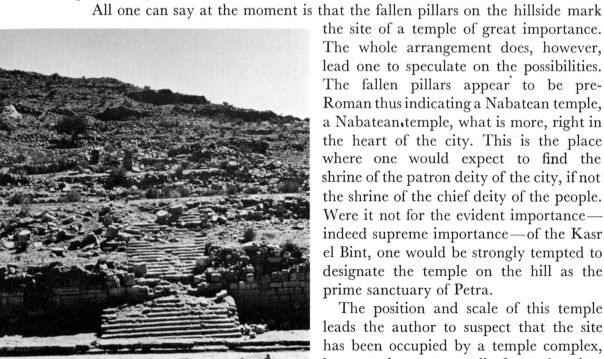

Fig. 82 The Propylaea steps which lead up to the fore-court of the Manathu Temple on the hill behind.

of the earliest urban occupation of the city area. The first real burst of architectural and civic energy probably occurred under the stimulus of Hellenism which arrived late in Petra. Before that it is likely that there was little organised effort in the sphere of civic development, and the city was one of those places which just happened to grow according to the exigencies of the site and the whim of the inhabitants; in character very much like any old Arab town today. Aretas III Philhellen probably imposed some semblance of order on this chaotic shambles.

The linking of the temple site with the main road of the city by means of a courtyard and Propylaea in the classical manner would have seemed a very proper thing to do (Fig. 83). The fact that the Propylaea might have been re-developed and made a few degrees grander when the Colonnade Street was laid out does not alter the basic concept.

It is generally contended that the Kasr el Bint was the temple of Dusares. Accepting this to be so, one is bound to ask, to which deity was the temple on the hill dedicated if it was as important as its position seems to suggest? It would seem natural to dedicate the main temple to either the principal deity of the people or to the patron deity of the city, to Al Uzza or to Manathu. A thorough excavation of the site will be the only way to establish whether this is the site of the MANATHU TEMPLE as the author suspects.

A yard or so beyond the foot of the Propylaea steps is one of the few remaining constructed monuments of Petra, the TEMENOS GATE (Fig. 84). It forms the first feature of the Temenos complex which has always been of special interest to the British School. It has frequently been referred to by other names, notably the 'Triumphal Arch', the 'Monumental Arch', the 'Roman Arch', etc., but recent research and excavation have confirmed that it formed the entrance gate to the sacred precinct of the Kasr el Bint, the Temenos. The existence of a curb running across the central opening, of sockets for both bolts and hinges, leave us in no doubt that at one time the structure was furnished with heavy doors, probably of metal clad or studded wood.

In front of the Gate there is a sort of 'piazza', a very apt name given by Mr Parr, which separates the Gate from the Colonnade Street proper: this is empha-sised by the fact that the Gate is set slightly squint to the street. The Gate cer-tainly formed a terminal feature to the street but also served both functionally and visually the purpose of a prelude to the Temenos. The 'piazza' would have accentuated this effect. (Colour plate 4, facing page 144.)

The Gate in its present form was built sometime after the completion of the Colonnade Street and may well have replaced a previous, possibly less grandiose structure. The fact that the adjacent paving-stones had been lifted and replaced with smaller ones helps to confirm this contention. Elsewhere in the 'piazza' a certain amount of the original paving still exists.

Fig. 83 A reconstruction, based on Bachmann's plan, of the central city area showing the Manathu Temple, the Lower Market (*left*), the Colonnade Street and the Propylaea Steps (*foreground*) and the Temenos Gate (*bottom right*).

It was possible during the 1959 clearance of the area to investigate the levels below the existing paving. This revealed that the Gate stands on a massive stone platform partly designed to protect the foundations from the ravages of the Wadi Mousa 'next door'. Forming part of this buried platform were the remains of

Fig. 84 The ruins of the Temenos Gate from the Colonnade Street. At the foot of each shaft can be seen the squared blocks on which stood the free-standing columns.

a substantial structural wall running at right-angles to the present Gate but certainly pre-dating it, which indicates that the present Gate, although Roman, was built on the same lines as a predecessor and not on a new 'corrected' line which would square it off with the new Colonnade Street. A number of architectural pieces were also found in the excavations including a handsome pilaster covered with moulded plaster in the true Nabatean manner. It is believed that the pieces came from buildings which were demolished during the redevelopment of the Gate and its adjacent structures.

The Colonnade Street had raised pavements which, at the point where they reached the 'piazza', stopped short some 15 feet from the front of the Gate. The colonnades finished as well, and two steps down brought the pavement level with that of the 'piazza'. It was a neat arrangement which would have created a rather intimate atmosphere. Massive proportions applied in confined areas can produce an oppressive effect, but the lightness and openness of the 'piazza' would have been both impressive and agreeable.

To the north and to the south, the Gate was flanked by tower-like buildings, the remains of which are still to be seen (Fig. 85). The north tower is just a bare four walls, all much destroyed. The south tower, which is still undergoing systematic excavation, has proved to be an interesting subject and holds promise for the future. It is now thought that it served as the principal vestibule of a

Fig. 85 The Temenos Gate from the Temenos, showing the South Vestibule to the Baths on its right. The area in the foreground is the Temenos or sacred temple precinct.

Baths immediately to the south of the Gate. From the Gate, however, all that is seen is a massive blank wall of finely laid masonry acting as a foil for the elaboration of the Gate itself.

The clearance of this area in 1959 established that on the east side there were free-standing columns on individual square plinths between each of the three openings, making the construction a much more architectural piece of work than it would otherwise have been. The Temenos, or inner, façade was much more static in appearance, depending for its effect on the fact that it stood recessed and framed between the two tower blocks, thus giving it an effective illusion of depth.

Bachmann provided a well-reasoned and still substantially correct reconstruction of the Temenos Gate, which he called 'Das Strassentor' or the 'Street Gate'. This reconstruction has been taken as the point of departure for the present reconstruction (Fig. 86) but it is not suggested that this reconstruction is definitive. It does, however, incorporate not only the free-standing columns but also the recently discovered zoomorphic capitals which capped them, both of which are totally missing from Bachmann's reconstruction.

The free-standing columns, being on the eastern façade of the Gate (Fig. 87), indicate that this was the principal façade, preparing the visitor or pilgrim for the experience of entering the sacred compound. They also provided an important clue to the dating of the monument, for such a feature in the fastness of the Province of Arabia is 'unthinkable' before the reign of Trajan (reigned A.D. 98–117). As H. Plommer has pointed out in his book *Ancient Classical*

4. The Temenos Gate

Fig. 86 A reconstruction of the Temenos Gate, based on a revision of Bachmann's plan, and incorporating features established by recent excavations and researches.

Architecture, 'the earliest surviving arch which shows this feature in Rome itself, is of Septimius Severus. But perhaps Trajan's arch there had made the innovation.' Caution must, however, always be exercised in trying to date buildings on stylistic grounds alone. Stylistic considerations are none the less valuable in

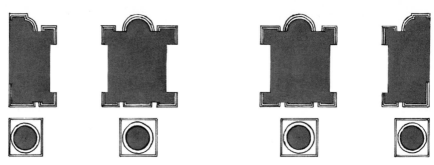

Fig. 87 Ground plan of the Temenos Gate.

providing a climate of knowledge in which other relevancies can be exercised. It was long held that the Gate and the Kasr el Bint were planned at the same time, possibly during the prosperous Antonine (A.D. 138–61) and Severan (A.D. 193–211) periods. Current belief, however, places the Kasr el Bint in the late Nabatean period and the Gate in that of the second phase of Roman alterations.

The architecture shows clearly that, for all the presence of Rome, the Nabateans never wholly deserted their native style which kept reasserting itself in new pseudo-classical guises. The panels on the pillars of the central arch and the zoomorphic capitals are good cases in point. The general 'feel' of the monument is certainly classical but it must be remembered that the classicism of the Nabateans was something well removed from the orthodox classicism of the Western world. The architect was, however, obviously determined to provide a Gate modelled on the Roman fashion of the three opening triumphal arch. To contrive this necessarily broad conception on a narrow and cramped site may have been one of the reasons for the slanted line of the old Temenos Gate, thereby gaining a few extra feet. The free-standing pillars would thereby be seen from the 'piazza' at a slight angle, creating a more exciting piece of architecture. Using this wall-like shape could have been the reason why the structure had to be locked between the two flanking towers as a very necessary measure of support; it would also account for the fact that the whole 'wall' was of continuous height. Given this awkward site, the architect made a remarkably effective architectural composition. Taken in its visual context, the Gate is an inspired piece of design; a structure of any greater depth than the 'wall' he provided would have been much less effective for it would have cut off the view into the Temenos beyond. As it is, when the gates were open the visitor would have seen through this imposing, architectural screen, across the broad paving and plots of the Temenos to the great mass of the Kasr el Bint. Even in its ruined state it is a fine and dramatic prospect (Fig. 23).

The soft pink ashlar facing seen today has been considerably restored and it is to the credit of the Department of Antiquities, and of Mr G. R. H. Wright who directed the work, that they have managed to strike a happy medium between blending in new stonework so that it is not obtrusive and not faking it up so that it attempts to deceive. The ground inside the Gate is strewn with an orderly array of architectural fragments which were unearthed when the area was cleared. Where all these pieces came from has not yet been determined—some indeed might have come from the Gate itself. Even though they are without exception rather badly battered, some are very beautiful and it is well worth not rushing past them. As it is, the heat of a Petra summer usually deters most people from rushing anywhere.

The north wall of the south tower is a massive cavity wall. It is in a very ruinous state except for the western corner where it still stands to a height of 4 or 5 feet. The masonry of the inner leaf is a little better preserved and stands to a slightly greater height (Fig. 85). The whole structure is what has been called the 'vestibule' to the Baths. Recent excavations have shown that, like the northern tower, its origins and structure are earlier than the Gate, the ends of which were incorporated into the previous fabric.

It would be premature to say too much about the function of the SOUTH TOWER but it is believed that it is related to the complex of buildings lying immediately to the south, i.e. the Baths. The existence of these BATHS has been known for many years—Bachmann made a preliminary plan and cross-section of the three domed chambers as early as 1917 — but it was only recently that they have been cleared and subjected to critical examination. Excavations are still continuing, so it would be inappropriate to speculate at this stage.

There are, however, one or two points which do deserve to be mentioned. It has always been assumed that this building complex was entered through a door in the Colonnade Street near the 'piazza', thus indicating a temporal establishment. The discovery of the south tower vestibule, with its imposing doorway into the sacred precinct, strongly suggests that the Baths played some part in religious rites. This does not mean that it was an homogeneous part of the plan for the area of the Gate, for all the buildings in this area appear to date from different times. The complex just accumulated over a period of time with all new additions being integrated into the existing fabric.

A small room inside the doorway was possibly the actual vestibule. This led through another door in the south wall into what appears to have been a pillared hall. This has only been partly excavated and only the top half of the pillars appear above ground level. It is much confused by later in-building of dividing walls, while a fine arched window on the western wall has been walled up. Even so it is possible, when looking down into the excavations from the higher ground level—which is roof level of the complex—to appreciate something of the plan of this hall which had four stout pillars set on the cross axis of the room. The lay-out of Baths in other parts of the Greco-Roman world always has a great hall fronting the composition, usually serving the purpose of the Frigidarium or Cold Bath. This hall might have served just that purpose in its original state. This would mean that in time excavations will reveal communicating doors with the other known rooms of the Baths: at present excavations are still not advanced enough to confirm or refute this.

The hall is, however, a room of sufficiently large dimensions, even by present evidence, to permit the possibility that the unimposing little doorway in the Colonnade Street also served as an entrance, albeit a secondary one. The asso-ciation of Baths, however, and a sanctuary is by no means unheard of, for there is much evidence of ritual bathing in both classical and ancient Near Eastern religions. Quite what form such bathing took in Petra, and the significance the Nabateans attached to it, we do not know at present.

Three main features of the Baths are known and have been partially exca-vated. Apart from the hall, the circular and square-domed chambers have only recently been cleared of the debris which precluded Bachmann from making a more detailed and penetrating study of them. The third feature is a square plan staircase, mostly collapsed, of monumental proportions. This appears to have connected the ground-floor level of the Baths with the level of the courtyard of the Manathu Temple. This raises the interesting question as to whether the Baths served as a venue for ritual bathing for both temples. Was there then any ritual connection between the Manathu Temple and the Kasr el Bint? Was the Temenos originally the private garden of the college of priests who served the Manathu Temple before the Kasr el Bint was built? One could go on to suggest that when Dusares began to become the paramount deity of the Nabateans, it was decided to site his shrine in the garden of the college, this being the only available place. This could explain the curious siting of the Kasr el Bint.

The three interconnecting-domed chambers are, at present, subterranean but it is not certain whether they were always so. They probably formed part of a single-storey construction, for they were lit by a central eye in their domes. The most likely explanation is that they were originally built near a small cliff which extended right down to just below el Habis, i.e. running parallel to the Temenos but set well to the south of it. The area between it and the Temenos was of con-siderable size, large enough to permit the erection of a residential quarter for the whole sacred college. This area would have filled up very quickly with sand once the city became deserted and the buildings began to fall down. At the moment there appears to be a steep hillside strewn with large blocks of stone and scrub-covered sand.

Of the three domed chambers, one is circular (Fig. 88) and two are square

Fig. 88 One of the circular chambers in the Baths: a complex of interesting buildings at present undergoing excavation.

with a door connecting them. Between them and the hall there is what looks like a narrow 'slype' but this has not been excavated. The wall of the circular chamber has eight half columns evenly spaced round it, between which are arched niches. The engaged half columns have capitals of an almost identical design to those on the pillars of the upper storey of the Khasneh but from this it must not be assumed that they are therefore of the same date. These capitals carried a bold dentilled cornice of plaster, suitably painted, above which rose the deep dome with its eye in the centre: it is highly probable that the dome and the walls were also plastered. As a room it is fairly straightforward but its interest lies in the closely related features. The first of these is the similarity of the capitals to those on the Khasneh, and secondly the fact that this room forms a part of the same fabric as the rooms next door and is therefore of the same date. The rectangular rooms are nothing more than square boxes over which are placed saucer domes. These are supported on deep, unadorned pendentives and depend for their effect, as well as their strength, on a precise understanding of the principles of dome construction. Domes on pendentives seem to have first appeared in Syria during the first century A.D.; the Hellenistic Near East pioneered many new architectural effects and features in the classical repertoire. This, then, gives us a date before which the Baths could not have been constructed. Were a date late in the first century to be ascribed to these two rooms, if not the whole Baths complex, one would be obliged to explain the occurrence of Nabatean-foliated capitals which appear to date from nearly two hundred years before.

It is not proposed to try and resolve this question in this work, for the site is still insufficiently excavated and what has been revealed has not been fully studied. A preliminary architectural study has been given in the 1969 Annual of the Department of Antiquities by Mr Safwani Tell, who suggests that the innovation of pendentives might have been made in Petra. It is perhaps too early to make concrete statements on this matter for the final picture will only appear when the whole Baths complex has been fully excavated. Where the foot of the staircase connects with the rooms has not been established. The steps themselves have collapsed into the well of the staircase but their original position is clearly marked on the walls and on the central pillar. These surfaces are still covered with their original plaster painted to represent veined marble of different colours. It must have been, in its pristine state, a very splendid affair probably with a set of clerestory windows flooding the upper flights of steps with light, leaving the visitor to descend into a cool, 'marbled', and dimly lit depth below.

Because excavations are still going on it is inadvisable to make these features accessible to the public, so at present the visitor has to be content with viewing from above the staircase and the hall, and regrettably, to miss the three domed chambers. Once work has finished the Baths will provide a notable and important addition to the sights of Petra; what is more it will be a monument very definitely associated with the living rather than the dead.

The vestibule in the south tower starts the TEMENOS proper (Fig. 89) which culminates in the massive Kasr el Bint. The northern line of the Temenos is lost because the Wadi Mousa has over the years eroded and obliterated all traces of the retaining wall which must surely have existed. The south side has fared better and, after being cleared of debris by the Department of Antiquities at various times between 1963 and 1964, the salient features of the temple precinct were revealed.

The clearance afforded the British School of Archaeology in Jerusalem a welcome opportunity to carry their investigations a stage further. The description presented here, culled in part from the Interim Report,* is necessarily incomplete and, as has been stressed in the Report, may even be inaccurate in detail. In particular the South Wall of the Temenos has not been fully examined and, although it is the most interesting feature second only to the Kasr el Bint, it would be inadvisable to adduce too much from its rather confused history. It had been repaired and partly rebuilt at a certain time in its useful life.

The south tower forms an intruding angle between the Gate and the South Wall. Abutting the western façade of this is the first of the 'structures' which comprise the salient features. It is a low DAIS one step high and about 9 feet deep by 49 feet long, with a simple seat or bench at the back up against the wall. Undoubtedly this would have been used by spectators at the religious ceremonies in the Temenos but its position so close to the Baths is interesting. It is tempting to associate the dais, always a seat of importance for dignitaries, with the supposed ritual bathing. It is conceivable, judging from the depth of the dais, that it was at one time the site of a purification altar which immediately confronted those emerging from the vestibule after a ritual bathe. The row of seats behind the altar would accommodate the priests while they awaited the arrival of the bathers. This is an imaginary reconstruction but does give some idea of the implications which could lie behind a rather ordinary looking low-paved dais.

Separated from the dais by an appreciable gap there is another PLATFORM of approximately the same dimensions (actually it is a little wider) but this time there is a row of seats or benches and the platform is reached by a flight of three steps. The suggestion put forward by Mr Parr, and alluded to by the Abbé Starcky, that it could be the remains of the staircase to the small 'protostyle' temple just to the south, seems the most likely explanation. The axis of the steps is the same as that of the temple but this theory would entail the steps originally passing over the top of the wall or through it if the wall had been carried to any great height. There is no indication in the stonework to suggest that a flight of steps was ever integrated into the wall or had abutted it, which leads one to conclude that the original steps were dismantled when the present Temenos South Wall was built, leaving only the bottom of the steps. The small temple would then have been isolated from the precinct and without direct access to it. This suggests that the temple and the platform under discussion are of an earlier date than the South Wall. The area behind the South Wall has not been excavated and at present there is little of the small temple to be seen other than a few fragments; sufficient, however, for Bachmann to devise its plan. Having once

* Annual of the Department of Antiquities, 1967–8.

Fig. 89 The Temenos from the steps of the Kasr el Bint. The South Wall (*on the right*) is a clear demarcation line between the excavated precinct and the unexcavated hillside.

been separated from the Temenos by the South Wall, the small temple may have
served as a private sanctuary for the college of priests. Before the construction
of the Kasr el Bint there may have been no wall at all so that the college grounds
extended from their southern limits right down to the edge of the Wadi Mousa.
With the Kasr el Bint there it became necessary to permit the public to invade
the privacy of the college grounds, and for this reason the South Wall would have
been built to divide the sacred compound into public and private areas. The
Temenos half thus became the forecourt of the temple with the area behind the
wall being reserved for the priests. This latter area has not been excavated but it
is quite likely that there is great depth of ruins buried there standing on the same
level as the Temenos.

Beyond these steps there is a small water basin served by a conduit through the
wall behind. Whether this channel is a drain or a spout for the supply of water
remains to be seen. The purpose of this basin at present is unexplained.

Beside the basin there is another flight of steps which coincide with an opening
—walled up—in the South Wall. Where these two steps lead or how high the
original flight went there is at present no telling, but these are obviously steps of
some consequence judging by their very spacious nature.

From this point the principal feature of the Temenos, a DOUBLE ROW OF
BENCHES, starts and extends westwards for some 80 yards to just short of the
Kasr el Bint. Behind the top row there is, in fact, an additional level which
served as a plinth or pedestal—possibly for statues—and cannot therefore be
properly called a row of seats. All these seats cannot be taken as a whole, for
there is a distinct difference in the construction and design of those in the
western half—the last 23 feet of them—which are much more poorly built than
the carefully dressed tiers to the east. There can be little doubt that the two
sections date from differing periods. The fact that the paving in front of the seats
fits neatly with the eastern length, but is short of the western, leads one to believe
that the eastern tiers are older than the western and that the latter were either
later additions or reconstructions.

What is certain, however, is that the western seats are later than the South
Wall, for they are clearly built up against it and are not integrated into it. The
whole length of the wall, unlike the tiers of seats, is of one construction and is
probably contemporary with the paving. The general contention is that the
eastern benches originally continued the whole length of the wall but that the
western end was dismantled and replaced by the present inferior work. This was
a curious thing to do for there seems to be little point in the exercise. Could it be
that those concerned had embarked upon an ambitious scheme to 'develop' the
western end of the Temenos, necessitating the removal of a certain amount of
seating, only to find that they had bitten off more than they could chew, and that

Fig. 90 A doorway in the South Wall close to the Kasr el Bint.
It is not known at present where this evidently important
doorway led.

in the end it was decided to restore the original seating arrangements?

It was on the western section, some 16 feet from the end of the rows of seats, that one of the most significant discoveries of recent years was made. As is so often the case in archaeology, relatively unimpressive objects can prove to be of major importance. On the plinth level, an ashlar block measuring about 13 by 19 inches was found to have a Nabatean inscription which had apparently been uncovered as early as 1964 but which was not subjected to critical study, by the Abbé Starcky and Mr John Strugnell, until 1965. The block of sandstone proved to be the base of a statue of King Aretas IV (8 B.C.–A.D. 40) and the inscription, judging from the mode of the script, could be dated to not later than the beginning of the first century A.D. This inscription is, in fact, one of many which formerly stood on this plinth level, and it is tempting to visualise that here there was a row of royal statues. The importance lies in the fact that the block of stone on which the Aretas IV inscription was found formed an integral part of the western plinth and seats, and was not a later addition. This gives a date of not later than the beginning of the first century A.D. for the seats. As the western seats are later than the eastern series and the whole of the South Wall, these latter features must date from well before the Aretas IV inscription. Having established a prospective date for the South Wall it becomes possible to consider a date for the Kasr el Bint, to which it is undoubtedly related.

Before considering this, the last two features of the Temenos before the Kasr el Bint is reached must be noted. The first is a monumental doorway set within a framework of engaged pilasters and quarter columns, which occurs immediately at the end of the row of benches (Fig. 90). It is not known where this doorway leads but it must have been to a building or compound of some importance judging from the scale of the entrance. It could have been an entrance to the college of priests but this is only guesswork, as was Bachmann's ground plan

which showed a range of rooms set round a pillared courtyard. There is no evidence to support this notion.

On the other side of the doorway, the wall continues very slightly out of line, for another 16 feet, in front of which are the remains of a massive pedestal. What stood on this again is not known.

Beyond the pedestal, the Temenos wall turns a right-angle to the south and apparently continues all the way round the back of the Kasr el Bint, reappearing again on the other side to connect with the Exedra, the remains of which can be seen beyond the Altar Platform. The wall thus makes a sort of shallow stone, three-sided well in which the temple stands. The name given to such a feature is a 'peribolos'. The actual arrangement of this area must await description until after the Altar Platform has been discussed: the whole question is intimately tied up with the perplexing siting and axis of the Kasr el Bint in relation to the Temenos as a whole.

The KASR EL BINT dominates the Temenos (Fig. 23 and 91); it was designed to do so. It has been persistently attributed to the Roman period but recent researches and archaeological excavations have caused this assumption to be seriously questioned. It is, in fact, now believed to be a late Nabatean work probably dating from the reign of Obodas II (30 B.C.–9 B.C.). The evidence to support this can briefly be summarised as being derived from three main sources of enquiry. It must, however, be emphasised that these arguments are to a great extent based on considerations of the respective plans and are, as yet, unsupported by any 'trench' evidence. The scale of operations during the last decade has not permitted, nor extended to, a complete excavation of this monument.

The principal piece of evidence is, of course, the Aretas IV inscription and its clue to the date of the South Wall of the Temenos. Although this wall is fractionally out of line on the other side of the doorway, there is no reason to suggest that this is later than the main section to the east. This being so, it is logical to assume that the peribolos is of the same date as well. The lay-out of the South Wall, the peribolos and the Temple are patently all part of a single design. The peribolos is, however, the important thing at this stage because, for it to make sense, the Kasr el Bint or some earlier building must have stood there when it was built. But even the limited excavations have shown that there was no phase of monumental building on this site before the present structure was put up. It is, therefore, possible to promote the theory that all these constructions are of the same date, i.e. not later than very early first century A.D.

On the same axis as the temple, at the foot of its steps, is a large rectangle of masonry (Fig. 92) measuring some 44 feet by 39 feet, and at present some 9 feet high. This feature is obviously an integral part of the Kasr el Bint complex even

Fig. 92 The Kasr el Bint and the Temenos from the top of el Habis. The plan of the temple shows up clearly as does the layout of the Temenos, particularly the Altar Platform in front of the temple.

Fig. 91 The great Nabatean temple known as the Kasr el Bint Faroun.

though it may be a slightly later addition. Mr Parr's excavations in 1965 established with reasonable certainty that this was an outdoor ALTAR or ALTAR PLATFORM. It was approached by a flight of steps extending the full width of the feature—possibly in its original design these steps were inset slightly—and was, like the podium of the temple, sheathed in veneers of marble. This feature is so much a part of the Kasr el Bint that it is best considered with that monument.

Brief mention should be made of the actual paving of the precinct. It is interesting that parts of the Temenos were never paved, certain areas at all stages being left free of flagstones. A particular instance of this is found in front of the steps of the small temple at the eastern end where a straight edge to the pavement

is clearly seen well away from the foot of the steps. Another is to the north of the Altar Platform. On the latter a trench revealed that at no time had a building of any substance or permanence stood on this site. The question then has to be asked, what were these unpaved areas used for? At present there is no way of telling but, as Mr Parr has pointed out, they could have been small sacred 'garden plots' to use a modern idiom, or places where sacrificial animals were tethered.

Passing behind the Altar Platform, the remains of the Exedra shown on the plan can be seen. It is rather like an ordinary curved stone wall but it is all that remains of the western Temenos wall, which would have originally stood to a considerable height and may have been decorated with architectural plaster-work.

The Kasr el Bint was constructed on a colossal scale (Colour plate 5b, facing page 192). It was built on a north/south axis and of sandy coloured stone which has a faint blush of pink to it. The exterior is square-looking and powerful and, like the interior, was probably at one time decorated with hard painted plaster so beloved of the Nabateans. Extensive runs of decorative plasterwork reminiscent of the architectural framework fantasies in the 4th Period Pompeian frescoes can be seen on the south and west walls of the temple. The temple stood on a high podium, the edge of which is set well out from the main walls, creating a spacious ledge several feet wide around the building. It has been suggested that a portico covered the eastern part of this, if not the whole, but this would have only ex-tended a little way up the wall of the main structure. The architectural plaster-work is small in scale and would probably have been wall decoration on the inside of this outward-looking cloister (Fig. 10).

Square panels of plaster decoration running up the faces of the pilasters which adorned all four corners have strong parallels with similar features on the Temenos Gate, though here the scale is infinitely larger.

Above the cloister, unrelieved walls of finely dressed and laid ashlar supported a bold frieze, cornice and parapet behind which would have been the roof. The frieze has 'rosettes' set between rather stark triglyphs. The flowers of these 'rosettes' are bold and have two rows of petals each instead of the usual single row. Elsewhere in Petra these rosettes are used as small decorative features in strings and thus may possibly be a continuation of the Hellenistic rosette feature — or, more interestingly still, be related to the highly stylised 'palmettes' of Assyrian and Babylonian architecture. It is believed that there were originally portrait busts within the frames of these rosettes, and the flower motif is, in fact, a later alteration. Such a bust has been found close to the Kasr el Bint. Parallels exist for this form of decoration at Khirbet Tannur which Nelson Glueck dated to approximately the same time as this temple.

Fig. 93 'Ruins of a Temple' by Léon de Laborde shows the south-eastern corner in the collapsed state of a few years ago; it has recently been rebuilt by the Jordanian Department of Antiquities.

The south-east corner—or at least the outer leaf of the fine cavity wall—had collapsed (Fig. 93) but has been rebuilt by the Department of Antiquities up to the level of the frieze in order to stabilise the south and east walls. No attempt has been made to 'fake-up' details, nor was it deemed fit to perpetuate the 'out-of-plumb' of the remainder of the east wall. This reconstruction was sensible remedial work and consists of plain, excellently laid masonry.

The north front was the principal one, facing as it did on to the western end of the Temenos (Fig. 94). It consisted of a huge pillared portico in antis, that is, the area covered by the portico was built into the body of the building and not made to project out in front of it. This device was very popular in Petra, inherited no doubt from the cave façades, for it creates areas of deep shade under the portico and must have been a deliciously welcome place of coolness in the throttling heat of high summer. Above the portico there rose the usual classical pediment.

Excavations on the steps which run across the whole width of the façade have shown that there was probably a change of plan, for the steps are built up against the podium and not integrated into it. The sides of these steps, and the podium on which the temple stands, were sheathed in veneers of marble. Considering that marble, of which the steps were also made, was even then a valuable mineral it is not surprising that there is practically nothing of them left now. At the foot of the steps a drain was constructed, but where this led has not yet been established.

Fig. 94 A reconstruction, based on the plans and elevations of Mr G. R. H. Wright, of the Kasr el Bint showing the marble-clad Altar Platform in the foreground.

The four great pillars of the portico are now little more than huge stumps. Beyond them, across the rubble-strewn portico, rises the massive main wall in which is set a high-arched doorway. In ancient times this main portal would have a lintel, and the arch we see today (Fig. 95) would have only been the relieving arch over it. There is evidence that the walls were covered with plaster in the Nabatean manner, though there is now no indication of how it was ornamented.

The body of the temple is still filled with fallen masonry (Fig. 96), but above this the walls rise to a considerable height. Inside the doorway there is, or rather was before the rubble choked it, a broad unobstructed chamber extending across the full breadth and to the full height of the building (Fig. 97). This was called the 'cella' or area immediately in front of the holy of holies. It was lighted by windows high up on the side walls; all wall surfaces were probably plastered and painted. In the case of the Kasr el Bint, the holy of holies is divided into three parts with the central one containing a flight of steps leading up to the statue— or god-block—of the deity to whom the temple was dedicated. These steps are now buried beneath the rubble, probably of the segmental arch which spanned the front of this section. The rear wall has a wide relieving arch in it which shows that the builders were concerned about the strength of this wall. The outer walls of this 'adyton', or holy of holies, are of enormous thickness and in all but one case contain internal staircases which funnel up, quite comfortably, in the cavity of the wall. The outer wall of the central section is thin by comparison, affording considerably more space inside. With the great height of this central wall, the builders were rightly concerned that such thinness would stay standing, so the relieving arch carried the load on to the thickness of the walls on either side: the remainder of the wall within the arch was quite capable of carrying its own weight.

The two flanking sections of the adyton were faced with screens of pillars which carried a balcony served by the staircases in the walls. The sockets for the wooden joists of the upper floors can be seen quite clearly. Screens of much shorter columns were placed in line above the lower ones, giving a most striking vertical rhythm across the face of the adyton which was emphasised by the cross-lighting. This two-storey colonnade on either side of the main 'chancel' provided a splendid counterpoint to the cavernous emptiness of the central space which has no window and was, in consequence, held in mysterious gloom (Fig. 98).

The Kasr el Bint has long been regarded as the shrine of Dusares and, as we have no evidence to the contrary, it is as well to accept this attribution. Suidas maintained that Dusares was worshipped in Petra as a block of stone. Knowing of the Nabateans' extreme conservatism, it is fair to say that in the early days of the Kasr el Bint this assertion would probably have been justified. But with the persistent pressures of the classical world, first through Hellenism and later through Rome, conservatism even in Petra would have been worn down and deities with human image would have begun to appear. Moreover, representations of this deity in the form of a man are known. Nelson Glueck has pointed

Fig. 95 The entrance arch to the Kasr el Bint was originally only a relieving arch over the lintel of the main door.

out that 'The Hellenistic–Semitic gods of the zenith of Nabatean development in the second century A.D. were far removed from the rough-hewn rectangular blocks of the Dhu Shara (Dushara, Dusares) deity of their earlier history'.* He was writing about Khirbet Tannur which is a remote and late period, religious site where anthropomorphic innovations were accepted. In Petra one would expect to find a much higher degree of restraint towards change, especially on religious matters: their architecture certainly indicates this. Even so, it is probable that such an image was installed in the Kasr el Bint together with or in place of the block. During the 1959 excavations of the podium, a fragment of a hand, about four times life size, was found. It is Greco-Roman in style and indicates a statue of 20 feet high: such a statue would fit comfortably into the central shrine of the *adyton*.

The siting of the Altar Platform outside is both curious and significant. Mention has been made of the unlikely siting of a principal sanctuary on the site occupied by the Kasr el Bint, and it is possible that this Altar Platform may provide a hint at a solution.

Nabatean temple plan, or as far as we know at present, derives like so much else in Nabatean civilisation, from the Parthians, or going back still further, from the Achaemeneans or Persians. Here the temples were oriented east/west so that, particularly at calendrical celebrations, the image of the deity would be seen amid the streaming splendours of the rising sun. The Kasr el Bint, however, like

some other Petraean temples, is oriented approximately north/south. It may have been that the builders in Petra were bound by a particular city tradition which demanded that the axis of their temples should be this way. The orientation of the Temenos is dictated largely by the lie of the land along the banks of the Wadi Mousa and is, in consequence, oriented east/west. If the civic tradition forbade an east/west temple, it would obviously be impossible to place it at the end of the Temenos. This would have resulted in either a totally blank side wall being presented to the worshippers in the sanctuary at festivals, or the creation of a totally new form of temple plan which permitted a right-angled turn between the

* *Deities and Dolphins.*

Fig. 96 Interior of the Kasr el Bint today.

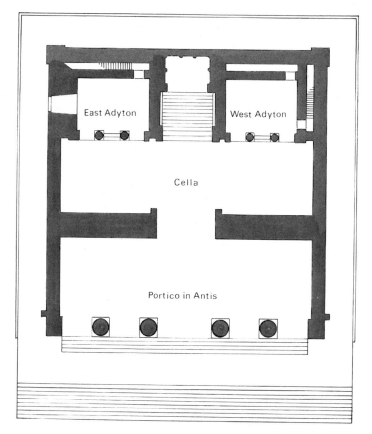

Fig. 97 Ground plan of the Kasr el Bint, after G. R. H. Wright.

principal door and the entrance to the shrine. The former was obviously out of the question but the latter would have been such a remarkable innovation that it is not surprising that this did not happen: there is no precedent for such an arrangement in the history of the Nabateans. The Nabateans were, in fact, curiously resistant to innovations of this kind. The only answer was to set the temple to one side with a grand portico giving on to the Temenos. The breadth of the Temenos at this point would not permit an assembly of any great size facing up the steps into the temple, so an open-air Altar Platform was constructed in front of the steps, towards which the throng of worshippers in the whole length of the Temenos could face. A temporary, portable god-block could be carried from the temple, with tremendous theatrical effect, to be placed on the Altar Platform for devotional display. By this means the predilection for worshipping east/west could be satisfied and the local tradition, if that be the case, for temples aligned north/south would have been maintained.

Mr Parr has also pointed out that, had the temple faced back up the length of

Fig. 98 A reconstruction of the interior of the Kasr el Bint.

the Temenos, the deity would have had a restricted view only of the city roofs. In its present position the deity enjoyed a superb view of the Gebel esh-Shara, the mountain of which he was Lord. What is much more significant in Mr Parr's words is the question, 'might not the orientation of the Kasr el Bint towards the north symbolise or commemorate in some way the connection of the deity with the mountain tops, and underline the predilection of the Nabateans for the high places?'*

The name Kasr el Bint, or more fully Kasr el Bint Faroun, means the 'Castle of Pharaoh's Daughter'. Quite how Pharaoh's daughter came to be associated with the building is not known, but Dr Margaret Murray has suggested that as

* P. E. Q., July 1960.

the temple was dedicated to Al Uzza, the mother-goddess, such an attribution should not be surprising. Be that as it may, Musil records a local legend that there lived in the Kasr el Bint a princess who was always complaining that there was no running water from a near-by stream or spring. She let it be known that she would marry the man who could bring water into the building. Various contenders came forward, one of whom claimed 'I will bring water for thee from Ain Haroun and I shall do it by the power of God, men and camels'. He succeeded and, of course, married the girl. As yet we do not know, but it would be interesting if it were found that there had originally been running water laid on in the Kasr el Bint.

III

el Habis, Wadi Siyagh, Umm el Biyara, el Sabrah

The cool shade of the tall, willowy trees in the area immediately beyond the western end of the Temenos is very welcome in the heat of summer (Colour plate 5b, facing page 192). These trees also add a touch of green to an otherwise dusty brown landscape. All around rugged mountains rear up along the skyline, while eastwards the boldly shaped low hills which carried the ancient, sprawling city rise on either side of the Wadi Mousa. Today they bear the rubble of its destruction. To left and to right was once a teeming mass of houses rising, thickly packed, probably on terraces, from behind the monumental buildings along the wadi-sides to the crests of the hills. The air was shrill with noise; colour flickered and flashed against the white-plastered walls. Now they are bare, silent hills choked with rubble and sand.

The hotel building of Nazal's Camp is most conveniently placed in the heart of Petra alongside the Kasr el Bint. It is also a building of quite unredeemed ugliness and is a monstrous modern intrusion in a crucial point in the old city. The present thoughts of removing it to the Wadi Siyagh are to be encouraged, for there it would be less obtrusive and be in a setting of unequalled natural grandeur. Behind the hotel is the sheer-sided rock of EL HABIS which Brünnow referred to as the 'Acropolis Hill' while others have named it the 'Citadel' (Fig. 184). It seems impressive close to, but from a distance and in relation to the towering, vast bulk of Umm el Biyara, it is like 'a cat beside a camel'. It is a scramble to reach the top, and an attempt should not be made without a local guide. On the summit there are precious few remains to be seen except for those of a fort which is believed to be either Byzantine or Crusader. The views over the whole city area with the Kasr el Bint immediately below are, however, very fine. The plan of the temple shows up particularly well from this 'aerial' vantage-point (Fig. 92), and its relation to the Temenos is clearly seen.

The eastern face of el Habis contains some interesting and perplexing monuments. The first, and most southerly, is still completely unexplained. It is called the COLUMBARIUM (Fig. 99). A columbarium is a place with tiers of niches for the reception of cinerary urns. The niches which cover every inch of the inner chamber and most of the walls of the recessed front, are not really big enough, being only about ten inches square, to hold funerary urns and so it is extremely doubtful that this was the purpose of this particular monument. The back of each niche slopes down inwards so that no tall object, like an urn, could stand on the rather narrow ledge. The whole arrangement looks like a Post Office sorting grid except that the niches have no depth to them. In Latin a columbarium is a pigeon-house or dove-cote, but any pigeon trying to perch here would quickly end up with a very stiff neck. As there is no evidence to suggest its original use, this monument may as well continue to enjoy the name of the Columbarium. Dr Post in 1888 described a comparable 'Columbarium' at Araq al Amir, near Amman, but even though it is remarkably similar to the Petra model, it gets us no nearer being able to deduce the original purpose to which they were put.

To reach the Columbarium it is necessary to climb the slope behind the hotel which is thickly covered with fallen masonry and boulders. Working one's way back towards the hotel, the next monument of importance is the UNFINISHED TOMB (Fig. 16).

From this monument we know how the Nabateans went about creating these carved monuments. Work was begun at the top and proceeded downwards, in this case until the whole entablature had been fashioned and the capitals of the pillars roughed out. The workers then cut deep into the mass of rock and hollowed out the interior before continuing with the façade. A small door has been cut at floor level, but it is arbitrarily set in exactly the place where a pillar would have stood, so we can assume that it is a later cutting of less sensitive times. Why this monument never received its final treatment we shall never know, but had it been completed it would have looked like a larger version of the Garden Temple in the Wadi Farasa. Such details as the Unfinished Tomb displays have the characteristics of Nabatean architecture, but the idea of a pillared portico in antis is something inherited

Fig. 99 The Columbarium, a monument the purpose of which is still unknown.

from Hellenism. It is possible that work on this large monument was cut short in A.D. 106.

Northwards the face of el Habis is riddled with caves of all shapes and sizes, some of which have been adapted as bedrooms and pressed into service with the hotel.

A wide sandy area on the bank of the Wadi Mousa leads to a gently graded flight of steps up to the Museum. At present these are adorned with a random selection of sculptural fragments, probably Roman copies of Greek, which have been found in various excavations in Petra, particularly in the vicinity of the Temenos Gate. It is too early to make any judgements of their artistic merit but they do show that the late Nabateans enjoyed a refined style of sculpture which leaned heavily towards the classical west. They are most probably imported works.

The steps become very steep before reaching a terrace in front of the MUSEUM. Various caves with stout wooden doors, which house workshops of the Department of Antiquities, are passed *en route*. The terrace is a necessary modern construction but is quite unobtrusive, unlike the bright red doors of the Museum. From the terrace there is an embracing view over the city, but somehow it seems to lack the curious sense of involvement which is to be had under the trees near the Kasr el Bint.

The museum is an important, façadeless monument distinguished by a series of windows. Kennedy referred to this monument as the 'Tomb with Windows', while Libbey and Hoskins called it the 'Rainbow Temple'. It is certainly singular in the fact that, of all the monuments of Petra, its interior is lighted by an organised and properly articulated series of windows instead of the usual reliance on such light as might penetrate through the doorway. The lay-out of the interior is also interesting. It consists of a high central hall, about 33 feet by 21 feet, flanked by side bays approached through wide, doorless openings of monumental proportions. The right-hand bay still has a stone-dividing floor; it is doubted whether the other, southern, end ever had one. The upper part of the screen wall of the northern end has been built up of large masonry blocks and not carved out of the solid rock like the lower part. Whether this indicates a later alteration or a fairly immediate change of plan, or even a remedy for a faulty stratum of rock discovered during the creation of the monument, it is difficult to say.

We do not know the purpose for which this monument was created. There are no graves or loculi to suggest a tomb, and if it was a living place it must have been the residence of someone of great importance. It is located at the beginning of an elevated gallery cut into the face of the rock high above the beginning of the Wadi Siyagh, which leads round to a notable sanctuary on the western side of el Habis. This is surely not without significance and seems to indicate that the 'Museum' was the start of a ceremonial processional way. In this case the 'Museum' could have been a temple—its plan is unlikely but the axis is north/south—or have been some form of pre-ritual gathering-point, or improbably the 'official office' of some religious dignitary.

Some of the 'finds' of Petra are displayed behind the massive, red metal doors, including a representative collection of pottery, jewellery and artefacts as well as some large sections of high relief decorative sculpture. The arrangement of the Museum is neither artistic nor particularly imaginative, but it is still worth spending time looking at the exhibits for they give some idea of the reality that was Petra. One of the most interesting is the collection of Nabatean earthenware water pipes which are all of a standard size and type, with connecting ends (Fig. 14). When one realises that the whole of Petra was probably served by an extensive system of such pipes, bringing water to all parts of the city, one begins to understand quite what an achievement the Nabateans' water engineering was. The design of such pipes has changed little in two thousand years. Some may be seen *in situ* let into the eastern wall of the Outer Siq at the point where it begins to widen out (Fig. 71).

Outside the door stands the headless statue of Hercules which came from the Theatre. It is Greco-Roman, but how appropriate to find this particular deity in Petra, for he was both the patron of drama and of trade.

The path beyond the Museum looks as though it disappears over the brink on to the stony floor of the Wadi Siyagh below, but a sharp turn to the left leads one on to the gallery which has a handsome stone balustrade. All this was carved out of the hillside, and unfortunately there is no way of telling when; the same may be said of all the flights of steps, couloirs and platforms with which the mountains of Petra abound. It is, in fact, almost impossible to move any distance in the mountains without coming across eroded flights of steps which lead off tantalisingly up into secret wadis and over shoulders of rock. Originally they led somewhere but all too often now the arduous climb up them can have the frustrating and exasperating result of a dead end with nothing to show. It is like driving in and out of culs-de-sac when you are looking for the main road.

From the gallery the multitude of caves on the far side of the Wadi Siyagh is particularly evident, and it has long been suggested that this was a rather fashionable suburb of the city. The area has not been systematically excavated but it can be said that, in the wider context of the city as a whole, every cave in Petra and the surrounding hills has been visited and inspected by one or other of the scholars who have recorded the place. Brünnow's work is the most re-markable for its sheer scope, even though by no means every cave is discussed or recorded. With staggering application the Germans must have visited nearly all the evident caves to see whether they were worth mentioning. Dalman seems to have done as much, one wonders whether with as much effort, for he relied extensively on Brünnow and Domaszewski, even though he spent most of his discourse trying to prove that they were wrong in nearly everything they deduced. Sir Alexander Kennedy and his party seem also to have clambered about in all directions, photographing and speculating on almost every curiously shaped rock and hole in the ground. His extensive review of the place is, however, a valuable collation of the facts known at that time and is a clear, readable exposition of the available material.

The gallery eventually debouches on to a broad strata-top of rock which forms a table-shelf behind el Habis. To the left the hill rises abruptly and on the right, with equal abruptness, the table-shelf tips down into the Wadi Thughra. The expanse of the table-shelf is confined by the towering mass of Umm el Biyara whose russet walls lead into a series of beautiful views of the junction of the Wadi Thughra and the Wadi Siyagh. These are probably the finest canyon views in Petra and if seen in the late afternoon, when the rays of the sun stream across the hollow heart of the gorge, it can be of an almost magical beauty (Fig. 100). The colouring pulsates with shades of carmine and gold, with the shadows sunk in deepest violet. Far below, the chiselled walls of the Quarries provide a precise counterpoint of hard, vertical lines and flat surfaces amid the bold, rounded tumult of nature. The white, stony carpet of the Wadi is wreathed in oleander as it dives mysteriously into the seeming depth of the earth.

A pleasant, and visually thrilling, afternoon may be spent walking down the Wadi Siyagh from the foot of el Habis. Except at midday, there is always plenty of shade and in any case there is usually a deliciously cool breeze in the wadi. It was probably this wind which in ancient times attracted the well-to-do citizens of Petra to use the wadi as a suburb.

The QUARRY is reached very shortly (Fig. 101). It is thought to be Nabatean but as quarrying techniques have changed hardly at all over the last four thousand years—except for the last hundred when the whole basic technique has altered radically—it is not possible to date the quarry by this means. Footholds, similar to those beside the Khasneh and elsewhere, are evident. An immense amount of stone has been excavated from the Wadi Siyagh quarry. Consider the cubic measurement of the space and imagine it in building blocks liberally scattered over the face of the city area and you begin to have some idea of the scale of the disaster which wrecked Petra.

Beyond the quarry, the oleanders grow thickly in the centre of the watercourse which starts to go downhill steeply between the enclosing walls of rock (Fig. 102). After something just over half a mile down, the wadi takes a pronounced turn to the north and the walls of the canyon seem to hang ominously large above your

Fig. 100 The Wadi Siyagh from behind el Habis.

Fig. 101 The Quarry in the Wadi Siyagh.

Fig. 102 The canyon-like Wadi Siyagh below the Quarry becomes a dangerous water course in winter during the heavy rains.

102

100

101

head. Here there is a DRIPPING WELL and pool of cold, clear water buried deep in the thicket of oleander. This pool has been a place of veneration from ancient times, and even today the local bedouin regard the place as the haunt of 'djins'. It is, however, far from being a spooky place especially when the sun radiates through the gently stirring oleanders and flashes on the incessant drops of water as they fall into the pool. The silence of this extraordinary place is broken only by the sound of falling water and the faint breeze sighing in the bushes. Very different is it in midwinter when an unholy gale howls up the gorge and moans its icy discontent round corners and into every nook and cranny. The Petra watershed pours its waters into the Wadi Siyagh, where they sweep down in a thundering cataract, dragging reluctant stones in their wake. The tough bows of the oleander are ravaged. That anything can survive this grey, frightening onslaught is a wonder, but each spring peace returns and with it the garlands of wild flowers of the desert.

Returning to the table-shelf, a small classical tomb marks the beginning of the ascent to the summit of el Habis. Whether this monument had any ritual significance is difficult to say; most likely it is just another patrician or wealthy merchant's tomb in a rather strategic place. The climb, or rather scramble, to the top should not be made without a guide.

The CONVENT GROUP of monuments takes the shape of a spacious rectangular courtyard dug into the floor of the table-shelf to a depth of approximately 15 to 20 feet (Fig. 103). Various individual monuments have been excavated into the walls and, although the dates vary, the group possesses a homogeneity of concept. The sunken courtyard is approached down a flight of steps from the south; originally an additional flight ascended from the Wadi Thughra entering the courtyard through a 'garden' in which there still is an enormous block of squared stone with a votive niche containing yet another block symbol. These steps are now so badly eroded that it is no longer possible to use them as a means of access. In the south-east corner of the courtyard is probably the oldest of the monuments in the group. It has multiple rectilinear carving over the door, the base of which is some six feet above the level of the courtyard. The steps which lead down into the courtyard have nearly cut this tomb off in the same way as later additions cut into the Theatre. Most of the chambers in the group are quite plain both in façade and interior except for the Cavetto I type in the north-west corner which has a manger grave.

The Convent Group was obviously conceived for some particular purpose. Unfortunately there is little evidence at present to help determine what that purpose might have been, but as there is such a noticeable feeling of intentional isolation or 'setting apart', the name 'Convent' could be not wholly inappropriate. Could this have been a communal habitation for those serving a particular holy site such as the small, well-preserved High Place which lies immediately above the corniced tomb on the western flank, overlooking the Wadi Thughra? Libbey and Hoskins, who discovered this feature in 1902, considered it to be a triclinium but Dalman recognised it as a holy place. The

Fig. 103 The Convent Group. An important set of monuments probably of religious character originally.

similarity between it and the famous High Place of Sacrifice on the Attuf Ridge is great even though the scale is much smaller; the el Habis High Place measures only 16 feet by 12 feet. All the essential characteristics are there including a block altar of the approved style: it should be remembered that in addition to being his altar, a block of stone was also the home of the deity, the Beth-el, as well as being the actual representation of the god. It might be that this shrine was a place of peculiar sanctity to which the whole of the el Habis processional way led, and which deserved its own college or convent of priests. Its position in a hidden but none the less spectacular spot perched above the Wadi Thughra

certainly has all the makings of a site that would have appealed to the imagination of early peoples who worshipped rock gods.

   Standing in the centre of the courtyard, surrounded by the rough and worn
walls, one gets an impression of what housing might have looked like in Nabatean
times. The form of common dwelling house has changed little in the remoter
parts of the Near East over the last two thousand years, with blank outside walls
protecting inner courtyards, not only from the sun but also from the dust of the
street. Rooms are still grouped round the courtyard with only small windows and
doorways. The walls are generally plain and unadorned. In the Convent Group
we have exactly this, but on a slightly larger scale and, of course, there is no
outside street. The city of Petra was thickly packed with houses which rose up
the hillsides behind the monumental buildings which lined both banks of the
Wadi Mousa. In all probability they would have been of this courtyard type.
Here, then, in the Convent Group, we have the only remaining indication of
what a living unit in ancient Petra might have looked like: in the city area such
complexes would have been built of stone and then plastered, here they have
been hewn out of the living rock. The group is now badly weathered and worn
but the impression is still there.

   Beyond the Convent Group there are no more monuments of note in the wall
of el Habis. Further on, past the end of el Habis, an important series of façades,
predominantly of the Assyrian II and Double Cornice I types, appears in the
wall at the foot of the towering Umm el Biyara (Fig. 104). One of the Double
Cornice II type has been so deeply carved into the slope that there are two
enormous buttresses frequently causing a deep diagonal shadow to fall across the
façade. The overall lines and character of this monument can best be seen from
Katute; close up, it is rather disappointing being so hideously worn and mutilated. A pair of round-headed façades appear again, set fairly high up the slope
(Fig. 43), but it is the author's contention, on stylistic grounds, that these are
later than those in the Outer Siq (see page 98).

   The Wadi Thughra at this point is just below the level of the main central
basin or valley and is joined by the Wadi Farasa which has come in across the
undulating country to the east. The area is covered with soft, powdery, purple
sand from which emerge large, smooth-surfaced slabs of grey rock. Beyond the
carved façades, a narrow gully seems to go straight up the side of the mountain,
its floor filled with a scree of large, sharp stones (Fig. 105). This is the beginning
of the ascent to the top of UMM EL BIYARA (Fig. 2).

   The initial climb up the screes is not so much a difficult or dangerous job as
an exhausting scramble up a very unstable surface. If one is in Petra during the
summer months this ascent should be made well after midday when the face of
the mountain is in shadow, otherwise the heat from the direct rays of the sun can

Fig. 104 The foot of the eastern face of Umm el Biyara is much carved with façades of all periods. The beginning of the ascent to the summit is in the dark cleft to the left.

make the climb intolerable.

Suddenly one comes upon a carefully smoothed ramp set between narrow vertical walls of equally smooth rock. The change from the scree surface to stable, hard rock is very marked, and the easy uphill walk is a delightful change. Above the beginning of this ramp can be seen the vestiges of an arch which at one time spanned this monumental approach to the heights (Fig. 106). The ramp leads up to a wide, spacious landing at which it turns and carries on uphill like some enormous double staircase (Fig. 107). The return ramp is protected by huge parapet walls which only cease when the top landing is reached.

Why a COULOIR of such magnificent proportions was necessary is a mystery when a single stairway of modest proportions would have sufficed at this admittedly difficult stage in the ascent. It is also perplexing why a ramp was preferred to the usual flights of steps: it would hardly have been necessary to lavish so much magnificence for the use of animals. The couloir was evidently created as much to impress as to

Fig. 105 The first part of the ascent, looking up to the great couloir.

Fig. 106 The Umm el Biyara Couloir, a massive double-flanking ramp carved into the mountain-side, formed a principal feature on the ceremonial route up the mountain.

be practical. Stepped ascents are common enough in Petra but nowhere on quite the same scale as this. One is led to the conclusion that on the summit there was a sanctuary of major importance. The gently sloping table-top of Umm el Biyara is covered with Nabatean ruins, including a temple (?) built on the very edge of a sheer drop overlooking the city below. As none of these Nabatean ruins has been excavated it is impossible to identify any important sanctuaries. An important Edomite settlement, excavated by Mrs Bennett, does exist on the top but it was a purely domestic site and does not bear directly upon the

Nabatean development of the summit. The purpose of the couloir must, then, remain a mystery but it is obviously religious in origin.

Beyond the couloir, the route up was at one time carefully engineered with a series of flights of steps with precipitous drops to one side occurring the whole time. This has become badly eroded and in places is quite dangerous. The ascent should not be undertaken without a guide, not only because of the dangers themselves but because the path is now difficult to follow.

Arrival on the top is abrupt. One suddenly peers over the top of the cliff, out across gently rising ground towards the highest point on the north-west. Almost in the centre of this scrub-covered plateau are the excavations of the Edomite settle-

Fig. 107 A birds-eye view of the Couloir.

ment. Less than a third of the extent of the settlement has been uncovered but sufficient was done to bring out some vitally important information on the little-known culture of the Edomites. This was a small, but flourishing, community of the seventh and sixth centuries B.C., of a people who had not worked out a centralised civilisation like their flanking neighbours on the Nile and Tigris/Euphrates. The Edomites were basically agriculturalists in this area; further north there is a suggestion that they were also actively engaged in mining and primitive metallurgy. Their wisdom was reputedly considerable even for their time, but it did not find expression in the construction of mighty architectural and engineering wonders.

In the excavated area there is one long, continuous central wall running approximately north/south, off which the various domestic units, houses, etc., were built (Fig. 108). In the main they were of the 'corridor' type with small rooms off a central passage. The dry-stone walls, built on the bed rock, are of the local stone which breaks very easily along its natural striations; no mortar was used and the stones are only very slightly trimmed. There is evidence of a certain amount of rebuilding and strengthening of the fabric which suggests later phases. Quantities of poor quality pottery were found on the beaten earth floors, in fact, many pieces can still be seen held fast in the sides of the excavation (Fig. 109). The charred remains of looms were found in two rooms, as well as over seventy loom weights. Usual domestic utensils such as lamps, storage pots and jars

(Fig. 110) were also found, suggesting simple farming folk rather than the ferocious subjects of Biblical diatribes. The whole settlement was ultimately destroyed by a fierce fire which burnt down to bed rock.

In its time, the settlement must have been sufficiently important in the reckoning of Edom to receive a missive from the 'king' of Edom. To all such communications the king's seal would have been attached, and an impression of this seal was found during the excavations (Fig. 111): again we do not know the contents of the letter or proclamation which the seal 'covered', for this was destroyed in the fire. The seal, being of clay, was baked hard and has thus been preserved. It shows a winged, aproned sphinx with some Phoenician text above it, 'belonging to Qaush-ga . . .'; the last letters are unreadable. This must be Qaush-gaber or geber who reigned at about the same time as Esarhaddon and the first year of Asurbanipal of Assyria (c. 668 B.C.). One other vitally important 'find' must be mentioned, that is a sherd of a storage jar bearing an inscription in cursive Phoenician, in black ink. It is difficult to make out, but the first word certainly means 'oil', and the text gives the contents of the jar and where it came from. This is the first recorded Edomite inscription.

Mention should be made of the eight cisterns cut deep into the rock which give the mountain its name, Umm el Biyara—Mother of Cisterns. If they are Edomite, as has been suggested, it would indicate that the Edomites were not only capable of the techniques of rock cutting but might have passed this skill on to the Nabateans. These deep, bell-shaped cisterns formed a highly effective water-storage system where even in hot weather evaporation would have been only slight. Early archaeologists lamented that they were filled with rubble and earth but one of these cisterns has now been cleaned out and its considerable size and depth revealed. Unfortunately there was not the yield of archaeological treasures which some people expected.

The eastern edge of Umm el Biyara overlooks a dizzy drop of 900 feet into the Wadi Thughra below. All along this edge are unexcavated Nabatean remains which command a magnificent view over the city. In the middle of them, where there is an uninterrupted drop to the rocks below, a broad flight of steps leads down to the very edge of the abyss. It has been suggested that this was the site of a temple, for a statuette of a deity was found very close by this spot. Until the site has been excavated it would be vain to speculate on why these steps were so perilously sited.

The north-western corner, being the highest point, affords a vantage-point for some of the finest views in Petra. To the south-west the massive, cliff-girt cone of the Gebel Haroun dominates the scene (Fig. 26), so great is its presence. On the summit the shrine of the Prophet Aaron gleams white against the intense blue of the sky. Westwards, lesser peaks and ridges jostle closely together, each trying

Fig. 108 The remains of the Edomite settlement on the plateau-top of Umm el Biyara. The walls were constructed without mortar to bond the undressed fractures of local sandstone.

Fig. 109 Edomite pottery and a pile of loom weights uncovered during the Umm el Biyara excavations.

Fig. 110 Edomite pottery from Umm el Biyara.

to peer over the other for a glimpse of the shimmering expanses of the Wadi Arabah below and beyond. The hazy distances of the Negev and Sinai complete the picture. To see this view at dawn is an experience which can seldom be rivalled. When Mrs Bennett was directing the excavations, she stayed up on the top for the seven weeks' season in 1963, without once coming down, and was thus able to see this gentle spectacle every day. The mountain has such a reputation for being haunted or 'possessed' that none of her locally employed Bdul workers would spend the night on the summit. Except for one worker from the Saidin, she stayed there alone. She has told the author of the beauty and intense silence when

Fig. 112 The central city area from the top of Umm el Biyara. The Temenos and the Colonnade Street can be seen clearly cutting across the valley with the Wadi Mousa to its left and the outline of the Markets and temples on the right.

Fig. 111 The seal of the Edomite king, Kaush, from the settlement on Umm el Biyara.

the sun goes down and the camp fires of the local bedouin in the valley below begin to wink their warm messages of comfort through the velvet shroud of the gathering night.

To the north lies a rugged terrain of jagged peaks closely packed together and scored by deep fissures. Their colour and character change imperceptibly throughout the day, not presenting the same face for more than a few minutes.

On the eastern side lies the city of Petra with the eastern barrier range enclosing the site upon the far side. The Kasr el Bint is seen in plan from this great height though perhaps not with the same clarity of detail as from the top of el Habis (Fig. 92). The undulations of the city site are clearly seen in this view with the Temenos and Colonnade Street seeming to sweep out across the valley like a band of white across the tawny hues of the ground (Fig. 112). In the western wall of el Kubtha, the huge Palace Tomb looks insignificant while an indelible shadow etched across the bland face of the mountain marks the Outer Siq. Above and beyond, the hills of Shara—the mountains of Seir—form a flat-looking backdrop with a smudge of dark green denoting the village of Elji. In the evening the whole view to the east is suffused in a golden light with the city area sunk in the gathering dusk and the bold,

angular shadow of Umm el Biyara cast on the face of el Kubtha. But as the sun is digested by the hot horizon there is a fleeting moment when the violet landscape embraces a limitless sky of the most intense yet limpid blue. The stars look like pin-pricks in the fabric of heaven through which Man glimpses the greater glory of an unseen paradise beyond. A few minutes later the magic has gone and night has replaced day.

To the south, the bumpy uplands cavort between the sterner hills of the flanking ranges (Fig. 113). On these steep hills is the suburb of el Sabrah which is as much a miniature Petra as el Barid in the north. Seen from the top of Umm el Biyara it is like looking out over a static rough sea in which the horizon is a rearing tidal wave.

The climb up the mountain can take nearly an hour, the descent can be done by the sure of foot in a little over a quarter of that time. Trying to do it in the dark is the only thing to be discouraged; there is a great temptation to tarry on the top watching the sun go down which can mean being caught by the sudden onrush of night.

To the south of Umm el Biyara lies el Barra, one of the rockiest groups of mountains, peaks and wadis in the district, above which the Gebel Haroun towers in a very foreboding way. Tradition has it that the shrine on the summit covers the last resting-place of the prophet Aaron (Haroun) and the site is still reverenced by the local people who are all Moslems. This has led to considerable prejudice against visitors climbing to the prophet's shrine: under present circumstances it would perhaps be unwise even to try to arrange a trip—which must be made with a guide. Those who have been to the summit say that the views over the Wadi Arabah are no better or magnificent than those to be had from the top of Umm el Biyara or from the Deir plateau.

Eastwards is an area called the SOUTHERN GRAVES which has apparently always been well outside the confines of the city with no sprawling suburb intervening. It is also debatable whether it was ever exclusively a 'graves' area. Habitations there certainly were here, even though the predominant remains today are those associated with religious cults and tombs. The area is astride the 'road' into Petra from the south and it is worth considering whether it was the

first caravanserai for travellers approaching from that direction. It has been suggested that el Barid in the north, and al Khan (now the Government Rest House) at the head of the Bab el Siq, were the northern and eastern caravanserais. The markets were in the centre of the city but these points could well have been goods depots. In some respects, the Southern Graves might have been the most important of these depots for it was at the end of the great spice route up from the south of Arabia.

Apart from a two-storey tomb which is almost unique in Petra, the most notable features are an important snake monument and another 'djin' block. The snake monument consists of a carved snake coiled up on the top of a high rock, while the near-by 'djin' block is placed on the top of a shelving platform of rock in which is carved a cave (Fig. 114). This treatment is unusual and tends to make the monument look top-heavy. These 'djin' blocks seem only to occur on the main approaches to the city.

Fig. 114 The 'djin' block at the so-called 'Southern Graves'.

The distant suburb of EL SABRAH appears to have been quite a sizeable town in its own right. It enjoyed the amenity of a neat, small theatre along prescribed classical lines (Fig. 115)—no doubt Roman—and there are the remains of what look like large barrack buildings, perhaps for a garrison defending the southern approaches to the city. We know little about the Nabatean army, although it is certain that they must have maintained a military establishment of certain size to protect the routes under their control. There is ample evidence of this in many

Fig. 113 The view south towards Sabra from Umm el Biyara.

Fig. 115 Léon de Laborde's view of the Theatre at Sabra. His interpretation of the surrounding country would be truer to England than to the Jordanian desert.

inscriptions at Hegra (Medain Saleh) and at other Nabatean sites. What form this establishment took is open to question but it is probable that the Nabateans, who were almost pathologically addicted to trade, would have tolerated better some form of Territorial Army or Ever-Ready force, than a full-scale standing army. This quickly mobilised reserve would have been able to support the professional force. The barracks at el Sabrah may, of course, be Roman, in which case they are almost sure to be for military use.

It must, however, not be forgotten that the hillsides about el Sabrah are riddled with mines. There is a view that the Edomites were really a mining and metallurgical people whose main sphere of activity lay further to the north; in that area Mrs Bennett is investigating the mining sites, including the famous Khirbet Nahas (Copper Ruin).

Until, however, el Sabrah has been excavated it is impossible to say whether the minerals there were exploited by the Edomites. There is no evidence of the Nabateans having been particularly inclined to extractive metallurgy but this does not mean that mining was not carried out. El Sabrah might have been a mining and industrial suburb of Petra complete with its own facilities and civic life, and the 'barracks' might be explained as having provided housing for the large number of expatriate workers needed to operate the mines, and presumably the smelters.

Unfortunately it is not easy to arrange a trip to el Sabrah, and it is imperative that a visit should be planned well beforehand and that suitable guides are taken. This is a day trip which should only be undertaken by those with plenty of time to spare and who actually like walking.

IV

Lion Tomb, the Deir

The area of the Kasr el Bint makes a good focal-point for most excursions, which require a certain amount of climbing. None of the climbs, however, is nearly as difficult or hazardous as the ascent of Umm el Biyara and, by and large, the going is relatively easy if a little exhausting in the summer heat. It is worth choosing the right time of day to see many of the monuments at their best. This is never more true than in the case of the Deir—or the Monastery. This monument of quite prodigious size is set aglow by the late afternoon sun. At other times of day its highlights contrast sharply with the deep, dark shadows and the ethereal beauty is not present.

Leaving the leafy shade of the trees by the Kasr el Bint, the route to the Deir first goes down into the bed of the Wadi Mousa and across the mouth of the Wadi Siyagh. The sand is very soft and powdery. Oleanders stand in bluey grey clumps which, if the time of year is right, are smothered with bright pink, white and red flowers. A few yards further on there is the wide rocky opening of the Wadi al Deir. Up this, flights of steps soon appear, cut into the rock. The route is at first quite gentle and makes little demand.

A small wadi appears on the left after a short while, but its unspectacular entrance, partly screened by bushes, could easily be passed by as of no consequence were it not for the Department of Antiquities' sign indicating the way to the Lion Tomb. This lies, with other interesting monuments, at the head of this small wadi.

The first thing that must be said of the LION TOMB (Fig. 116) is that it is not a tomb, but a triclinium. It is a small classical work possibly of the early Roman period. Even so it is most decorative with its flanking corner pilasters and elaborately carved frieze and capitals. The latter in Nabatean architecture are generally left quite plain, but here the designer has indulged himself with some very stiff, formalised floral scroll-work. The frieze is divided into the usual alternation of *triglyphs* and *metopes*, freely interpreted, the latter having very masculine buttoned discs or *paterae*, except for those above the pilasters which are adorned with masks of a Medusa character. This simple composition is topped-off with a low-pitched pediment. The extraordinary keyhole-shaped aperture above the door is a freak erosion and would once have been a separate window. There are traces of slender pilasters at the door and these must have carried an architectural feature like nearly all the other classical and post-Assyrian types.

Fig. 116 The Lion Tomb. The keyhole effect has been produced by erosion of the door lintel and the frame of the window. The monument takes its name from the carved lions which flank the door (*see* Fig. 117).

Fig. 117 A restored elevation of the Lion Tomb.

The Lion Tomb gets its name from the lions which face each other from either side of the door (Fig. 117), but they are now badly worn and many people have difficulty in seeing them at first. A sculptured lion appears again on the way up to the High Place of Sacrifice on the Attuf Ridge (Fig. 140), and it would be interesting to determine the significance of this animal to the Nabateans. In ancient Mesopotamian religions, from which it is contended that so much of the Nabatean culture and possibly religious ritual might be derived, the lion is the animal of the paramount female deity, while the horned bull was the supporting beast of her male equivalent. Lions appear in Nabatean sculptures standing for the goddess Al Uzza with whom the crescent moon is also associated. She equates in the classical calendar with Venus. Appropriately, bulls were the beasts of Dusares, the leading male deity who was originally a fertility god; the brute strength and tremendous virility of this animal were at the command of this god. There are interesting parallels here with the Golden Calf of the Wandering Israelites in the barren wilderness.

The southern Arabians, however, appear to have stuck to their habit of putting the lion in second place, thereby emphasising that they regarded the MALE moon deity, whose sign was a bull, as being in the first place in the pantheon. Here of course we have a clash between the theistic ideas of the Parthians and of the Arabians. The Nabateans appear to have resolved this conflict and it would be fascinating to know how they actually did it: once again we have an example of the Nabatean genius for compromise and adaptation within the rigid bounds of their conservatism.

Immediately to the left of the Lion Tomb is a Dusares block set in a rectangular niche. Further to the left are two very simple, small tombs with excellently preserved rectilinear carvings. The left-hand one, with a 'chalet' gable, is particularly noteworthy (Fig. 31), while the right-hand one, which is slightly larger, shows a development of the rectilinear idea with a suggestion of pilasters on either side of the main composition. They are rare instances of such decoration which has survived intact. As late as 1924, the graves inside these tombs still contained bones.

From here on, the road to the Deir is every bit a processional way. Great

flights of steps, in places evidently recut even in Nabatean times, carry one up
through the narrowing gorge. Twists and turns lead round shoulders and up
otherwise unscalable heights. On the right of the wadi, shortly after it has taken
a turn to the west, there is a beautiful classical monument of almost diminutive
proportions (Fig. 118). On the pediment sit three bulbous urn finials looking
rather like a row of bottles on an apothecary's shelf. This monument is a bi-
clinium, an unusual arrangement of only two benches, while a manger grave has
been cut in the floor at the back, probably at a later date.

When it seems that the climb is never going to end, the left-hand wall of rock
peels away to reveal a wide, sunlit ledge from which one can look down into the
depths. On the other side of this narrow chasm rise steep-walled mountains, their
crowns torn and serrated into strange shapes (Fig. 119). Beyond looms the re-
ceding cliff-girt eminence of the Gebel Haroun. This view down into the gloom-
shrouded floor of a narrow chasm is so suddenly come upon that it is all the more
spectacular.

The ledge forms a superb balcony on the mountainside which the weather has
eroded into weird and lunatic shapes. At times it is as though nature had poured
a coating of rock over a sandwich of geological history cake like icing, leaving it
to hang and drip in petrified dribbles. Intrusions of various rocks can be seen
here adding many different colours to the overall pattern of dusty gold.

In the top of a steep-sided pinnacle, a couple of caves can be seen (Fig. 120),
on the inside of which are carved some crosses. This has been given the name of
the HERMIT'S CELL or the HERMITAGE. Undoubtedly Petra came in for its
fair share of anchorites during the fanatical periods after the Byzantine occupation. Certainly these caves were visited by early Christians but it is impossible
to say whether this was actually a hermitage. If it was, then the hermit who
occupied it must have had one of the most sought-after views in Christendom.
Nothing needed to be left to the imagination here if mortification of earthly
delights, isolation and denial were the thoughts a hermit was to have when
looking at a view.

At the far end of the ledge the path squeezes through the narrow space between two boulders, drops down a short pebbly slope for a few feet, and comes
out into a wide, open saucer-shaped space. There is a moment's anticlimax in so
pedestrian a view after such a build-up until one turns to the right and sees
the DEIR (Fig. 40).

People have extolled the beauty of the Khasneh with the sun on it but the
surprise view in Petra must surely be the sudden revelation of the Deir. It may
not be such good architecture as the Khasneh, and its enormous size alone does
not necessarily commend it, but it dominates and resolves its setting in a way no
other monument in Petra does. As early dusk sets in, the sun bathes its great

Fig. 119 The view from the Deir plateau showing the ruggedness of the mountain terrain.

Fig. 118 The Wadi al Deir Triclinium.

Fig. 120 The Hermitage.

façade with golden light, sending a shadow slowly up its face, folding up its glory. As there is no distant view from here one is aware only of the scale and the complete harmony of the monument.

The façade is 132 feet high by 154 feet wide, and is carved in deep relief out of a great shoulder of the mountain; the doorway is 26 feet in height, and anyone standing in it seems little more than a speck. Architecturally it is a progression of the Khasneh via the Corinthian Tomb, but all decoration has been eliminated and one is left with a bare, simple architectural statement expressed in mighty and expansive terms. The Khasneh is essentially a statement of Man's ordered creativity and inventiveness, while the Deir intones the elementality of the stone itself with architecture becoming the vehicle by which Man expresses his devotion to the ageless power of God. It is as though the Khasneh were a demonstration of what Man can do, but the Deir speaks of what Man is aiming blindly at.

The temple has only one large chamber, 38 feet by 33 feet, lit by the light coming in through the door. On the far side there is a wide niche with steps leading up to it and a segmental arch over it. A groove following the line of this arch indicates that at one time there was probably an architectural coping, perhaps of a different coloured stone, inserted in this position. The niche would have contained the representation of the deity to whom the temple was dedicated. The interior is otherwise quite plain and unadorned but might at one time have been covered with painted plaster: if this is so, the plaster must have come off sometime before the Christian era, for the crosses which have been found on the walls are on the stone and not on plaster.

A temple of this fantastic size indicates a site of particular sanctity for the Nabateans. A vast circuit of ground in front was levelled as well (Fig. 121), and one can only assume that it was to accommodate the great congregations which

came to witness the rituals. Due to this the saucer edge rises rather abruptly and sharply to the rim of the plateau, forming a great amphitheatre. There can be no doubt that the Deir was a prominent festival venue, with an elaborately staged ascent to it and a vast 'court' in front.

The area to the left of the monument is lined with caves and cisterns of one kind or another. In this area there is, not far from the Deir, an interesting low-relief carving showing two camels and men; a direct allusion to the Nabatean traders.

In a cave in a rocky hummock on the far side of the 'court', in front of the Deir, there is an elaborately worked niche resplendent in Hellenistic garb (Fig. 122): the modelling of the panels containing human heads in the frieze is curiously reminiscent of the frieze discussed by Mr Parr, on the Urn Tomb. There are obviously stylistic lineages here, as there surely are between the Khasneh, the Corinthian Tomb and the Deir. In the previous chapter it was suggested that the Deir was the final Nabatean expression of the Hellenistic theme as first uttered in the Khasneh. It is not possible to attribute a date to this but its creation must be very close to the period of Roman occupation.

It is quite an easy climb to get up to the finial which sits on the top of the central kiosk. The path is on the buttress to the left of the court. The climb is steep but the view from the top looking down between the columns to the sand and scrub below is worth the effort. People walking about below seem like miniatures of the human race below this Brobdingnagian work. Even when sitting or standing on the tent roof of the kiosk, the horned Nabatean capital, surmounted by what looks like an outsized soup tureen, seems to tower above one in a thoroughly unfriendly way.

Many writers have found the Deir dull and monotonous in comparison with other monuments, for it has neither fineness of detail nor decorativeness, but maybe these are not the terms by which it should be judged.

One incidental feature is the tree which has grown for more than three-quarters of a century on the wide ledge to the right of the central kiosk (Fig. 35). Even in the earliest photographs it is shown clinging to its unlikely perch—how it gets enough water is a mystery—and, as it in no way detracts from the drama or the architectural satisfaction of the monument, it is to be hoped that this charming and delightful anachronism will be allowed to remain unmolested by tidy minds. If a reason is wanted to justify its continued survival, then it should be pointed out that the tree gives the Deir the aspect of a Piranesi engraving.

It is only a short walk up to the edge of the plateau overlooking the Wadi Arabah, against which the Gebel Haroun once again rears up. These views to the west are substantially the same as those from the top of Umm el Biyara. In fact, for those who want to see them without scaling the heights of Umm el Biyara, the

Fig. 121 A distant view of the Deir showing how it has been carved from a shoulder of the mountain (*see* Fig. 40).

Deir plateau is the place. The only disadvantage is that there are no views to the north, south or east.

Fig. 122 This pilastered niche in a cave near the Deir is important for its undamaged representation of the Nabatean decorative idiom.

To get back to the area of the Kasr el Bint it is necessary to retrace one's steps the whole way down. This is not quite such a bore as one might expect, for a totally different aspect of the Wadi al Deir is seen on the descent. Occasionally, dramatically framed views of the central city area occur and one is aware of the 560 feet one has had to mount to reach the Deir.

V

Faroun Pillar, Wadi Farasa, Roman Soldier Tomb, Attuf Ridge, High Place of Sacrifice
Behind the Kasr el Bint the ground rises steeply towards the south but one suspects that this is not the original contour and that one is walking over deeply buried ruins. The fallen masonry and rubble which covers the sandy ground could well, therefore, be the tip of an archaeological iceberg.

A little further up the hill the path cuts across the hillside in a south-easterly direction, passing over terraced fields which in spring are gay and bright with the ravishing blooms of the desert flowers. Eventually it levels out and one comes to the lone standing column known as the FAROUN PILLAR (Fig. 123). Another pillar of the same size and type lies on the ground, its disjointed sections resting exactly where they fell centuries ago.

These pillars present something of a problem for they appear to be totally unrelated, physically, to the temple entrance which is clearly visible on the steep hillside behind (Fig. 124). Bachmann's plan shows them standing alone and of greater size than the other pillars associated with the courtyard, immediately opposite the entrance across an almost square courtyard. One can probably dismiss the idea that they were an architectural caprice, or means of emphasising a particular feature such as in the terminal apses of the Severan Basilica at Leptis Magna, for they are much too independent of the design as far as we know it today. Whether there is any connection here with the two independent standing pillars at the entrance to the Herodian Temple in Jerusalem is difficult to say. The First Book of Kings relates that on the platform on each side of the steps (leading up to the temple door) was a pillar of brass, one called 'Jachin', he shall establish, and the other 'Boaz', in it is strength. The brazen pillars were, of course, of copper. In the model of the Temple in the Louvre, these pillars are shown in the form of obelisks, a very likely idea. These obelisks probably find their origins in Early Bronze Age Egypt, in the form of male and female fertility deities. However, five thousand years ago, twin pillars were set up before the temple of the Moon-god in Ur in Lower Mesopotamia. There are many other instances of stone pillars/obelisks being venerated across the Near East in ancient times (the practice even extended as far as the Indus Valley) but a lot more research, and excavation of the Faroun

Fig. 123 The Faroun Pillar with its fallen pair.

Fig. 124 The Faroun Pillar, with its pair, were important parts of a temple courtyard; their significance is unknown but they are aligned with a ruined entrance on the hill behind (*foreground*).

Ruins, will be necessary before we can know that these pillars fit into this pattern.

The bedouin had a notion to explain away the strange phenomenon of a pillar standing alone on a hillside. As all such unaccountable objects were the doing of Pharaoh, it was assumed that the pillar was his phallus. For that reason it was dubbed the Zibb Faroun (Phallus of Pharaoh). Pharaoh of course had nothing to do with the Faroun Ruins, but to regard the standing pillar as a phallus, the sovereign symbol of fertility, is interesting, for if there is any substance in the idea of the two Petra pillars relating to Jachin and Boaz, which were originally fertility deities, the bedouin might not have been all that far from the mark.

Bachmann's plan of the Faroun Ruins is particularly interesting in one major respect. The rear wall of the temple on the hill behind is shown lying at an obtuse angle and not at a right-angle to the side walls as one might expect (Map 4, facing page 136). It is very difficult to verify this on the ground, but since the German's work shows remarkable fidelity to the facts in other cases which can be checked it may be assumed that his observations at the Faroun Ruins are not inaccurate. One is bound to ask, therefore, why the back wall of the temple was at so odd an angle. The probable answer is that it fitted in, not so much with the exigencies of the site and geography, but with the street plan. If one were to carry the line of this wall north-eastwards it would touch the south-east corner of the courtyard of the Great or Manathu Temple, from where there is a known flight of steps down into the Lower Market, and from where access to the tethering ground, or Middle Market as Bachmann would have it, was easy. To continue the line southwards it would strike the South City Wall near a point at which the Horsfields believed there was a gate in the defences. Even today a path winds northwards from the area of the Southern Graves, up and across the Wadi Farasa, to enter the ruins of the city at about this point. Could it be that this track lies along the line of the ancient trade route from the south up into the markets? If this were so, it would mean that the odd angle at which the rear wall is set is due to it abutting a main arterial street.

5*a*. El Kubtha from below Moghar al Nassara

5*b*. The Kasr el Bint

On the summit of the ridge above the Faroun Ruins, there is a High Place which commands the whole of the central area, and which would doubtless have been an important sanctuary.

A short distance beyond the Faroun Ruins, on the track which leads to the Wadi Farasa, lies the KATUTE site, excavated by Mr Parr in 1958–9. The ground here is noticeably less covered with rubble, due in some measure to the deep deposit of sand over the remains, as well as to the existence of an extensive rubbish dump.

The area was chosen for excavation because the Horsfields had deduced that the line of the South City Wall ran under it. A few blocks of limestone had lain on the surface, which perhaps suggested to the Horsfields the idea of the wall. In fact, they turned out to be fragments from the upper courses of a wall forming part of an annex to a large building a few yards further south. The occurrence of this large building came as a complete surprise—if archaeologists are ever prone to complete surprise—and it turned out to be a structure of considerable consequence, perhaps the house of a wealthy merchant. The annex building in its present partly excavated state is a long narrow room, or series of rooms, nearly 60 feet in length and 16 feet wide; excavations so far have revealed the south-western corner of what could prove to be a very extensive complex of buildings of a temporal character. There is a suggestion of a courtyard with a beaten earth surface, to the west of which a door led into the annex. The interior of the building was partitioned by subsidiary walls but there is no evidence of any communicating doors. This arrangement is curious and poses the question of the original use. The walls, both interior and exterior, are built of the soft sandstone found locally, with the main wall still standing to a height of approximately nine feet. These are built of evenly laid courses of masonry, though the interior face of this wall is noticeably coarser. The upper courses have been badly eroded on the interior side and the whole has suffered badly from the shock of an earthquake causing the top two courses to lean well out of vertical. The wall we see today (Fig. 9) is, in fact, a rebuilding of an even more ancient one: a fragment of this can be detected in the larger blocks used in the construction of the extreme south-western angle.

In the interior face to the wall there are curious large slots which possibly helped to carry the roof of a portico running down the outside of the building. As it is generally believed that this wall is on the line of the South City Wall, the purpose of a portico or loggia in that position is strange, even though the character of the building gives no indication that it was a defensive structure. Within the building the debris contained a great deal of moulded plaster which must have sealed and protected, as well as adorned, the interior. That it was a building of no mean importance is certain from the character as well as from the position it had. It could have had two storeys, judging by the kind of buttress which projects from each of the partition walls in the main building.

A date in the first half of the first century A.D. has been ascribed to the present walls, though traces of an earlier structure lie beneath them. A small sounding was made beneath the foundations of the present building, and the footings of an earlier wall were revealed. In addition, almost another nine feet of occupation levels unassociated with any structure were found, and still bed rock has not been reached. The importance of this depth cannot be over-emphasised, for it facilitates the securing of a long type-series of pottery, among other considerations. Basically it means that this site had a long period of presumably unbroken occupation before any buildings were built, thereby giving a standard by which other evidence can be measured.

The Katute site ceased to be occupied shortly after the Roman annexation, though the reason for this is not clear. Mrs Bennett has visualised 'the proud, wealthy Nabatean owner . . . resenting the loss of his capital's independence and removing himself to an area where the Roman presence was not so acutely felt'.* There must indeed have been a fairly large movement away from the city at that time, for Mr Parr's excavations in the northern sector have also shown that that part of the city contracted about then. During the years after A.D. 106, it would have been difficult for anyone in the Near East to get away from the acute presence of Rome unless he went south into Arabia or north to Palmyra. This is quite likely what did happen for the Nabateans would have been moving back into their real homeland, and ancient Hegra, present-day Medain Saleh, could well have been the place to which the disillusioned emigrated. Likewise, there is evidence of a Nabatean community in Palmyra.

One cannot, however, ignore the fact that the Katute site is partly covered by the so-called TOWN RUBBISH DUMP. The material of this huge dump has not been fully studied but it is fairly certain from surface traces that the spoil is of the first century with little of anything later than the second century. It is very tempting, as Mr Parr suggests, to believe that when clearing the site for their civic improvements in the centre of the city, the Romans dumped the rubble and rubbish over the South City Wall. Presumably this would have been the place in which least offence would have been caused.

The sad picture then emerges of a 'proud, wealthy Nabatean owner' of the Katute building being told that the land next to his fine house was going to be used as a rubbish dump. There would have been little he could do about it. With the new Roman administration determined to push through their improvements whether the citizens wanted them or not, the only alternative would have been

* _Archaeology_, Vol. 15, No. 4.

to depart leaving his house to moulder away until it finally collapsed. The dump eventually engulfed the wreckage though squatters had used it occasionally and part of it was used for a time as a Christian cemetery.

The Rubbish Dump now spills down the south-western side of the hill, into the deep cut of the Wadi Farasa. It is clearly distinguished from the surrounding terrain by both its lighter colour and by its smooth surface.

The path turns away eastwards towards the Attuf Ridge and down into the upper reaches of the Wadi Farasa. All around now are the bare, featureless low hills of the central valley, with the jagged heights of the barrier ranges beyond. Far away to the right rise the tumbling rocks of the el Barra and the fortress of Umm el Biyara. To the left, the red-ochre walls of the Attuf Ridge rise in tiers, adding on pinnacles and ledges until the summit is lost to sight behind the lower cliffs. The path makes straight for the wall of rock and then bends gently southwards along the line of the cliff.

The area has many monuments, principally of the Cavetto I and II types, arranged in a haphazard fashion, sometimes standing on three levels, superimposed one upon the other (Fig. 125). There is one curious one, facing north, which has torn away and slipped over sideways and still remains at this rakish angle.

It is some way further on that one comes upon one of the most individual monuments in Petra. It stands alone facing west, its tall façade topped by the now familiar low-pitched pediment on which sits the usual urn finial. Its great glory is the architectural framework to the doorway which shows a certain virtuosity in its design (Fig. 38a). There is a similarity between the segmental open pediment which crowns the composition and that which appears as part of the façade of the Corinthian Tomb (Fig. 156) and the Sextus Florentinus Tomb (Fig. 161).

This monument has no name, but the elegance of the doorway is so much like the work of the Italian Renaissance that the name RENAISSANCE TOMB does not seem wholly unreasonable. It would be pointless to give a monument a name just for the sake of doing so, but where a façade shows particular characteristics, a name to help distinguish it does serve a useful purpose.

The Renaissance Tomb (Fig. 126) faces out across its own courtyard with a generous open space in front, across which the path runs. Whether this was

Fig. 125 Carved façades in the Wadi Farasa.

the site of a suite of sepulchral buildings or not is uncertain but it is generally believed that each important tomb was encompassed by its own set of rooms, gardens, reservoirs, triclinium, etc. The greater the tomb the more pretentious these ancillary structures would have been. The area in front of this tomb has not yet been excavated.

A short distance further on, just where the Wadi Farasa gorge begins to close in, one is confronted by the BROKEN PEDIMENT TOMB (Fig. 127). This stands on a ledge, facing north, above the level of the path. By any standard it is a small-scale façade but it is architecturally an important one, for in it are resolved some of the ideas which the Nabateans were obviously perplexed about. Façades of the Nabatean Classical type display a multiplicity of lines and projections, and broken pediments get lost in the plethora of architecture. Here the concepts have been stripped of their superfluous string courses, additional architraves, extra cornices, etc., to produce a design of simple, masculine clarity.

The monumental façade is approached by a broad flight of steps which end up on a platform as broad as the front of the tomb. Into this platform are cut two tanks, one square and the other octagonal. The interior arrangement is interesting, for the right-hand wall has been marked out for cutting a series of loculi of which only the rear four were actually executed. One is tempted to think that this was a kind of family mausoleum which, for some reason, was never fully occupied. As Sir Alexander Kennedy has pointed out, for work on such an

overtly pretentious tomb to be discontinued the reason must have been very serious. The almost total lack of Nabatean feeling of this façade leads one to suggest that it falls into the Roman period rather than into the Nabatean. As the next tomb complex to be encountered in the Wadi Farasa indicates, this area was developed more under the Romans than under 'native' rule.

Before continuing into the upper part of the Farasa Gorge, a small diversion can be made into the wadi immediately to the south, which lies deep at the foot of the Gebel al Najr. In this wadi is a Roman tomb with a façade which closely resembles the well-known Roman Soldier Tomb. The main differences lie in the fact that this AL NAJR TOMB (Fig. 128) has not got a 'first floor', which is such a distinctive feature of the Roman Soldier Tomb. The whole façade is, in consequence, lower and more compact and strikes one much more as a truly classical temple façade. One

Fig. 126 The Renaissance Tomb, one of the most sophisticated of the carved façades.

Fig. 127 The Tomb with a Broken Pediment, a small but architecturally interesting façade with an un-completed interior behind. **Fig. 128** The al Najr Tomb.

curious feature is that the apex of the pediment is rounded off, while the string-course of the attic storey is thrown forward at this point to form a kind of baroque acroterion or pedestal.

This monument has hardly ever been visited and even more seldom mentioned. It may be because it does not lie on the route to anywhere and because the Roman Soldier Tomb is much grander and larger. This, however, is an important classical monument which deserves to be better known.

The path into the upper part of the Wadi Farasa, or the Farasa Gorge, clings closely to the cliff, while ahead the wadi looks as though it is barred by a stone wall (Fig. 129). Seen beyond this wall, and very much at an angle, is the ROMAN SOLDIER TOMB. The narrow wadi here has been made relatively level by the retaining masonry wall forming a natural courtyard, reached by a broad flight of steps almost overhung by the towering mountainside above.

The Roman Soldier Tomb has a forthright classical façade (Fig. 41), classical in the western Mediterranean tradition rather than in the Nabatean; only the capitals and angle pilasters have the usual Nabatean detailing. The pediment is low pitched and backed by a plain parapet. The central doorway (Fig. 130) is decorated with pilasters supporting an entablature and pediment almost identical to that on the classical monument at the mouth of the el Barid Siq (Fig. 131)

Fig. 129 Approaching the Roman Soldier Tomb; the retaining wall on the right holds the level of the area in front of the façade (compare with Fig. 135). **Fig. 130** The doorway to the Roman Soldier Tomb, a standard pattern that has close parallels with other major tombs in Petra.

and the central doorway of the Urn Tomb (Fig. 132). The framed niches at first-floor level are important, for the central one houses the headless torso of a statue in Roman armour; the other two also have statues but in a less presentable state. It is difficult to say whether the bust in the central niche, like the one in the central aperture of the Urn Tomb, is a representation of the dignitary for whom the tomb was made, or is just the central feature of a trophy of arms. The 'cuirass anatomique' was a distinction reserved for the use of those of the highest rank in Imperial Rome, but whatever its application here, it is this which has earned the tomb its name. We do not know for whom it was made though the scale and magnificence, not only of the tomb itself but of the sepulchral complex, leads one to acknowledge that it was for a person of very considerable rank and importance.

The interior of the tomb consists of two large chambers (Fig. 133), the main one having a series of segmental arched recesses, presumably for the reception of corpses or coffins. Like all other tombs, it could well have been plastered and painted but there is now no remains of this. The stone is also much blackened by the centuries of fires by which the bedouin have tried to keep warm during the bitter winters in Petra.

Fig. 131 The doorway to the temple at the entrance to the el Barid Siq (Fig. 181).   **Fig. 132** The doorway to the Urn Tomb (Fig. 152).

Before discussing the complex, it is worth noticing the line of five niches carved into the planed wall of rock immediately above the tomb (Fig. 41). The enormous rectangular cavern which sits above and slightly to the left of the niches is probably all that remains of a monument which lost its façade when the Roman Soldier Tomb was created. We have seen in the Theatre the effect of this mutilating process which has led to those huge 'projection rooms'. The top of the tomb is marked by a terrace running across the top of the attic storey; this may be the reason why the pediment has such a low pitch.

High up on the wall to the right of the tomb are two small Dusares obelisks incised in very low relief into the face of the rock.

Directly opposite the tomb is a magnificent TRICLINIUM. It is not known whether this is related to the tomb but the odds are very much in favour of it being so. The monument has no façade. It is, however, the large-scale interior, approximately 35 feet square, which is the main attraction, for it contains the only carved interior decoration in Petra (Fig. 134). Engaged half-columns, beautifully fluted and reeded, divide the side and rear walls into five bays, each with a square-headed niche between the pilasters. The capitals to these pilasters

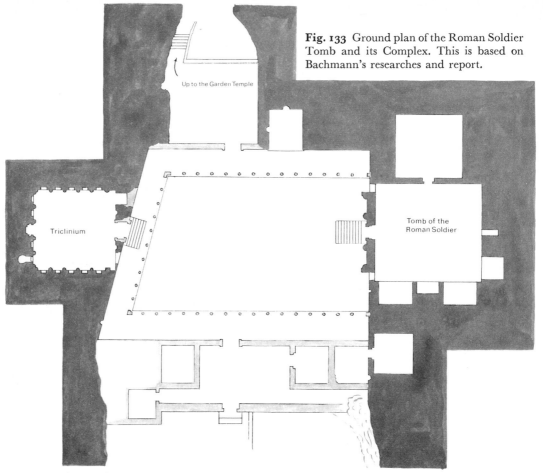

Up to the Garden Temple

Fig. 133 Ground plan of the Roman Soldier Tomb and its Complex. This is based on Bachmann's researches and report.

Triclinium

Tomb of the
Roman Soldier

are a curious kind of Tuscan Order which looks forward to Ionic. The colour of the extremely soft sandstone is a particularly attractive blend of mauve and dull red streaked with silvery grey, which creates a delightful atmosphere of mystery in the half light.

It was in triclinia such as this that the funeral feasts took place at which guests sat at long tables placed round three sides of the room—hence the word 'triclinium'—all facing into the centre. The remains of the dais which went round the room can still be seen but due to the softness of the stone it is very badly worn.

It is not easy to understand why this, of all the numerous triclinia of Petra, should have been singled out for such elaborate treatment. The date, like that of the tomb opposite, is possibly the early Roman period, in which case it could well be an example of the Roman preference for magnificent interiors. The majority of triclinia in Petra were probably constructed, and have subsequently been destroyed. It is possible that their interiors were elaborately decorated with architectural plasterwork in the usual Nabatean manner which could mean that

Fig. 134 The Triclinium of the Roman Soldier Tomb Complex is alone in Petra in having an elaborately carved architectural treatment for the interior. The splendour is enhanced by the dramatic colouring of the veining of the stone.

this Triclinium was not originally so special. In any case a great number of triclinia could well have been outdoor sites and not rooms in the accepted sense of the word.

We know from the inscription on the Turkamaniya Tomb what went to make up a sepulchral complex, and Bachmann probably took this as the basis for his reconstruction of the elaborate Roman Soldier Tomb complex (Fig. 135). The levelled area between the tomb and the triclinium was surrounded on three sides by a colonnaded portico, the rear wall on the western side being carried on the retaining wall which can still be seen. There was no colonnade across the front of the tomb, but the face of the triclinium was protected by the northern portico. Above the rock into which the triclinium is carved was a natural ledge, which was utilised to accommodate a large cistern, and a terrace overlooking the courtyard. A large hall, some 25 feet wide with an arched wagon roof, was carved into the hillside behind the cistern and must have been an important cultural site. The line of the roof can clearly be seen on the rear wall, and the springing of the masonry vault is also evident on the remains of the side wall. The so-called

Fig. 135 A reconstruction, after Bachmann, of how the Roman Soldier Tomb Complex might have looked.

Garden Temple (often incorrectly called the Garden Tomb) may have formed part of the Roman Soldier Tomb complex (Bachmann certainly shows it as doing so) but there is reason to believe that it is earlier than the tomb, possibly late Nabatean, and was thus incorporated into the complex when the tomb was laid out.

A flight of steps curls up out of the courtyard area into the narrow upper part of the Wadi Farasa (Fig. 136). The mountainsides rise steeply on either side. Facing up the wadi is the GARDEN TEMPLE (Fig. 137) above the roof of which are the terrace, hall and reservoir or cistern which E. L. Wilson measured to be 20 feet by 60 feet and 12 feet deep. All these are reached by a steep flight of steps to the right of the Temple.

The temple faces out on to a levelled area, in front of which is what appears to be a 'garden plot'—hence the name. The façade is simple, as is the plan

Fig. 138 Ground plan of the Garden Temple.

g. 136 The steps leading from the Roman Soldier
omb to the Garden Temple.

Fig. 137 The Garden Temple.

(Fig. 138). Two free-standing columns between two engaged ones form a portico in antis about 24 feet by 24 feet, beyond which there is the shrine, 18 feet square. Even though the entablature of the façade is now worn it is still an attractive, small-scale monument in one of the most delightful positions in Petra (Fig. 139). The wadi has a nice, discreet, tucked-away atmosphere with awe-inspiring views of sunlit pinnacles high up in the shimmering blue sky. There is always some green in the wadi but it is in the spring that the area lives up to the name associated with the temple, 'the Garden'.

The ascent to the High Place of Sacrifice on the Attuf Ridge is a steep and a tiring climb. At many points the Nabateans carved flights of steps into the rock to help one round or over difficult patches. The care taken to make the ascent safe and as easy as possible shows that the routes up, particularly the alternative which rises from the Outer Siq near the Theatre, were regarded as religious processional ways rather than as mere means of getting there. This route can, in fact, be regarded rather as the back-door ascent, for the Outer Siq route is much grander and more ceremonial.

About a third of the way up is the LION MONUMENT (Fig. 140). As has already been mentioned, the Lion was the creature of Al Uzza and its appearance here was doubtless to put the worshipper in the right frame of mind for the impending ceremonies at the High Place. The 15-foot beast is shown side on with its head turned at right-angles to face the visitor. There are traces of a water channel in the rock above the Lion's head, with indications that the water from this flowed down through a pipe to come out of the Lion's mouth. Presumably, therefore, this monument was a public drinking fountain on a sacred route and there can be little doubt that it was much appreciated by the perspiring pilgrims who struggled up in the heat of midsummer. There would originally have been some sort of basin to catch the falling water and to carry it away to a reservoir— perhaps the one above the Triclinium in the Wadi Farasa.

There are other sacral reminders on this route, in the form of votive niches, altars and the like, including one block altar measuring some 6 feet high, which marks a turning (Fig. 141).

On a route up from the northern side there is a deity block, 18 inches by 7 inches, set deeply into a small rectangular niche between two pillars, 4 feet high, surmounted by a crescent moon with its points uppermost (Fig. 142). It will be remembered that the crescent moon in this position was not only the symbol of Al Uzza but also, with the addition of a star, of the Edomite deity, Qaush. The scarab found at Tawilan showed this crescent moon supported on the top of a pillar, so it is interesting to consider whether this reflects a connection between the pantheon of the Edomites and of the Nabateans. It could be that the Nabateans adopted Edomite deities who were local gods rather than tribal

Fig. 139 Léon de Laborde's view of the Garden Temple shows the Roman retaining wall as well as the steps up to the terrace above.

ones. The Nabateans came from southern Arabia (the generic name Nabathu is south Arabian) and even if they brought their own gods with them they could well have adopted and assimilated the Edomite ones as well.

The top of the Attuf Ridge is clearly divided into two distinct parts lying roughly north and south of each other with a small, jagged ravine as the separating factor. The southern part is known as the OBELISK RIDGE and consists of a relatively level area on which stand two obelisks approximately 100 feet apart (Fig. 143). They are both just over 20 feet high and are aligned

Fig. 141 An altar shrine on the route up to the Attuf Ridge.

Fig. 140 The Lion Monument, probably intended originally as votive drinking fountain on the route up to the High Place on t Attuf Ridge.

Fig. 142 Votive niche.

Fig. 142 The 'Moon' Shrine on the Attuf Ridge.

east/west of each other. There appears to be nothing particularly remarkable about them until one realises that in order to create these, the whole mountain-top had to be carved away (Fig. 144). Even if the summit had consisted of only two pinnacles instead of one huge one, the labour of excavation would still have been prodigious. One must ask what was their significance to merit such herculean exertion. With the limited knowledge of Nabatean religion we have at present, it is almost impossible to provide an answer. There are one or two facts which suggest possible ways to a solution.

143   144

Fig. 143 The obelisks on the Attuf Ridge are each over 20 feet high and were created by carving away the mountain-top. Their significance has not been established.   **Fig. 144** One of the obelisks; note the typical Nabatean style of diagonal hatching of the stone surface.

The obelisks are almost certainly representations of a deity or of two deities; the Dusares block was often expressed in this form. However, it was not confined to the use of the male deity for it was also used by Al Uzza. Even as far away as Cyprus this form of representation was used, for on coins struck at Paphos (the chief shrine of Aphrodite who equates with the Roman Venus and the Nabatean Al Uzza) the goddess is shown as a conical obelisk set in a temple framework. Do, then, the two obelisks on the Attuf Ridge represent the two major deities of the Nabateans, Dusares and Al Uzza? If they do, is there a relationship between them and Jachin and Boaz? Jachin and Boaz were originally male and female fertility deities of the Early Bronze Age in Egypt, if not older, and the Edomites must have known of them. They may even have adopted them into their own mysterious pantheon, which raises, of course, the whole question of Edomite influence on Nabatean religion, to which there is regrettably at present no answer.

The orienting of the obelisks east/west also leads one to speculate on their connection with Al Uzza, for her planet was Venus which was frequently referred to in ancient texts as the 'star which rises in the east'. Venus was greatly feared, and yet loved, in the ancient world, particularly by the peoples of Mesopotamia. Babylonian writings can be interpreted that the planet (the word 'planet' comes from the Greek 'planetes'—the Wanderer) Venus was originally regarded as a 'stray sheep' or a wandering star which appears to have settled down rather late in life. Most of the other bodies in the heavens were, or seemed to be, fixed and were stable, and their movements predictable. Naturally those which were unpredictable were regarded with peculiar suspicion and had to be placated. It was probably in Mesopotamia that Man first began to make a 'science' of the way in which the fixed and 'wandering' bodies interacted and how they affected human life. The resulting science of astrology was an integral, indeed indispensable, part of life in all the civilisations of the ancient world, as it still is in many parts of the eastern world today. Is there, then, some significance in the fact that the obelisks stand aligned to the east where the feared Venus, alias Al Uzza, rose?

The man-made plateau on which the obelisks stand was, until quite recently, known by the bedouin as Zibb Attuf, the place of the Merciful Phallus. The name 'Attuf'—Merciful—however, is extremely interesting, for its very unusualness must denote an inheritance from the past. Why should modern bedouin term these obelisks 'merciful'? In so far as they were symbols of fertility they would originally have been regarded as merciful, but the fascinating thing is that this concept has come down to us through all the centuries, enabling us to believe that these obelisks were originally representations of fertility deities.

On the northern side of the ravine are the tumbled and broken walls of a 'fort' (Fig. 145). A date cannot be given with any certainty to this ruin; it has been variously described as Crusader, Byzantine and Nabatean. It is an appalling muddle of fallen masonry, with the fractured and distraught remains of walls projecting from the confusion like broken bones from a wound. A steep track leads up past the ruins on to the northern plateau of the Attuf Ridge. The area is not great and is almost wholly occupied by the remarkably well-preserved HIGH PLACE OF SACRIFICE.

This High Place, or 'Madhbah' in Arabic, is the best preserved of all such sacred places which have survived from the religions of the ancient world (Fig. 146).

The cutting of the stone is still remarkably sharp considering its extremely

Fig. 146 The High Place, showing the shallow 'courtyard' area before the Altar platform. This is probably the best preserved High Place to have survived from Biblical days.

6. The Urn Tomb colonnade

exposed position approximately 3,400 feet above sea-level and 625 feet above the level of the Temenos. The plateau consists of a roughly oval platform, 210 feet by 65 feet, in the middle of which is the sanctuary. The site was levelled to form a shallow courtyard measuring approximately 48 feet by 21 feet. A triclinium was thus formed with places for seats on the north, east and south sides facing the altar platform on the west (Fig. 147). It was at this altar that the blood sacrifices were made.

The nature of blood sacrifice, indeed sacrifice of any kind, is probably very different from what the majority of people today think. Popular fiction has always presented it as a kind of barbaric practice attended by brutal pagan rites. The painful and unpleasant sides, the element of denial, have always been stressed, as has the loss of life of the victim, the ultimate denial, so that sacrifice becomes a payment by suffering. Even the use of the word 'victim' implies suffering. Yet in ancient times, when symbolism was understood by even the most uneducated, sacrifice engendered feelings of joy and happiness at the working of Grace. It was seen as a renewal of the close relationship between Man and the deity, a sort of mystical

Fig. 145 The fort which guarded the approach to the High Place is now almost completely ruined.

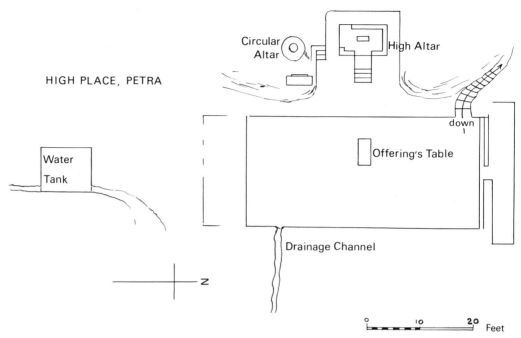

HIGH PLACE, PETRA

Fig. 147 Ground plan of the High Place.

union with God. Blood, in popular terms, is the symbol of suffering but in ancient times it was the symbol of life, indeed, was the source of life. By the use of blood in the ritual sacrifice, the congregation expected a renewal of life and divine protection, but because blood was the sole property of God, certain uses, such as drinking it, were taboo. But by having blood ritually sprinkled on his family, his house or his goods, a man would be invoking the deity for a continuance of his prosperity.

Although there were sacrifices of atonement, thanksgiving, entreaty and worship, in none of them was the actual physical suffering of the 'victim' an essential part. The actual death, the immolation, was not the crux of the act, it was just a necessary preparation for the renewal of life through the agency of blood which symbolised life. From this it will be seen that the existence of a place such as the High Place of Sacrifice does not mean that the Nabateans were a bloodthirsty people; for them it was a means and instrument of Grace.

The Abbé Starcky disputes that the Nabateans practised human sacrifice and contends that they stuck to animal sacrifice only. There is, however, a Nabatean inscription at Hegra which reads 'Abd-Wadd, priest of Wadd, and his son Salim, and Zayd-Wadd, have consecrated the young man Salim to be immolated to Dhu Gabat. Their double happiness.' Al Uzza in her role as the Morning Star is also known to have received the sacrifice of boys and girls. In particular, the

Fig. 148 The 'Mensa Sacra' or Offerings Table lies before the Altar platform which is approached by a flight of three steps.

pagan philosopher Porphyrius states that once a year a boy's throat was sacrificially cut at the oasis of Dumat some two hundred miles from Petra. One can usually discredit Byzantine accounts which, because of a violent conflict of religious beliefs, were very partisan and prejudiced. But in this case there must have been sufficient fire to account for quite so much propaganda smoke.

Where there is human sacrifice, however, there is always animal sacrifice. The former, in fact, probably arose out of the latter. The altar at the High Place is well fitted with drains and basins for the blood-letting and the necessary washing afterwards. The altar stands about 3 feet above the level of the Court and is approached by three steps (Fig. 148). It is situated in a specially made recess in the solid rock. A square hole about 4 inches deep is cut into the top of the altar: this was probably a socket into which the deity block was slotted. To the south of the altar enclosure, and approached by four steps, is a circular platform in which there is a basin 3 feet 9 inches in diameter (Fig. 149). This was provided with a drain which discharged on to the steps, and it was possibly used for libations of some kind. An inscription at Palmyra—written by a Nabatean cavalryman—refers to Dusares as 'a good god who rewards his people, and does not drink wine'; this may be interpreted to mean that wine was not used as a libation on the altar in his particular rites.

Another hole, on the eastern side of the altar platform, could have been a 'piscina' for the washing of sacred vessels. Likewise, a large tank about 4 feet deep a short distance to the south of the actual courtyard would have provided the essential supply of water. Where there were blood sacrifices taking place, large quantities of water would have been necessary for the washing of both priests and altar. The invitation to disease from unattended pools of blood would have been an ever-present threat to the Nabateans. There are, incidentally, no

signs of the continuous and intense fires needed for burnt offerings at this High Place, nor at any of the other, lesser High Places in Petra.

Fig. 149 The Round Altar at the High Place.

Coins dating from the third century A.D., found at Bozrah, the capital of the Roman Province of Arabia and an important town in the Nabatean empire, refer explicitly to the games associated with the worship of Dusares. This is very much a classical tradition, whereas Epiphanius records that on 6 January there was a ceremony in Petra in celebration of the birth of Dusares to the virgin-mother-goddess. It is unlikely that either of these ceremonies took place at the High Place, for there is only enough room for a few officiating priests, let alone a crowd of spectators and competitors.

In front of the altar, set within the shallow sunken area of the courtyard, is a small platform standing only 5 inches above the level of the courtyard (Fig. 148). Its position indicates that it was important to the ceremonies performed here. There can be little doubt that Dalman was correct in assuming that it is a 'Mensa Sacra' exactly equivalent to the shewbread table on which the bloodless offerings were laid in Israelite temples. The dogmatic measurements for such a table are 'two cubits shall be the length thereof, and a cubit the breadth thereof'; the 'table' measures 5 feet 1 inch in length by 2 feet 8 inches in breadth. The table of the shewbread was always placed in the congregation area of the temple, 'without the veil', and the courtyard at the High Place in which the 'table' is set, can be taken to represent the 'public' area or congregation place of this sacred precinct. The implicit relationship here of Nabatean religion with that of the Promised Land is extremely interesting. No date can be given to this sanctuary but it is believed to be Nabatean work entirely on the strength of the high quality of the stone working. Its origins could, however, be earlier, for the Edomites are believed to have worshipped in High Places. This site may, in fact, be of very great antiquity as a place of worship even though the setting-out was a comparatively late development.

From the northern tip of the ridge there are magnificent views down over the central city area, with Umm el Biyara glowering sullenly on the other side. All about you are serrated peaks glowing hotly in the sun. From here one really appreciates that the city of Petra lay in a valley, approximately half a mile wide, guarded to east and to west by towering mountain ranges. To the north the uplands of the Ma'aiserat and Turkamaniya rumble until they are lost in the blue distances of the el Beidha ridges. To the south, the rolling low hills, with their deep dividing wadis, slip furtively away to the el Sabrah ridge and down to the pass which leads to the distant Wadi Arabah. It is a place, this, impregnated with mystical history and the resounding silence of clamorous forgotten rites. The simplicity of the site, with its primitive strength and closeness to nature, acts not as a leash to restrain but rather as a stimulus to the imagination. As the sun goes down it is eerie with sinister ghosts creeping in with the gathering shadows and clutching at your arm with the biting cold of a desert night. The slightest noise is magnified by the imagination while the great vault of heaven, full of glittering, gliding deities, enfolds you in its timeless grasp.

The route down to the Outer Siq takes you back first to the ravine in front of the obelisks and then down, across the face of breathtaking gorges. Spacious couloirs have been cut (Fig. 150), in addition to long runs of steps at various parts, and all the way down there are ravishing views of rock and distant highlands.

Just before the path debouches on to the track in the Outer Siq near the Theatre and the 'Streets of Façades', there is another large quarry with some more of those tantalising footholds going up to nowhere.

VI

Royal Tombs, Moghar al Nassara, Conway Tower, Turkamaniya, Ma'aiserat Ridges
Some distance down the track from the Theatre a path leads off up in the direction of the URN TOMB (Fig. 151) which has always vied with the other 'Royal Tombs', the Khasneh and the Deir, as the most spectacular of Petra's monuments. Its enormous height and deep courtyard give it an air of stately

importance which is enhanced by its elevated position (Fig. 152). It is the first of the so-called 'Royal Tombs' and has been dubbed with a variety of names from 'Urn Tomb' to the 'Royal Courts of Justice' (the vaulted substructure is then regarded as the dungeons where prisoners languished). Quite what justification there can be for the latter is not clear for there is nothing about the monument to suggest a Law Court.

As with nearly all the carved monuments, it is very difficult to ascribe a date to the Urn Tomb. The Abbé Starcky has suggested that it is the tomb of Malchus II who died in A.D. 70, and stylistically this would seem plausible, for even though there is strong Roman feeling about it it is still essentially Nabatean architecture. The carvings which have been recently examined by Mr Parr display markedly Hellenistic characteristics. It is reasonable to suppose that both influences would have been apparent around A.D. 70.

Fig. 150 The eastern descent from the High Place is furnished with some finely made couloirs such as this, carved from the steep mountain-side.

The main chamber, on the courtyard level, is a massive single room of approximately 56 feet deep by 62 feet wide and must originally have served more as a funerary chapel or triclinium than as a tomb

153

Fig. 152 The Urn Tomb. The courtyard originally extended forward upon masonry foundations and supports, the remains of which are the arches shown here. This is the first of the so-called 'Royal Tombs'.
Fig. 153 Ground plan of the Urn Tomb.

(Fig. 153). The remodelling and rearranging of the interior for its adaptation as a Christian church in A.D. 446 effectively obliterated the original layout. The various loculi shown in Domaszewski's plan, those we see today, need not necessarily be part of the original plan. Less important burials, of court officials perhaps, might well have taken place in this chamber, making it a kind of court necropolis for a particular reign.

The courtyard, measuring 70 feet across with its two flanking cloisters behind plain colonnades, is the grandest of several similar arrangements in Petra (Colour plate 6, facing page 208). Al Khan, over which the Government Rest House is constructed, is comparable. Apart from any processional adaptations it may have had, its primary function might well have been that of an open-air triclinium. Above the courtyard rises the Double Cornice II type façade of the tomb, with the only architectural enrichment on the lower stages being the central doorway (Fig. 132) and the worn lower parts of the pilasters. The flanking colonnades impart an impression of great depth to the courtyard by means of their lowness and the wide spacing of the pillars; as a foil to the soaring height of the main

Fig. 151 The point at which the Outer Siq debouches into the central valley. Taken from above the Theatre and showing the Urn Tomb with its low colonnade on the mountain-side to the right.

façade they could not be more effective. Above them can be seen some additional loculi incised into the walls like those high above the main façade. They are later insertions which bear no relation to the general design in either scale or positioning.

The three apertures high up between the columns of the façade have been mentioned by most writers. Many have assumed they lit a correspondingly large single chamber above the 'ground floor'. Examination by Mr Joe Brown has shown this is not so, for each opening serves a separate, independent chamber. The outer ones were found to be unadorned boxes let into the rock, with a rectangular grave cut into the floor of the left-hand one. The deep reveals, sockets, and some lead packing which was found in one, have been interpreted as evidence that at one time these chambers were securely closed, but by what means we have no way of telling.

The central aperture, however, has aroused most interest, for its mouth is blocked by a large stone which originally depicted the head and torso of a man wearing a toga. This is set within the remains of a frame and if, as seems possible, this is a royal tomb, this aperture is the royal loculi and the carved 'man in the toga' represents the deceased—in the Abbé Starcky's contention it would be a portrait of Malchus II.

It can be said without doubt that these three chambers are loculi and that their placing high up in the façade was fully in accord with the Nabateam funerary practice. Their 'inaccessibility' would make them inviolable, safe from scavenging animals and casual grave robbers. Loculi placed high out of harm's way are common enough in Petra, but the Urn Tomb is practically unique in that they form an integral part of the architectural character of the tomb façade. In the majority of cases the loculi are housed inside the monument. Here the loculi form a fully articulated trio and are treated architecturally with suitable decoration round the apertures. The placing of funerary chambers in an architectural 'tower' has many parallels in the Greco-Roman Near East, not least at Palmyra and Dura. These Mesopotamian kin are, however, different from the Urn Tomb in some important respects, particularly in that they have their loculi placed lower down in the structure where they are carefully disguised to afford protection. The loculi of the Urn Tomb are blatantly obvious and placed high out of reach.

The urn which gives this tomb its name is high up on the very top of the pediment: why this particular monument should have been given the name of Urn Tomb when so many others have an identical feature is a mystery.

The recent climbing activities of Mr Brown allied to Mr Parr's photography have revealed some hitherto unnoticed and unrecorded decorative details. These are to be seen in the main architrave immediately above the four pilasters which adorn the façade. They project slightly from the entablature and consist of four heads—presumably deities. They have been savagely eroded and it is impossible to recognise any features at all. They interrupt the line of the cornice above them in a similar way to the reliefs which adorn the angle pilasters of the Temenos Gate and the ornate little votive niche in the cave opposite the Deir (Fig. 122). In all these cases the busts are mounted in medallions placed in the frieze above the pilasters, and they cannot be far removed from one another in date. Recent research has pointed to a date in the early or middle second century A.D. for the Temenos Gate in its present form, which tends to upset the notion that the Urn Tomb was executed for Malchus II. It does not necessarily demolish the theory, however, for it is possible that the tomb, if it was for the king, was carved after his death. The carvings on the Temenos Gate would then be derived from those already in existence on the Urn Tomb.

The carving and part of the cornice on the extreme right hand has been shielded from erosion but shows signs of having been intentionally defaced. Similar defacement is apparent on the Khasneh and on the Temenos Gate, and Mr Parr has put forward the theory that as the defacement of human images in Petra is of a consistent, thorough and widespread nature, there was 'a deliberate, once-and-for-all, iconoclastic frenzy in Petra'.* The carvings which fell from the Temenos Gate and the Kasr el Bint do not appear to have been similarly defaced. It has been suggested that the final destruction of Petra occurred in the catastrophic earthquake which wrecked both Jerusalem and Jerash in the mid-eighth century A.D. If these carvings fell undefaced and became covered with sand, the iconoclasts must have worked after this date. This would tie in with the famous decree of the Caliph Yazid II (A.D. 720–24) which ordered the destruction of all human images and pictures in Muslim lands. The fact that the job was done with great thoroughness in Petra could signify that the city was sufficiently famous and important to attract this scale of attention from the iconoclasts. Unfortunately for this argument none of the early Muslim historians even mentions Petra and since the time of the Hegira (A.D. 622)—some hundred years before—nothing had been heard of the Nabateans.

Little can be said of the partly ruined subvault which carries the edge of the courtyard. It has beautiful, if massive, proportions which impart a tense, muscular elegance to the composition—no excavated information is available. The view, however, from the edge of the courtyard above is superb and commands the whole of the city area with Umm el Biyara dominating the scene (Fig. 1). It is seen to best advantage as dawn is breaking, for then Umm el Biyara seems to shine with the soft glow of pale gold against a washed and limpid blue sky. The floor of the valley is still deep in mauve-blue shadows and the

* *P. E. Q.*, January 1968

mountain is like a beacon. Soon afterwards, however, it dons a hard, relentless ochre-brown which only yields to a hazy violet as the afternoon draws into evening and shadows steal across its craggy face. At dusk the dark mountain is a massive silhouette against a golden sky.

No monuments of importance are encountered on the path round the western face of el Kubtha until the 'SILK TOMB' is reached. This is set well back in a deep excavation and one thus has a good view of the whole monument (Fig. 154). Architecturally it is not particularly special but its bands of brilliant colouring set it apart from almost all the other façades in Petra. It has not been given any name before but the colour wafts so lightly across its face reminding one strongly of watered silk that the 'Silk Tomb' does seem appropriate (Fig. 155).

The monument is a typical Double Cornice II type with a much worn set of four pilasters supporting the familiar double cornice and single-divide crow-step. Of all the monuments in Petra, this one has solicited most comment on its colouring: well could it have been the inspiration of Edward Lear's cook who went into such gastronomic ecstasies of description.

A short distance further on one comes to the so-called CORINTHIAN TOMB

(Fig. 156). Many of the early writers thought the pillars which adorn the upper part were of the Corinthian Order; they are in fact variations of those adorning the Khasneh. Falls of rock and its exposed position to all the winds that blow in Petra have led to this monument being grievously mutilated. In parts only the barest outline can now be discerned, making what has survived look as though it were struggling to free itself from the wall of rock.

Architecturally it is unsatisfactory, for the upper and lower parts stem from different traditions. The upper is a direct imitation of the Khasneh, while the lower was the inspiration for the Bab el Siq Triclinium, with the usual Nabatean Classical multiplicity of lines and incidental projections. It is also related to the Broken Pediment Tomb and the Renaissance Tomb. It could be that the architect was trying to combine the unadulterated Hellenism of the Khasneh, which no doubt he admired, with the local architectural tradition with which he felt much more at home.

Fig. 154 The Silk Tomb has the most dramatically coloured façade of any monument in Petra.

Fig. 155 A close-up of the bands of sandstone which range in colour between white, blue, salmon, grey and bright red.

The exercise has not come off because the language of Hellenism was not allowed to speak freely and the local style became cramped and tongue-tied by being forced to cohabit and converse with its unlikely partner. The doorways inserted into the left-hand bays of this 80-foot wide façade totally disregard the symmetry of the classical language and are disturbing; they are not compensated for by the niches which are supplied to the other bays.

Through the ravaged central doorway is a chamber, 30 feet by 40 feet, which is unconnected with the smaller chambers served by the other two doors (Fig. 157). For all its defects and imperfections the Corinthian Tomb serves as a link in the architectural chain of development which was inspired by the Khasneh and reached its ultimate resolution in the dramatic simplicity of the Deir.

Fig. 156 The Corinthian Tomb has been severely battered by falls of rock but still its great debt to the Khasneh can be clearly seen.

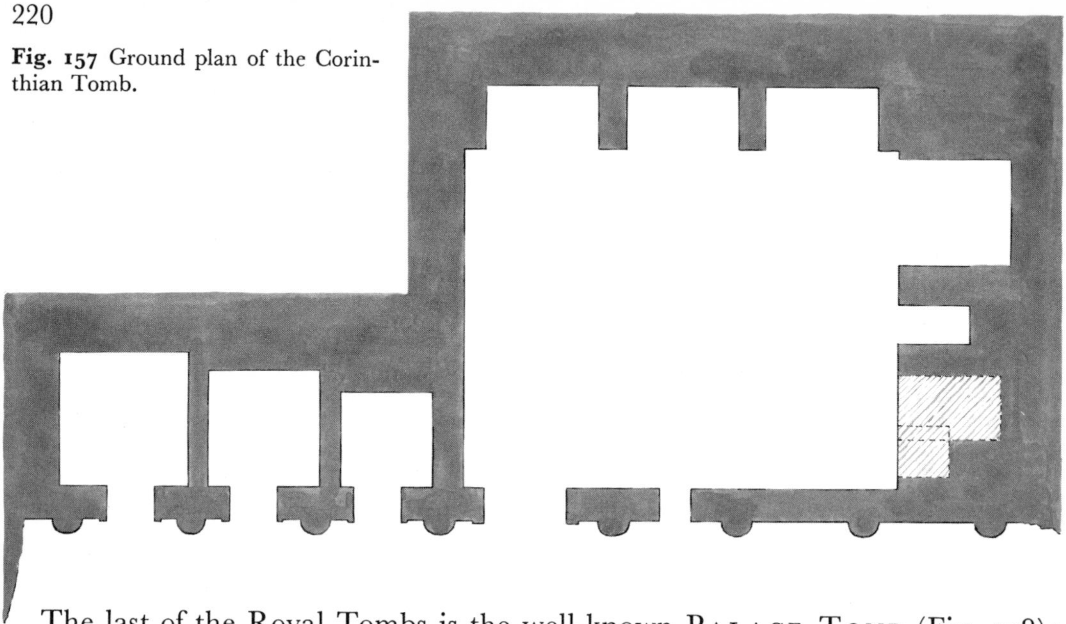

Fig. 157 Ground plan of the Corinthian Tomb.

The last of the Royal Tombs is the well-known PALACE TOMB (Fig. 158): it has in fact been known by other names such as 'Les Trois Etages' by the French, the 'Stockwerk-Grab' by the Germans. Olin referred to it as the 'Corinthian Tomb', which would have been very misleading. The reason for its present name lies in a supposed similarity to Roman palace design with particular reference to the Golden House of Nero. Whether such a claim could be substantiated is beside the point, for the architectural vocabulary is wholly Nabatean. This does not mean that a date in the Nabatean period can be given with certainty, for like so much else in Petra, it displays features which persisted well into the period of Roman occupation, as exemplified by the Sextus Florentinus Tomb.

It is one of the largest and most imposing façades in Petra. Whereas the Urn Tomb relies for its effect on enormous height in a confined area, accentuated by a simple, vertical architectural treatment, the Palace Tomb commands attention by means of its great breadth in an open site and its complicated architectural rhythms. The massive, clear and individual articulation of the ground floor does not correspond in either scale or vertical alignment with the two storeys above (Fig. 36). These consist of unevenly spaced engaged half-columns, eighteen of them, supporting recessed and advanced entablatures over alternate bays. This complicated counterpoint is repeated in the top storey, but the clear punctuation of the theme by the pillars is missing and the effect is, in consequence, confused. Much of this top storey had to be built of masonry, for the cliff into which the monument was carved proved to be too low. A great deal of this construction has collapsed and so one is not immediately aware of the considerable height of this tomb and the resulting top-heaviness.

Fig. 158 The Palace Tomb is the largest of the Royal Tombs and is reputed to resemble a Roman palace, some say, Nero's Golden House.

The two top storeys are divided from the ground floor by an unrelieved plinth which is important to the design, for it serves as a neutral zone between the two conflicting treatments. There is no evidence, other than the inexplicable difference in the stylistic treatment of the two storeys, to suggest that there was a change of design when the tomb was only half completed. Such a change in design, however, would provide a solution to the uncomfortable mixture of scales. It is possible that the 'architect' realised that the scale, in particular the spacing of the columns, of the second storey would be far too cramped when it came to providing the necessary portals on the ground floor of what is patently a monument of the first importance. For so important a monument as this, large-scale openings would have been called for. The 'architect' needed only to look at the design of the Khasneh to see how in the hands of a designer of genius the transition between two totally different architectural concepts could be made quite smooth and, indeed, effortless. The plinth divides and yet unites the two disparate characters. At the Khasneh the result is wholly successful and there is a feeling of near poetry, but this is not the case at the Palace Tomb, for not only is the rhythm changed but also the scale.

The four pedimented portals of the massive and boldly sculptured ground floor are set between projecting pilasters which have suffered horribly at the hands of the elements. But in the right-hand corner, close in the angle of the protecting cliff from which the monument has been carved, the detail remains wonderfully crisp and fresh (Fig. 159). The scale is here seen to have been enormous and the original effect of the complete monument must have been staggering. The interior, which consists of four huge, unadorned chambers (Fig. 160) of which only the middle two interconnect, would undoubtedly have

been plastered and possibly painted in the accepted Nabatean manner. The largest of these chambers is 33 feet by 23.

Of all the carved classical monuments, the Palace Tomb has a decidedly theatrical air about it. It is not only the stage-like platform on which it stands that gives this impression but the whole *scenae frons* appearance of the façade. No other façade is so wide in proportion to its height, nor so flat in its sculptural rhythms: the Deir may have great width but the boldly articulated five-part invention of its first-floor level creates a totally different impression. It is almost as though the Palace Tomb was designed as a backdrop for State funerals with all their pageants, processions and rituals of Oriental intensity. If the 'funeral services' of the Nabatean kings were affairs of sumptuous and vivid proportions, then there could hardly have been a more fitting venue than the Palace Tomb.

The six niches which appear on the first floor of the façade were investigated by Mr Brown and Mr Parr in 1962. Domaszewski shows them on his elevation of the tomb, but in his discussion of it he avoids explaining their irregular and 'accidental' siting—as well as their possible use. Mr Brown discovered that the

spaces within were quite small, while the third from the left has in its lower part an aperture giving access to a vertical shaft connecting with the top of the cliff behind the actual façade of the tomb. Its purpose remains unexplained, but could it have had anything to do with sacred ritual drama—possibly as part of a funeral rite? These niches surely have been afterthoughts. The fact that care was evidently taken to orient them to the original design indicates that the tomb was still venerated and in use at that time. Mr Parr suggests that they might have been designed to hold flat commemorative stelae but the comparative shallowness would make their use for housing a statue seem improbable. The provision of recessed emplacements for commemorative inscriptions is, however, certainly not unknown in Petra, nor in Medain Saleh. These originally contained small panels of either bronze or marble which could take the elegant epigraphy more legibly than the soft

Fig. 159 Though seriously mutilated, there are still some parts of the Palace Tomb façade which retain the original crisp carving.

sandstone of Petra. All these tablets have long since vanished—more is the pity
—but the places where they once were housed can still be clearly seen on many
tombs.

When, during the Byzantine period, the city contracted in size, a new wall
was built to defend the reduced northern sector (Map 3, on pages 120–1). This
Byzantine Wall started close to the platform of the Palace Tomb and
struck out towards the nearby Wadi Mataha, which it crossed before ascending
the hill on the far side to join up with the original first leg of the Nabatean wall.
The line of this wall can be seen from the platform of the Palace Tomb as a lump
in the ground, liberally scattered with tumbled masonry, ploughing off into the
wadi.

To reach the last of the important monuments in the western face of el Kubtha,
one has to follow a sandy track along the side of the mountain which now dips
gently down into the wadi. The height of the cliff drops drastically until it becomes along, low promontory (Colour plate 5a, facing page 192). Carved into the
end of this is the Sextus Florentinus Tomb (Fig. 161).

This is the only tomb in Petra which it is possible to date with reasonable
accuracy from historical evidence. Over the door, on the main entablature below
the bold, nearly semi-circular pediment, there is a Latin inscription which reads:

> To Lucius . . . ninius, Son of Lucius Papirius Sextius Florentinus, Triumvir
> for coining gold and silver, Military Tribune of Legion I Minerva, Quaestor
> of the Province of Achaia, Tribune of the Plebs, Legate of Legion VIIII
> Hispania, Proconsul of the Province of Narbonensis, Legate of Augustus,
> Propraetor of the Province of Arabia, most dutiful father, in accordance
> with his own will.

Professor Yadin of the Hebrew University found in the 'Cave of the Letters' at

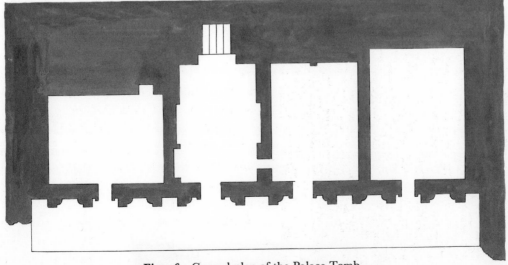

Fig. 160 Ground plan of the Palace Tomb.

Nahal Hever, overlooking the Dead Sea, documents written on papyrus which relate to Nabatean affairs and which mention Sextus Florentinus. From these he was able to suggest that Sextus was the Roman Governor of the Province of Arabia in about A.D. 127, but as the inscription on his tomb shows, it was his son who had the tomb made. This would have been about A.D. 130, for by then Sextus had been succeeded by one Haterius Nepos as Governor.

The façade is a complex but yet a very simple design in which the Nabatean penchant for a multiplicity of lines and projections was handled with great restraint and sureness of touch. Although a work from the Roman period, it is among the best and most fluent statements of Nabatean architecture (Fig. 39). The surmounting pediment is of a slightly higher pitch than usual but this could well be due to a strong Roman influence. The semi-circular pediment which dominated the façade from its central position over the door is a curious feature, however successful it might be as part of this wonderfully integrated design. As contended in the previous chapter, there are parallels here with the tympanum of the Vegetation Goddess at Khirbet Tannur and, on a much humbler scale, with the two round-headed monuments at the foot of Umm el Biyara. An eagle

sits on top of the semi-circular pediment with wings outstretched in the drooping Imperial Roman style as opposed to the about-to-take-off American style.

The Nabatean origin of the style raises some interesting speculations as to the character of Sextus Florentinus. Was he a man who came to have a real and deep affection for Petra, and for the subject Nabatean people, so much so that he wished to be buried in their city and to be commemorated in their 'style'? Or was he, perhaps, one of those strange, enlightened servants of empires who find greater peace in the far outposts than in the power vortex of the metropolis? The inscription definitely quotes his will as having specified that he wanted to be buried here.

The tomb is badly battered, and as it faces north it seldom has the sun on it. It is by no means a large monument but it achieves a monumental stature simply by means of its architectural impact.

Fig. 161 The Sextus Florentinus Tomb was made for a Roman Governor of Petra, and is alone in bearing an inscription by which it can be dated.

The wadi behind the tomb rises back into the heart of el Kubtha. The caves in this little gorge may once have been the workshops of smelters and metal-workers, particularly in iron. Abundant traces of that metal have been found on the ground in front of the caves. A path climbs up beside the narrow bed of the wadi, which is now filled with natural and artificial terraced fields, bright with patches of rich green vegetation. On the top of the promontory it enters a couloir to take it round a shoulder of rock before beginning the sharp ascent to the summit of el Kubtha. This is an easy enough climb with no dangers, ending up with fine views down on to the city area, with the Theatre describing a crisp arc immediately below. There is on the top another High Place and an important reservoir with one rather flimsy masonry elliptical arch still in place, all that is left of the roof which once covered the whole reservoir.

North from the Sextus Florentinus Tomb is the 'CARMINE TOMB' with its strange colouring. Striking herring-bone patterns in a rich carmine with feathery bands of blue and white waft across the eroded façade. Like the Silk Tomb, there is nothing particular about it other than its curious and dramatic colouring.

From a point near here the original Nabatean North City Wall went west-wards across the steep terrain in front of the pinnacle-capped prominence of Moghar al Nassara (Map 3, on pages 120–1). The city walls of Petra have been the subject of a study by Mr Parr but his researches are not yet complete, so it would be premature to say much about them. The general map of Petra in this book shows the approximate line of the walls, both north and south.

Although it looks so close, it is a surprisingly long way up to the heights of Moghar al Nassara (Fig. 162). This suburb lay just outside the walls and was given the name because of the crosses found on many of the monuments in this area. It was assumed that these were Christian and that, therefore, this was a Christian 'ghetto' or the Christian quarter of Petra. The word 'Nassara' corres-ponds with Nazareth in Arabic.

Al Nassara is a rock outcrop of great extent on the top of a hill commanding a fine position to the north of the city: why it was never incorporated into the city proper is difficult to understand. The smooth, sandy slopes are broken abruptly at the crown of the hill by a series of low, jagged cliffs in which are

162 The hill-top suburb of ghar al Nassara, or the Chris- Quarter, from the Sextus entinus Tomb.

carved façades of nearly all types, ranging from the Assyrian II type through to the classical. It is not proposed to describe every façade here but one or two are of special interest.

A classical tomb, with four pilasters and a refined pedimented doorway on its front, has lost completely the upper part of its façade (Fig. 163). It looks as though there are four pilasters supporting nothing: there is a comparable—if not identical—instance of this on the Ma'aiserat Ridges. The probable reason for this is that the superstructure was built up of dressed masonry. As with other monuments which have been treated in this way, e.g. the 'djin' blocks in the Bab el Siq, the Palace Tomb, etc., the stone used would probably have been much harder than the soft sandstone.

Also facing south out over the city is a group of tombs, one of which has a levelled forecourt in the same manner as the Deir. The scale is much smaller, almost miniature, in fact. The main monument in this group, a Double Cornice Intermediate Triclinium, has an unusual refinement to the attic storey, for between the four squat capitals are placed a group of shields and trophies and two Medusa heads (Fig. 164). The façade overlooks a hollowed-out stretch of the road to el Barid which will be referred to later.

At the northern end of the outcrop there is what appears to be another High Place around which are grouped the earlier tombs of this area.

For those visitors who have time to spare, an enjoyable and interesting afternoon could be spent exploring the whole of Moghar al Nassara. The crown of cliffs goes back a long way and some interesting façades are to be found on the northern faces: in a way it is like el Madras and the Ma'aiserat Ridges in that there are monuments of nearly all types here. Mr Lankester Harding, however, gives a warning to visitors who enter the caves to look out for the fleas left after the seasonal visits by the bedouin; this warning sounds rather like a *cri de cœur*, for the fleas are described as being 'rather hungry'.*

Moghar al Nassara, both from a distance and close to, has the appearance of a deserted and desolated hill-top town in the manner of those in Apulia. It has several attractive advantages which would commend it to settlers, except for the fact that it stands out like a sore thumb, and it would be interesting to know whether this natural defensive site was exploited by the early settlers, Nabatean or Edomite. All the other sites are less obvious, with the notable exception of Tawilan.

On the western side are the remains of the main rock-cut road north to the commercial suburb of el Barid. If it is true that el Barid was the main caravanserai on the northern side of Petra, a depot for goods, this road south into the city

* *The Antiquities of Jordan.*

Fig. 163 A classical monument at al Nassara which has lost its entablature. **Fig. 164** An important monument at al Nassara which has a series of trophies carved in the frieze.

would have been of great importance. It would have been from al Nassara that the merchants got their first view of this desert city, sprawling across the hill on either side of the Wadi Mousa.

The Wadi al Nassara runs close to the hill with the result that the western slopes are very steep. The escarpment on either side was crowned for much of its length by part of the city wall (Fig. 165) which reached its most northerly point in the vicinity, at the so-called Conway Tower. The wall had come up from in front of the Kasr el Bint along the line of the ridge which lies between the Wadi Turkamaniya and the Wadis Mousa and Mataha. This was a perfect location for a line of defence, the only weak part being opposite the Kasr el Bint.

The northern point of the wall is known as the CONWAY TOWER or CONWAY HIGH PLACE, after Mrs Horsfield (*née* Agnes Conway), who assisted in the initial excavation in 1929, directed by her future husband, Mr G. Horsfield, then Adviser to the Director of Antiquities in Jordan. In 1934, however, Mr Horsfield invited Professor W. F. Albright, Director of the American

Fig. 165 Nabatean walls below al Nassara with the mountain of el Kubtha beyond. Note the scale of the Palace Tomb carved into its base.

School of Oriental Research in Jerusalem, to undertake further excavations on the site.

The tower consists of a strong ring-wall—or bastion—built round a massive central 'sacred' rock. The rock itself was partly paved and was approached by a stepped processional way which also encircled the rock like a kind of ambulatory. The line of the wall, stretching back to the Kasr el Bint, is clearly discernible from here.

A short distance down the wall is the site of one of the trenches put down in 1958–9, at the same time as the Katute excavations on the south side of the city. This examination trench was known as TRENCH V (Fig. 166) and showed that the deposits were considerably shallower than at Katute and, therefore, no comparable sequence could be established. The fact that the wall is 6½ feet thick and founded in manually levelled bed-rock would undoubtedly make it a defensive work (Fig. 167). The masonry is consistently poor, but it is interesting that the outer faces showed signs of having been dressed with hard plaster. This would not have made the wall any stronger structurally but it would have protected it from the weather and thus prolonged its useful life. This indicates that the Nabateans were aware of their shortcomings when it came to handling masonry and tried to find remedies rather than cures. As the evidence concerning these North City Walls is still not available, it would be inadvisable to ascribe a date.

One feature at Trench V does, however, call for particular mention. This is a small, circular cobbled area around which are placed the bases of eight pillars. At one point its similarity to the circular room at the Baths led to the suggestion that this was another Baths, probably for private use. Its position on the thickness of the walls makes one favour the alternative suggestion of a gazebo. Its elevated site overlooking the Wadi to the north would have placed it right in the way of any draught of wind. A shaded, north-facing spot, fanned by whatever breeze there might be, commanding a majestic panorama would have been a delightful

Fig. 166 The excavations at Trench V.

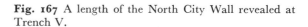
Fig. 167 A length of the North City Wall revealed at Trench V.

adjunct to any palatial residence. Only further excavation will determine what it was and to what it was related.

Some way down the wall in the direction of the Kasr el Bint, at a point where the Wadi Ma'aiserat al Wasta comes in on the right, there is the partly excavated site of a Nabatean cemetery. The full extent of these TURKAMANIYA GRAVES has not been plotted but once this has been done a clearer picture will be had of the limits of the residential parts of the city at particular times. It is reasonable to suppose that these burials were outside the city bounds, but was there a suburb here at any time which came to be abandoned when the city contracted in size? Most of the burials here are of the later period of the city's history when, in fact, the city was contracting.

This contraction would account for the fact that a further burial site was found just inside the North City Wall (Trench V) which proved to be relatively rich in grave goods. It was the grave of a young person whose body had been curiously mutilated by the amputation of both feet and, strangest of all, by the total abstraction of the pelvis. Quite how these factors relate to late Nabatean funerary practices, if at all, we cannot at present determine. The body was found lying in a stone-slab walled grave with a sort of gable roof, also of stone slabs. A certain amount of jewellery was found in the grave.

Some distance further on below the Turkamaniya Graves, on the thin nose of land which rises steeply between the Wadis Turkamaniya and Mousa, are the remains of what could have been the terminal tower of the wall. Some authorities regard this as having been a water cistern, though it is difficult to see what good purpose could have been served by having a water cistern terminating a city wall. There are practically no remains now except for the foundations. Viewed from this low vantage-point, one can appreciate the defensive advantage of the ridge in protecting the northern flank of the town (Fig. 168).

It has been suggested that the route from the north entered the city at approximately this point—on the axis of the Kasr el Bint, with the temple as a stately backdrop or termination of the vista from the gate in the walls. This would have made a difficult entrance, and to some extent an impractical one. Putting aside the question of defence against attack, one should consider the known layout of the city from a practical point of view. If, as is believed, the Temenos was the venerated sacred enclosure set before the main temple of the city, it would surely have been kept as such and not used as a trunk route for all the traffic entering the city from the north. The markets are believed to have been sited off the south side of the Colonnade Street, so entry from the north opposite the Kasr el Bint would have entailed the riotous tumult of trade shattering the cloistered serenity and calm of the sacred Temenos. It is possible that a seldom used ceremonial entry to the town existed at this point, on the axis of the temple and crossing the Wadi by one of the bridges.

Admittedly the traders could have turned left along the north bank of the Wadi Mousa and entered the commercial part of the city by the bridge in front of the so-called Lower Gymnasium. Alternatively, they could have gone right

Fig. 168 The northern half of the city from the top of Umm el Biyara. Wadi Turkamaniya lies on the left, overlooked by the site of the North City Wall which stood on the ridge above.

and circled round the Kasr el Bint under the wall of el Habis. The known existence of a fine road extending north from Moghar al Nassara in the direction of el Barid, militates against both these alternatives. From the practical point of view—and to the Nabateans that would surely have meant from the commercial point of view—the northern entry would have been much better for easy access to the markets in the commercial part of the town. By that route the quiet of the Temenos would have also remained undisturbed.

Thickets of oleander seem to bar the way up the track in the soft sand of the Wadi Turkamaniya. The ridges of the Ma'aiserat area begin to gather in on the left and although the wadi is not very deep, the banks shut out any view so that one only sees the tops of craggy mountains. A short way up, on a rocky plateau overlooking a sea of oleander, is the square white box with windows which is the 'village' school. With no other habitation in sight it is at first a wonder where the pupils come from. But come they do as the boisterous sounds during break will tell. It is then that one remembers that many of the caves—not those of architectural note—are occupied for most of the year by settled bedouin families. It is indeed in this area that one sees a number of caves with their entrances walled up and boasting a startling modern door and, in one instance, what looked like a Georgian sash window. This school, though utterly unprepossessing, is a marvellous antidote to the feeling of creeping morbidity which can affect one in this dead city. The yelling, tumbling life of young, uninhibited people who are totally undepressed and undaunted by the historic site in which they live, is a refreshing tonic.

Just over half a mile up the otherwise uneventful wadi, there is the so-called TURKAMANIYA TOMB, or TOMB WITH THE NABATEAN INSCRIPTION (Fig. 169). It stands on the left bank, cut into the wall of the Ma'aiserat Ridge, overlooking a very wide part of the wadi. It is situated right down on 'water level' which may well account for the fact that its lower part has been completely worn away: the top half of the façade seems to hang rather perilously on to the cliff. Between the inner two pilasters which adorn the façade is a long Nabatean inscription (Fig. 11) which is worth quoting in full, for it gives some vital information concerning the ancillaries of a tomb.

Fig. 169 The Turkamaniya Tomb, important because of its Nabatean inscription (Fig. 11), has had its base completely eroded by the winter flood-waters sweeping down the Wadi Turkamaniya.

This tomb and the large and small chambers inside, and the graves made as loculi, and the courtyard in front of the tomb, and the porticos and the dwelling places within it, and the gardens and the triclinium, the water cisterns, the terrace and the walls, and the remainder of the whole property which is in these places, is the consecrated and inviolable property of Dusares, the God of our Lord, and his sacred throne(?), and all the Gods (as specified) in deeds relating to consecrated things according to their contents. It is also the order of Dusares and his throne and all the Gods that, according to what is in the said writings relating to consecrated things, it shall be done and not altered. Nor shall anything of all that is housed in them be withdrawn, nor shall any man be buried in this tomb except him who has in writing a contract to be buried according to the said writings relating to consecrated things, for ever.

The cutting of the beautiful script is still very sharp, as are the architectural details near the inscription. Above, however, the façade becomes very worn and battered. This is a large-scale façade, and within there is a spacious chamber 30 feet by 20 feet with an inner chamber of 8 feet by 20 feet which contains a single loculi (Fig. 170). There is no sign of the triclinium, porticos and other buildings mentioned in the inscription and it must be assumed that these have been swept away by the spate waters of the Wadi.

What comes out most clearly is the considerable size of a Nabatean tomb complex in its original state; they were not just isolated façades such as we see today. With all the ancillary appurtenances mentioned in the inscription, one can credit Bachmann's reconstruction of the Roman Soldier Tomb (Fig. 135). The other thing which stands out in this inscription is the sacred character of Dusares' throne. Here we have on a late monument a reiteration of the Beth-el concept by which the block of stone was not only the deity himself, but also his abode and his altar/throne. How dearly one would like to have a sight of the original writings which are mentioned, but these, like all other 'soft' goods, paper, papyrus, etc., would soon moulder and disintegrate in the damp winters of Petra.

The other buildings mentioned must have

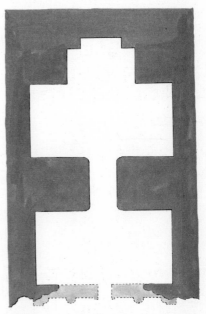

Fig. 170 Ground plan of the Turkamaniya Tomb.

stood in front of the tomb, extending into what is now the wadi bed. It is likely that the water course was originally located much more towards the opposite bank, but in time, without the hand of man to restrain it, it has spread out to engulf the whole bed of the wadi that we see today, hence the disappearance of the buildings. It is, however, interesting to note that there were dwelling-places attached to the tomb; could they have been used by a 'chantry' of priests?

The Ma'aiserat Ridges are a dramatically pitched series of plateaux dominated by raw pinnacles of rock jabbing the skyline. Like Moghar al Nassara, there are monuments of all kinds here which are worth seeing although it would be pointless to enumerate them all, even though they are, by and large, better preserved here than in most places in Petra. The overall conglomeration is fascinating.

One of the first monuments to confront someone climbing up out of the Wadi Turkamaniya, is a large Double Cornice I type, the back of which has been cut away to form a deep couloir (Fig. 171). This particular feature stands out conspicuously from the Kasr el Bint.

Mention has already been made of the classical monument which has lost its architectural top (Fig. 172). This forms a pivot for two other monuments, a deeply recessed courtyard, looking like a 'fives court' to use Sir Alexander Kennedy's description, and a courtyarded monument. The 'fives court' has carved out of its back wall a row of large, shallow niches. The back wall which is some 30 feet high was the end of a massive roofed courtyard for which the niches, measuring about 6 feet high and 3 or 4 feet across, were slots to carry the huge beams which would have been required. This was served by an impressive couloir which runs off at an angle to connect with other monuments: the whole complex has the stamp of an important sanctuary served by a processional way.

To the north of the 'fives court', on a higher level, is a notable example of a Double Cornice I type monument facing on to a two-level courtyard. The upper part of this courtyard is cut deep into the rock, resulting in high smooth walls on either side. This must have been a site of some religious and ritual importance, comparable with the arrangement at the Deir and at Moghar al Nassara.

Most interesting of all the sites on the Ma'aiserat Ridges is the High Place (Fig.

Fig. 171 Pinnacles and carved façades on the Ma'aiserat Ridges.

Fig. 172 The Ma'aiserat Ridges are a complex collection of façades and monuments from most periods of the Nabatean occupation of Petra.

173). This is situated on the top of a small, snub-nosed pinnacle, into the face of which a Cavetto I type façade has been cut. The top of this rock is so curiously formed that it looks like a few very flat cushions piled one upon the other. The area is scarcely large enough for four men to stand together, yet it is approached by an impressive, though worn, flight of steep steps. The view this platform commands is superb with the Kasr el Bint directly in line far below. The importance of these High Places has been discussed already but the sheer number of them impresses upon one the religious fervour of the Nabateans. Perhaps it is that in the desert one is nearer God and one's need for God is greater. The High Places cited in this book, from the great site on the Attuf Ridge to the small complex behind el Habis, were all important 'public' shrines and no account has been taken of the countless 'private' High Places which abound in the hills around Petra.

The Ma'aiserat Ridges were evidently highly developed, a development which covered the full gamut of Nabatean architectural activity. Double Cornice monuments seem to predominate but there are handsome examples from all other periods. One particularly fine sweep of façades of the Double Cornice Intermediate type is that which overlooks the Wadi al Gharbieh, while this is approached by an equally fine set of Assyrian II type façades. For those who wish to study the architectural development of style in Petra, the Ma'aiserat Ridges are an ideal exploring ground.

VII

el Beidha, el Barid

The 'road' up through the Wadi al Wasta to the el Beidha tract is beautiful and impressive with high ridges rising steeply on both sides of the wadi. There are tantalising glimpses of façades continually coming into view on the slopes above. The further north one travels the closer the mountains become and the more remote the terrain seems to be (Fig. 174). Soon the façades stop appearing and one is left with the wild magnificence of nature. This is a serene world in the early morning, for the colours have a softness and cool clarity which is so pleasing.

Abruptly the mountains give way to broad expanses of absolutely flat upland encircled by a ring of high ridges. In summer the ground is hard-packed mud with thick tufts of wiry grass and tough shrubs like the astringent smelling *shiah* (desert sage) with its tiny yellow flowers (Fig. 175). The essence of *shiah* is reputedly very good for stomach disorders and is used by the bedouin as an homeopathic remedy. In the cool of the early morning, before the heat has had a chance to stifle all fragrance from the air, its bitter-sweet scent pervades this upland sierra in a deliciously refreshing way.

Away to the east the bleak, blank face of the Shara hills persists rather monotonously along the distant horizon. It is possible to reach this high plateau by the Wadi Turkamaniya and, of course, by the Nabatean 'road' from Moghar al Nassara.

On the far side of the plateau is the wadi which leads up to el Beidha. EL BEIDHA is in fact a whole district in which are two distinct sections of archaeological interest. The Nabateans would never have regarded what we now call el Beidha as separate from el Barid. To them the whole area was probably the northern caravanserai at the end of the trade route into the markets of Palestine and Syria. As Sir Alexander Kennedy has observed, the Siq of el Barid, which is the easiest position to defend in this area, would have been 'the principal business street of the suburb'. It is approached from the south by a long winding wadi in which are the shattered remains of terrace walls. The stream, when in spate, has gouged out a deep water course of glistening white, round stones which contrast sharply with the golden brown of the rocks and the greens of the desert grasses.

At the head of this wadi, just before it debouches out into a spacious area of level ground with white limestone outcrops, is the famous site of the Neolithic village of SEYL AQLAT perched defensively on the top of a steep bank surveying the surrounding terrain. It was discovered by Diana Kirkbride (Mrs

Fig. 173 The High Place on the Ma'aiserat Ridges; in a spectacular position overlooking the central valley.

Fig. 174 The Wadi al Wasta, early morning.

Fig. 175 The jagged hills of the el Beidha tract.

Helbaek) with the aid of local bedouin in 1956, and excavations began in 1958. It was hoped to establish a link with Pre-Pottery Neolithic Jericho. The result was that, after eight seasons, the parallels with Jericho were considered close enough to place Seyl Aqlat in the same civilisation even though there are differences in practice and forms. One of the main reasons for the importance of the el Beidha village is that it contains a uniquely complete record of architectural evolution from the early Neolithic period (*c.* 6800 B.C.), and there are indications of Mesolithic levels below that, which have not been fully investigated. Although there was a gap between the occupation of the site in the Mesolithic and Neolithic periods, the evidence of the former culture means that the site was inhabited for at least part of the year, for many more centuries before the Neolithic remains we see today. These remains are of the Pre-Pottery phase of Neolithic (when flint and stone implements were still used). It is interesting to note that crude clay manufactures have been found, including one delightfully lively representation of a massively horned ibex and a bowl. These show the beginnings of human awareness of the potential of the material, an advance that was to lead, in time, to the discovery of how to make pottery. The 'finds' are, however, firmly rooted in the Pre-Pottery period and consist of querns (Fig. 176), a vast array of worked bone implements and tools. The collection of flints is also enormous, containing beautiful arrowheads, blades and scrapers of many kinds.

The site is a natural one from the point of defence and so it is not surprising that no defensive wall has been found. Subsequent excavations, in 1967, revealed a long wall encircling the Level VI and subsequent villages. In parts it stands to a height of about 3 feet and is built against and to retain the soft aeolian sand on which the village is founded. This was more in the nature of a retaining than a defensive wall but would, none the less, have presented a fine defensive barrier should the need have arisen. Much of the wall was damaged, if not destroyed, by Nabatean agriculture; the entire south-eastern stretch has, however, been excavated.

The excavations of the village area show a complex of walls, some built on or across others of an earlier level, which make it visually confusing (Fig. 177). There are, however, six clearly defined levels of permanent buildings covering the whole period of Neolithic occupation, about five hundred years from c. 7000 to 6500 B.C. Each level seems to have lasted for approximately seventy years. The top level, the most recent, has been almost wholly eroded but, from fragmentary evidence available, the buildings seem to be approximately the same as those of Level IV. The buildings of Levels II and III are a set of rectangular structures containing six small rooms, three on either side of a central corridor (Fig. 178). It is now held that these small rooms were workshops, and

Fig. 176 Querns from the Neolithic village at el Beidha. Corn was ground in these some 8,500 years ago.

the massive walls of such enormous thickness supported a light superstructure in which were the living quarters. These 'corridor' buildings were all arranged about large, single-roomed houses and set of courtyards. The large building, containing a hearth, was probably a communal mess; there are no hearths in the workshops.

Level IV saw the phase of the finest building techniques and is the culmination of a totally different architectural concept from the 'corridor' houses. It is believed that the 'corridor' houses of Levels II and III came about due to an intrusion of an alien people bringing with them their own architectural tradition. Before this, an indigenous tradition had been developing represented by Levels IV, V and VI. Level IV is, however, crucial, for here the walls of the earlier polygonal and round houses begin to straighten out into a rectangular space with gently curved walls and rounded corners. This is a most important advance, for

Fig. 177 The excavations of the Pre-Pottery Neolithic village at el Beidha. Seven levels of occupation had been built one upon the other creating an exceedingly complex site. However, the 'corridor' houses of Level II are clearly recognisable as are some of the 'round' houses of earlier periods.

Man was moving adventurously away from the structural security of a circle towards a straight wall, which requires much more skill in design to keep it standing up. Walls and ceilings were plastered, in fact the whole of this Level speaks of a high degree of early civilisation, with interiors being kept scrupulously clean, resulting in a dearth of 'finds' for the archaeologist, and signs of a developing social order with big fine houses for the bosses and smaller, less fine ones, set respectfully apart, for the 'lower orders'. Roofs seem to have done away with the central support post of the earlier periods, in itself a considerable adventure, while internal hearths were introduced.

In Levels V and VI we come to a clearly recognisable descendent of the round bough and mud huts of the school textbook on Prehistory. Level VI houses are actually polygonal (Fig. 179), the stretches of wall between the posts being straight instead of curved as in Level V. These are post-houses, but the main difference lies in the fact that the Level V houses are free-standing while the earlier Level VI ones are in clusters for mutual structural support. Instead of forming a cone like the mud hut, these were more cylindrical with the space be-

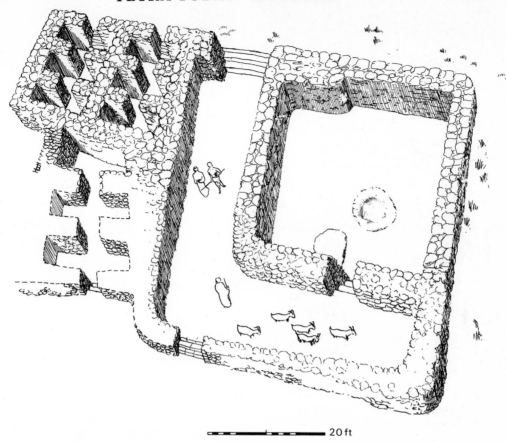

20 ft

Fig. 178 A schematic reconstruction of a 'Corridor' house and its communal mess at el Beidha. It is not known how these partly subterranean dwellings were roofed, possibly with dried mud on branches. The central hearth and large stone by the door of the mess building are to be seen in Fig. 177.

tween the wall-posts being filled with stones. The flattish roof was supported by the centre post and was made of brush-wood heavily plastered (Fig. 180). The fire hazard was enormous, as evidenced by the number of burned properties found. For this reason, it can be supposed, there are no hearths in the houses of Levels V and VI.

There are, in fact, Levels VII and VIII which do not contain the remains of any permanent buildings but there is evidence of plastered floors.

Some forty yards away to the east a 'sanctuary' area was excavated in 1967, which proved to contain buildings of a very special type. Possibly the most interesting feature found in this area is the 'standing' stone set in one of the many rounded enclosures which have carefully paved floors. One enclosure had flag-stones, another was metalled with small, angular pieces of stone giving something of the effect of a rough and random tesserae. Both floors were underlined with

Fig. 179 The remains of a Curvilinear post-house at el Beidha. The slots all round the inner wall originally held upright posts. A close descendant of the 'prehistoric' bough houses of school text-books.

an unidentified iron deposit which has not been found anywhere else in el Beidha. The evident care with which these 'shrines' were made attests to their having a special and important purpose and makes one suggest a sanctuary. The material was hand-picked, the workmanship is fine and the whole kept in a state of absolute cleanliness: there are also the remains of a fire and food possibly indicating a ritual meal.

The excavations at el Beidha have not been finished and the results to date not yet mulled in sufficient detail for too much to be said about this remarkable site. These few lines are, perforce, inadequate but bearing in mind the importance of the site, and its close proximity to Petra, it would have been quite wrong to ignore it.

When one considers that Man was starting from scratch when the permanent buildings of Level VI were put up, the development he managed to make in the next five hundred years was truly remarkable. The fact that this is so clearly and concisely shown on one site is the greatness of el Beidha. After 6500 B.C. the site was never occupied again for permanent buildings. The Nabateans put terrace fields across the site for farming but never actually built anything here. It is believed that it was the increasing aridity of the area which finally led to the abandonment of the site.

10 ft

Fig. 180 A schematic reconstruction of a Curvilinear post-house group, which shows how these partly subterranean houses were clustered together for mutual structural support. Compare with Fig. 179.

The SIQ OF EL BARID lies only a short distance further on. It is a narrow gorge, preceded by a classical temple (Fig. 181)—perhaps imitating the placing of the Khasneh—before the slim gap in the rock face. The gorge contains a beautifully simple temple with a portico in antis, with one of its two free-standing columns most curiously worn (Fig. 182). The main interest in the 'Street' lies in the so-called PAINTED HOUSE (Fig. 183), where there are extensive remains of a plastered and painted interior. It is in bad and dirty condition with far too many Arabic graffiti scrawled on the painted surface. Some of the plaster has come away, particularly on the walls, but on the ceiling nude classical figures and winged Cupids with bows and arrows cavort among a mass of vine leaves and bunches of grapes. Birds fly in and out of the flowery boskage, while the centre is taken up with a circular medallion with incised markings. This bower theme would have been a popular one all over the Mediterranean basin in classical times, so too much emphasis should not be placed on it, particularly with these paintings in such an undeservingly shabby state.

The great number of storage caves, offices, houses and the relative scarcity of

Fig. 181 A well-preserved temple at the entrance to the el Ba
Siq, might have been made in imitation of the Khasneh.
Fig. 182 A monument with a portico *in antis* in the el Barid

181 182

sepulchral works, together with the great number of water cisterns and reservoirs of considerable size, indicate that the el Beidha tract was of considerable importance in the work-a-day life of Nabatean times.

It is a long trek out to el Beidha which requires the best part of a day if it is to be done in any sort of comfort. An early start is called for if one is to avoid walking in the heat of the day across the desert flats and up through the mountain passes. It is advisable to take a guide, not that one would get lost very easily, but his presence always helps when one meets with the local bedouin who are naturally suspicious of complete strangers walking about off the beaten track, particularly under present circumstances.

From here it is possible to return to the Government Rest House by taking the track which leads past Al Fajja, up and down wadis,

183

The Painted House
el Barid.

Fig. 183 The 'Painted House' in the el Barid Siq, has best—indeed almost only—preserved painted interior in the Petra area.

Fig. 184 The drawing by David Roberts, 'The Acropolis', shows very clearly the shape of el Habis which is frequently lost against the huge bulk of Umm el Biyara behind. It has been referred to as 'The cat beside the camel'. On the top of it the Crusaders built a tiny fort.

and which comes out eventually near the ruins of AL WU'AIRA. It is a long, silent walk but one full of interest. The Al Wu'aira ruins consist of the remains of a number of buildings with rounded arches, barrel-vaulted chambers and battlemented walls which are believed to date from the Crusader period. The most interesting of these is what could have been an apsidal basilica. This, however, is the last leg of the ancient history of Petra for these ruins mark perhaps an early warning station in advance of the great Crusader fortress of Shobak and for which the forts on the summits of el Habis and possibly the Attuf Ridge were outposts. Petra then was a ghost town (Fig. 184), a tumbled spectre of a metropolis which kept its ghoulish secrets to itself. Men came and went, crossing like phantoms the empty stage of silent history. The sun shone on them from a limitless blue sky above golden rocks in lonely, remote valleys, as it still shines on those who come and go today.

Bibliography

Archaeological Appreciations

Bachmann, W. von, *Petra, Wissenschaftliche Veröffentlichungen des Deutsch-Türkishen Denkmalschutz-Kommandos* (Berlin and Leipzig, 1921).

Brünnow and Domaszewski, von, *Die Provincia Arabia*, Vol. 1 (Strasburg, 1904).

Dalman, G., *Petra und Seine Felsheiligtumer* (Leipzig, 1908).

Dalman, G., *Neue Petra Forschungen* (Leipzig, 1912).

Jaussen and Savignac, Fathers, *Mission Archéologique en Arabie*, Vols 1 and 2 (Paris, 1909 and 1914).

Kennedy, Sir A., *Petra, its History and Monuments* (*Country Life*, 1925).

Musil, A., *Arabia Petraea*, Vol. 2 (Vienna, 1907).

and articles and Reports in the *Palestine Exploration Quarterly*, *Revue Biblique* and other journals of learned Societies, by: Mrs C.-M. Bennett, P. J. Parr, G. Lankester Harding, G. R. H. Wright, Miss D. Kirkbride (Mrs. Helbaek), Abbé J. Starcky, B. Rothenberg, Y. Yadin, A. Lucas, M. E. Kirk, A. Millard, J. Potin, G. and A. Horsfield, P. C. Hammond, A. Kammerer, G. F. Hill and Others.

Studies

Glueck, N., *The Other Side of the Jordan* (New Haven, USA, 1940).

Glueck, N., *Deities and Dolphins* (Cassell, 1966).

Harding, G. Lankester, *The Antiquities of Jordan* (Lutterworth Press, 1967).

Libbey and Hoskins, Drs., *The Jordan Valley and Petra* (Putnam's, London, 1905).

Murray, Miss M., *Petra, the Rock City of Edom* (Blackie, 1939).

Rostovtzeff, M., *Caravan Cities* (Oxford U.P., 1932).

Historical Accounts

Bartlett, W. H., *Forty Days in the Desert* etc. (London(?), 1849).

Burckhardt, J. L., *Travels in Syria and the Holy Land* (Murray, 1822).

Crichton, A., *History of Arabia and its People* (Nelson, 1852).

Doughty, C. M., *Travels in Arabia Deserta* (Cape, 1921).

Irby, Capt. the Hon. and Mangles, J., *Travels in Egypt and Nubia, Syria and the Holy Land* (Murray, 1868).

Laborde, L. de, *Voyage de l'Arabie Pétrée* (Paris, 1830).

Layard, A. H., *Early Adventures in Persia, Susiana and Babylonia* (1840) (Murray, 1887).

Roberts, D., *The Holy Land* etc. (Moon, London, 1842/9).

Robinson, E., *Biblical Researches in Palestine* (Murray, 1860).

General

Macaulay, R., *Pleasure in Ruins* (Weidenfeld & Nicolson, 1953).

Huxley, J., *From an Antique Land* (Parrish, 1954).

Hooke, S. H., *Babylonian and Assyrian Religion* (Blackwell, 1962).

Unless otherwise stated, all works in this Bibliography were published in London.

Historical Authors and Sources

The Old Testament

Diodorus Siculus.

Josephus, *Antiquities of the Jews and Wars of the Jews*.

Pliny, *Natural History*.

Strabo.

Herodotus.

Index

References to illustrations are given in italic figures